About the A

"JRY" is a dyed in the wool Yorkshireman. He worked as a consultant surgeon in North Devon ("doing missionary work") for over thirty years. His surgical specialty was otolaryngology (ear, nose and throat) and he was perhaps best known in this field for his work on the sexual aspects of the nose (a subject in which he says there is little competition)!

He has written seven other books. The first was a study of the "*Inns and Taverns of Old Norwich*" which he wrote when he was a houseman in that fine city in 1972. He has co-authored a couple on surgery and some other obscure subjects include a short book on Military History and an illustrated book on Devon Church Architecture. Perhaps the most arcane title was *Poetry, Physick, Pestilence and Pox; Medical Ideas in English Poetry to the End of the Seventeenth Century.*

He has always enjoyed battling with hospital administrators since qualifying as a house surgeon at Doncaster Royal Infirmary in 1971. He has continued giving them a hard time right up until he retired in 2013. They tried to get rid of him after his controversial book about their gross incompetence, *The Hospital Revolution* but he always managed to keep one step ahead and they never succeeded in sacking him.

He has always had military connections and was formerly the Commanding Officer of a TA Field Hospital based in Plymouth. He retired from the Army List holding the rank of substantive Colonel.

He lists his hobbies as long distance walking, fishing, shooting, making stained-glass windows, cabinet-making, woodcarving, Punch and Judy, growing prize-winning Sweet Peas, British Bulldogs and Arabic/Farsi calligraphy.

He is married to a retired paediatrician and they have five children, lots of grandchildren and a bulldog.

To my long-suffering wife,
Elizabeth

John Riddington Young

THERE'S A NASTY CANCER IN THE HEALTH SERVICE

THE BETRAYAL OF THE NHS

AUSTIN MACAULEY
PUBLISHERS LTD.

A CIP catalogue record for this title is available from the British Library.

ISBN 978 1 78455 212 1 (Paperback)
ISBN 978 1 78455 214 5 (Hardback)

www.austinmacauley.com

First Published (2015)
Austin Macauley Publishers Ltd.
25 Canada Square
Canary Wharf
London
E14 5LB

Printed and bound in Great Britain

Acknowledgments

I must first thank my wife, Dr Elizabeth Young for all her help (not only with Dr Snoddy, but also with the proof-reading) and her endless patience in putting up with me while I wrote the book. I am also grateful to our three daughters, Alice Hammett, Mary Hacker and Dr Anne Jinks for their help with the midwifery section. I also owe a debt of gratitude to quite a few non family members, without whose help the text would have been considerably less interesting.

They are Moslem Abdullah FRCS, John Bennett FRCS, Laura Bretherick (my old landlady), Don Brooker (former editor of the *Barnsley Chronicle*), Alan Cockman (for his help with the computer), Bryan Cley Morgan (my old Catering Officer), John Aylett, Dr Colin Colville FFARCS, Rachel Corby, Seumas Eckford FRCOG, Trevor Farrington FRCS, Edward Fisher FRCS and his wife Mary, Andrew Gibson FRCS, the late Bill Gill FRCS, David Griffin FRCOG, Michael Hardingham FRCS, Melvin Heald, Simon Hickey FRCS, Iain Mackenzie BDS, the late Dr Robert Morton OBE, FRCP, Steven O'Malley FRCS, Edgar Parsons (my old Classics teacher), Victoria Rhead RGN, Professor Alexander von Rokitansky MD, Anthea Salihoglu (my old secretary), the late Lt.Col. Ivor Sewell FRCS, Nicholas Markham FRCS, Dr Andrew Bull FRCPath, Dr Guy Rousseau (my old anaesthetist), Dr John Quinton-Tulloch FRCGP (my GP), J.Pamela Cherrington (née Ward) SRN,SCM, Laverne Fagan SRN, Louise Silverton RCM, Jennifer Steeples RGN, Michael Timms FRCS, Nicholas Treble FRCS, Angus Wadell FRCS, Richard Griffiths (local BMA representative) and Paul Anthony from the North Devon Hospital.

Contents

CHAPTER 1

ALL CHANGE IS FOR THE WORSE

I was to learn later in life that we tend to meet any new situation by reorganising; and a wonderful method it can be for creating the illusion of progress while producing confusion, inefficiency and demoralisation.
Petronius (60 AD)[a]

Change whatever else it might bring really ought to bring progress.

CALL THE MIDWIFE
The midwife slapped your footsoles
Sylvia Plath, *Morning Song* (1961)

At the beginning of 2012, the BBC televised another highly successful period drama. It was an immediate success and soon had over 11 million viewers, all avidly watching the screen adaptation of a real midwife's memoirs.[1]

The author, Jennifer Worth had actually been a district midwife in Poplar, East London just after the War. The tabloid press was full of letters. There has been a popular interest in medical stories since Chaucer's time but this one seemed to have had a very special appeal. Why did the public want to watch the bad old days when women actually still had terrible pain during labour, when a significant number of infants as well as mothers still had a definite chance of dying in childbirth? One of the comments in the Daily Mail suggests why:

---

[a] Gaius Petronius Arbiter (c. 27 – 66 AD) was a Roman courtier during the reign of Nero. He is credited with writing the satirical Latin novel, *Satyricon.*

Perhaps we are comforted and even dazzled by the thought that once upon a time, nurses and doctors and midwives would do their absolute very best for you, no matter what. In every sense of the word, they cared. They would — I know this sounds incredible — even come to your house if there was an emergency. They would bang on your door and charge up the stairs, without so much as a box to be ticked or a form to be filled or a health quango to assess the health and safety risks. Theirs, not yours. And when they arrived at your bedside, there was a fair chance that they would know your name, your medical history and exactly who you were and what you did for a living. All the important stuff. The possibility of them speaking English was also high.[2]

The overwhelming popularity of this uncomplicated programme underlines very eloquently the dissatisfaction that has developed towards the once wonderful National Health Service. The patients are fed up to their back teeth with the fact that they can no longer get to see a doctor, particularly out of hours, but the people who are even more depressed about it are the NHS workers themselves.

I spoke to one grand old lady who was definitely a nurse of the *OldSchool*. She was nearly ninety and had been a student nurse in the pre-1947 era. She said that she could actually recall being on duty the day the black payment boxes were removed from the wards and the NHS was born! Just after World War II, the man in the street associated anything slightly right-wing with Adolf Hitler and the Germans and for the first time in Britain, the socialist Labour Party swept into power. The new Minister of Health, Aneurin Bevan, made medical treatment free and the wonderful National Health Service was born. Before this, patients had to put their money for hospital treatment into a box in the middle of the ward as they left.

This old nurse had recently been an in-patient herself and had not been very impressed with the experience. She had the *NewSchool* nurses enthralled with all her stories about what it had all been like in the *OldSchool* days. It was her impression that it was probably much harder work then, but she considered that it was far more rewarding. You actually spent quite a lot of time with your patients. She had noticed whilst she had been on the ward that nurses had so little actual contact with the people they were supposed to be nursing.

She had been very saddened about how the way the training of nurses had changed for the worse over the years. She had no doubts that it was much better for both the patients and the nurses in the old days. She said that the student nurses then provided the bulk of the workforce, and were proud to do so. The Nurse Training School where she had trained in Hertfordshire was attached to the local hospital and the nurse tutors went and worked with the student nurses on the wards. That lasted for around fifty years until an ill-advised new government initiative called Project 2000 was introduced. The old lady said that this was not just potty but disastrous. When the training schools were moved away from the local hospital, the close attachment to the community was lost. Her daughter, who had followed her into nursing felt frustrated at being in the classroom during the whole of her first year of training instead of being with patients on the wards and she says that there was a high drop out rate when this happened in Stevenage.

Things do appear to have all gone badly wrong.

But not just with the National Health Service, but with everything.

GRUMPY OLD MEN

Old men will die and children soon forget.
Black Letter Ballads (1647)

I am sure the philosophy I have just expressed puts me firmly into the category of a Grumpy Old Man. He is not an Invention of the 21st Century: he has always been around. I never considered my father to be a Grumpy Old Man, and yet it was he who told me that sadly all change is for the worse. I certainly did not think that that grand old fellow, the Poet Laureate, Sir John Betjeman was anything other than a benign old gentleman. During a wonderful television programme, bewailing the passing of the steam locomotive, he was asked if he thought that there were any recent changes which had actually been for the better. The old fellow considered for a moment and without a flicker of emotion,[b] replied "*Yes.*" After a short wait, the interviewer pressed him, "*Well, what do you think has improved then?*" Another brief interval preceded his answer, "*Dentistry!*"

Sadly, not even this is now true. In the sixties, when I broke a tooth, I would invariably be seen the same day. Now my dentist, who is a personal friend, has advised me to tell the receptionists that I have been on morphine all night if I want to be seen that same week! He also bewails the handcuffs of managerialism which have crept into dentistry – and all in the spurious guise of providing a better safer service for his patients. He too has had to spend countless hours (when all totted up at the end of the month) ticking boxes instead of getting on with the job in hand of fixing people's teeth.

In 2009 in order to provide protection for people with special educational needs under the Mental Health Act, a well-meaning organisation was created called the Care Quality Commission. What a pity they didn't just stick to protecting the interests of the intellectually less well-endowed.[c] They have extended their remit to sticking their noses into almost all aspects of public life! It all sounds like a good idea, but they have been shown to be spectacularly incompetent on more than one occasion. They did have the good grace to apologise for their blunders in the investigation of the Maternity Services at the Morecambe Bay Hospital Trust. They had found that *there were no major issues* with the baby care at the hospital, but the unit was later found to have the highest death rate in England. After an enquiry into an alleged cover-up of the deaths of

---

[b] Sadly Sir John was seriously smitten with Parkinson's disease in his later years.

[c] Any terms used for this condition are subject to a process called the *euphemism treadmill*. This means that whatever you call it, it will eventually become perceived as an insult. *Mentally retarded* was first used in the middle of the 20th century, because the previous set of terms (*eg* imbeciles and morons) were now deemed as highly offensive. By the end of the 20th century, inevitably this terminology itself had come to be seen as disparaging and politically incorrect and in need of replacement.

fourteen babies,[3] the CQC admitted, *"We let people down, and we apologise for that."*[4]

They let people down very badly again *when five elderly people died after suffering a devastating catalogue of neglect at a care home rated good by the CQC.*[5]They have been accused of incompetence in other care home investigations.[6]

I certainly would not even trust them to take my dog for a walk.

I was not at all surprised when in early 2013, their boss admitted that they were not *fit for purpose*[7]. I consider them to be Stasi in lamb's clothing and after this damning admission by their new head, I cannot understand why they were not disbanded.

They now *regulate* NHS, local authorities, private companies and voluntary organisations - whether in hospitals, care homes or even in people's own houses; all seem to come under the scrutiny of CQC. It claims to be independent but is quite clearly not: hardly surprisingly it is funded by the taxpayer. I do have to admit that the best thing about them is that they seem to put the fear of God into the Stasi, who see them as a very serious threat to their own supremacy. Perhaps I should at this point explain just who the Stasi are. In recent years, disaffected doctors have adopted pejorative nicknames for hospital administrators. These abusive epithets differ from region to region. In the South West, where I worked, *Stasi* seems favourite. In an audit of Surgeons in Training, the worst "pet-name" seems to be *The Filth* (used in Trent Area – one of the most draconian). Others include *Woodentops, Pigs* (unfair to the species), *Them Upstairs, WIGS/MIGS* (acronym for Women/Men in Grey Suits), *Control, the Archers* (?), *Control Freaks, Weasels, etc., etc.*

The layman has little or no awareness of the intense internecine power struggle that is going on in hospitals between the medical staff and the administrators. The public are often amazed to learn that in most hospitals, these administrators are paid higher salaries than the most senior and experienced surgeons. Very few lay people are aware of the minimal academic qualifications and lack of any proper Civil Service training of these so-called managers and are incredulous of the excessive power that they wield. The word Stasi also forms a fortuitously appropriate acronym for *Staggeringly Tactless And Simpletons Intellectually*. The real Stasi[d] were in fact the hated East German Secret Police.

The last time I broke a tooth, my dentist was tearing his hair out about how the CQC's complete lack of specialist knowledge had not prevented them making drastic changes to his dental practice and then shortly afterwards changing it all back again. Those horrible pliers for extracting teeth are evidently not often used in modern dentistry and the CQC (for no reason based on clinical evidence) decreed that they must be stored in sealed bags off-site! Not only this, but (for another reason evidently plucked out of thin air) they needed to be re-sterilised every 21 days. Then in the next edict from this draconian organisation (set up initially remember with the noble intention to protect the human rights of the mentally handicapped) the time period was increased – once again utterly arbitrarily – from 21 days to 365.[8] It appears that this directive has probably been invented by someone with no knowledge base in academic bacteriology (quite probably a nurse). It is similar to the potty command about short-sleeved white coats (which we will explore later in the book). The very fact that they are able to change their ruling overnight from just three weeks to a year underlines just how crass things have become. Another example of uninformed overkill was the edict that after the floor in the dental surgery had been mopped down with antiseptic floorcleaner, the mop then had to be destroyed.

It is not just medicine and dentistry that have gone to the dogs;[e] it would seem that almost all State-run services have in the past ten years or so taken a grave turn for the worse. I have relatives who work as teachers and police officers and they are constantly lamenting the spiralling deterioration in , these services, which they and their colleagues are being allowed to

---

[d] Stasi is a contraction of the German *Staatssicherheitsdienst* (literally State Security Service).

[e] 19th Century expression based on decrepit horses sent to the knackers' yard to become dog meat.

provide. It seems that, like the NHS, they too are being dragged seriously off-course by the increasing demands of second rate managers, who have no real powers of leadership and truly believe that they can genuinely overcome their total lack of knowledge by being politically correct. This of course is something they can cling to with that irritating self-righteousness of the dull, thick bureaucrat, who is now so commonplace.

Nursing has been absolutely and completely hijacked. The police appear to be rapidly heading the same way. In the past, student nurses, like police cadets served an apprenticeship to get into a career which they both understood would provide an essential public service. They did not want to be academics: if they had been of a scholarly, bookish intellectual personality, they would have chosen to go to University to study Medicine or Law. This has all changed. Nowadays under the so-called egalitarian philosophy that everyone should have a degree, they are made to pretend they are something which they are not. The BBC recently stated that, *"Police should be considered as a profession on a par with medicine or the law."*[9] My older brother and my younger son (both police officers) laughed out loud when I played this video clip to them. Evidently the manager who had proposed this did not know that the *OldSchool* definition of a profession requires it to be *"self-regulatory"* or he would never have gone on to suggest that police superintendents be brought into the "Service" who are not "Bobbies" at all and never have been.

Horror of horrors – they are to be management consultants!

That is guaranteed to do exactly the same for morale in the police force as it did for the NHS. The discerning reader will have picked up that their author has chosen to use the *Old School* term police *force* in favour of the *NewSchool* politically correct term *service*.[f]

---

[f] But with the same intelligence, we have come to expect, in 2012 they formed the *UK Border **Force**, evidently a "law enforcement command within the Home Office."*

In my lifetime (albeit quite a long time ago) the Royal Mail would proudly claim that any letter (and in those days there was no First and Second Class Mail: everything was First Class and could not be improved upon) posted before the last collection at around 5 o'clock, would be delivered anywhere on the British mainland the following day. And it was true; if you posted a letter in Land's End, you had no doubt that it would arrive the following day in John o' Groats (if, of course, that was the intended address).

Of course this is no longer true and hasn't been for years. But much worse than this are those "letters of doom", which you find on your doormat telling you that the postman couldn't leave some mystery item because either the stamp had fallen off or that not enough stamps had been put on (or worse of all that it requires a signature) and you have to traipse to the post office to collect what might very well be junk mail, which you don't really want.

TEN LITTLE NIGGLES[g]

Send to us power and light, a sovereign touch,
Curing the intolerable neutral itch
W.H.Auden. *Sir, No Man's Enemy* (1930)

I am not just referring to those irritating little niggles as the demise of old fashioned good manners. When I was a young lad, my mother taught me that, when on the tram or bus, I should always yield my seat to ladies and elderly people. "At least," she said, "when you get old yourself, then people will give up their seat for you." And do they? Recently whilst in the metropolis and travelling on the tube, I noticed a (grotesquely fat) juvenile weaving and dodging like a snake to occupy a vacated seat, whilst a frail old lady remained standing. As soon as he reached the seat, he started to eat small doughnuts from a greasy paper bag. I was the only person in the carriage who took him to task. I told him that he should give the seat to the

---

[g] Section title adapted from 1939 Agatha Christie novel, initially changed to *Ten Little Indians* and then to *And Then There Were None.* Originally the title was a traditional nursery rhyme.

old lady. Everybody (including the Fat Boy of Dickens[h]) steadfastly ignored me and his obese backside remained firmly on the seat, whilst he stuffed his gross face with sugared buns. Even the dear old dame told me that it didn't matter and not to make a fuss because she was getting off at the next stop. I consoled myself in the supposition that the others were probably all foreigners and could not understand English.

The television does little to help. I personally have no problem at all with sex and violence (or indeed with obscene language[i]). What irritates me are the little insidious things, like watching a so-called respectable couple (the characters were a barrister and his wife) eat their dinner using a fork held like a fish-knife in their right hand (like Americans, who cannot be expected to know better). If one doesn't like nudity, foul language and mayhem, one could always turn it off (or switch from the BBC and ITV to *Russia Today* or *Al Jazeera*), but one would hardly take such extreme measures to prevent one's children witnessing poor table manners. Perhaps one should.

My older son has a theory about cell phones[j] being a major factor in the decline of courtesy and good manners in modern society. He reckons that in the past, when you had arranged to meet somebody in say, Trafalgar Square, they would always turn up. Nowadays you arrive at the base of Nelson's Column and a minute or so before your appointed rendezvous, your cell phone goes off with usually a text message to say that they are not coming after all. What is more, they don't think they are letting you down or being hopelessly unreliable, because they have let you know!

Other little irritations are finding that *Bernard Smith* has been listed under B rather than S in the official British

---

[h] Mr Wardle's servant, Joe in "Pickwick Papers." He consumes great quantities of food and constantly falls asleep in any situation at any time of day; Joe's sleep problem is the origin of the medical term *Pickwickian syndrome* which ultimately led to the subsequent description of *Obstructive Sleep Apnea Syndrome.*

[i] Which they call *strong language*, even though it is clearly obscene.

[j] Often, for some inexplicable reason called *mobiles.* They might take photos, but even the smart all-singing, all-dancing do not actually move; *i.e.* they are certainly not mobile.

Telecom Telephone Directory (and of course one has given up any hope of being able to find the 'phone number of a post office or railway station). In fact with respect to this latter, I have recently even heard BBC News reporters refer to *train* stations and indeed mispronounce the word *schedule* (as well as the words *waistcoat* and *Majorca*[k]). I expect that soon, they won't even say *station* and will start saying *depot.*

I don't watch many games or sport on television, but when I do inadvertently turn on Match of the Day, I still cannot get used to Association Football players cuddling each other when they score a goal. I even saw them kissing on one occasion. Whatever happened to *sangfroid* and *stiff upper lip?* While on the subject of TV games I have completely given up on the BBC getting the difference right between *Sport* and *Games.* I know it is far from straightforward, but one would think that the British Broadcasting Corporation would strive to set a good example.

Another daft intrusion which has only turned up recently is the facial contortions of musicians. I cannot ever remember *OldSchool* professional musicians appearing to be having some sort of orgasm, when playing an emotionally uplifting piece of music. Then, when they take their bow at the end of the performance, they always give a full-on Japanese *ojigi*, with a 90 degree bend at the waist, rather than a proper restrained English bow of the head.

Christian names too (or in our new diverse PC society, *forenames*) are amusing and would only be irritating if one discovered one's grandson was about to be christened (should I say *named*) Chardonnay, Tyler or Madison.

CHANGES FOR THE BETTER
Change of pasture makes fat calves.
Heywood (1546)

Some change must definitely have been for the benefit of mankind.

---

[k] I will assume my reader knows that they are *weskit* and *madge-orca.*

No one would deny that important and sometimes life-saving medical discoveries are made with every passing week. It would be absurd to say that groundbreaking progress has not been made in almost all branches of medicine in recent years. Just one example is the development in the treatment of AIDS. Twenty years ago, acquiring the HIV virus was thought to be a virtual death sentence. The media spoke of the "Gay Plague," but when it became clear that heterosexuals could contract it too, the greater public began to panic, fearing a pandemic. Now, thanks to medication, AIDS is not the devastating condemnation to inevitable death that it used to be. Medication with new antiretroviral drugs have revolutionised treatment, which initially was fairly ineffective. Not only that; HIV positive patients who are on the drug (and take it regularly) do not transmit the disease to others. This is just one example of many recent advances in medicine which have saved countless lives.

And of course there are many others.

Things in the National Health Service should therefore be getting better and better. So why then did so many people die, whilst in the presumed safety of an NHS hospital in the Mid Staffs Disaster? Why then did a 20-year-old boy die of dehydration for want of a glass of water whilst lying in the ward of a top London teaching hospital?

We clearly have a paradox: things in the NHS should be improving and they are not. Morale amongst the professionals should be getting better and better, working during a period when great advances in medicine and surgery are evolving with every passing day. Morale however is dire. It has never been worse. GPs are earning more money than ever before and probably more than any other family doctors in Europe and yet they are bitterly unhappy and cannot wait to retire. Hospital doctors have never been at a deeper nadir than they are now. They are leaving at a greater rate than since the beginning of the NHS.

I believe that all of the blame for all this dissatisfaction can be laid fairly and squarely at the door of the execrable NHS management.

It is my opinion after working for nearly fifty years in the Health Service that the blame is wholly and exclusively theirs.

In a previous book, about hospital administration, I compared that management to a malignant cancer growing in the centre of the service. I think it is an excellent metaphor. Just as a patient with cancer does not know for quite a long time that a disease is present, the vast majority of the British public is unaware of the true cause and extent of the sickness in the NHS.

A cancer grows at the expense of the healthy tissues around it without serving any useful function. To the detriment of the doctors, nurses and surgeons, the administration has grown bigger and bigger and it has certainly not served any useful purpose. But they are worse than that; just like a cancer, their presence is actually harmful to the wellbeing of the whole.

Cancer grows and grows until it sometimes becomes bigger than the organ from which it has arisen. Cancer eventually kills its host by an insidious process of infiltration and spread. The administrators have certainly done that. Twenty years ago there were just a handful, but now there are thousands. By their own exorbitant salaries and continuing mismanagement and misuse of money, they have diverted precious funds and have made our once thriving Health Service into an emaciated shadow of its former self. Sometimes cancer causes bleeding. Then the blood flows away and cannot be replaced quickly enough by the ailing body. Doctors and nurses (the life blood of the NHS) have never before been leaving (or taking early retirement) in such unprecedented numbers. They are going because of the administration, which has made them all feel absolutely and utterly unvalued.

WHERE DID THE NASTY CANCER COME FROM, DOCTOR?

If Florence Nightingale was carrying her lamp through the corridors of the NHS today, she would almost certainly be searching for the people in charge.
Roy Griffiths (1983)

From before the inception of the NHS in 1947, the medical profession had been completely self-regulating (as we have said, part of the definition of *a profession* is that it must in fact be self-regulating, otherwise it is not a profession). There had been a couple of abortive outside attempts to manage or regulate British doctors. The first was the Salmon Report[10] of 1966, which marked the definite death knell for the professionalism of nurses and abolished NHS hospital matrons.[1] The writer of this report, Brian Salmon was (and this is true!) the managing director of J. Lyons (the tea-room people) and of course, not medically qualified. There were no practising nurses on the Salmon committee, only administrators, *and it was not difficult therefore to forecast that its report, when implemented, would enhance the status of administrators and depress the status of practising nurses.*[11] What is interesting is that this is the first time I can find when the Stasi Nurse Administrators actually paid themselves more at the expense of the practising nurses. This is exactly what would happen over and over again in the future.

There was an inconsequential "damp squib"[12] called the Merrison Report in 1979[m] and in 1982 another Tory attempt at rearranging the deckchairs on the Titanic with the highly innovative and original title *Patients First.*[n] Not a lot happened, however, until 1983 and the Griffiths Report.[13]

Mrs Thatcher had sailed into power and because her father had been a grocer in Grantham, her Minister of Health, Norman Fowler probably thought that she would be very happy indeed, if he asked another grocer how to run the NHS. Like most members of the Iron Lady's cabinet, Norman Fowler strove to keep her happy. Although Roy Griffiths was not your everyday grocer, he was the deputy managing director of

---

[1] Matrons do still exist (see Chapter 7)

[m] Sir Alex Merrison, Vice-Chancellor of the University of Bristol himself admitted his report had *"no blinding revelation which would transform the NHS".*

[n] Consultative Paper on Structure and Management of NHS, HMSO, 1979.

Sainsbury's° and since the whole ethos of Mrs Thatcher's administration was that of the marketplace, he should be the right man for the job.

It was also the fact that Griffiths had no medical (or even nursing) qualification and had never worked in a hospital which also made him so eminently suitable for the job. Manfred Davidmann (a management style analyst of international repute) said of the Report, *'what is completely missing from the enquiry team is grass-roots representation of any kind from those who would be affected by the inquiry's findings, namely from doctors, and nurses.'* He also correctly predicted the mayhem that acceptance of the report would cause over the next thirty years.[14]

This was the shape of things to come.

This marked the turning point.

Griffiths suggested appointing lots and lots of administrators, preferably with experience in retailing. Mrs Thatcher loved his proposals. She concurred with him that the differences between the care of the nation's health and the economic management of a chain grocery store are inconsequential; clearly the principles are the same. Unfortunately at the beginning of the eighties, British industry was in a serious state of decline and shedding lots and lots of managers. More and more industries went to the wall in a Darwinian manner. The best survived, but the real dullards were all sacked and looking for jobs. This was just the very time when at Griffiths' suggestion, the NHS was seeking managers.

You've got it.

Incompetent clods (presumably all with no medical experience) entered NHS administration in their droves. Neither the Iron Lady nor Griffiths conceded or even realised that general management by untrained personnel is inappropriate for the hospital service where the main "commodity for sale" is the knowledge, experience and technical skills of professional (albeit often pompous and self-opinionated) consultants and nurses. Neither did they foresee

---

° A well-known British supermarket chain.

(or perhaps care) that these experienced and highly skilled personnel might not take kindly to school leavers telling them how to organise their operating theatres.

This ingress of failed redundant managers, who had lost their jobs in industry, would begin a real power struggle against the consultants. They actually said that they would *run the show from now on*[15] and what's more, they would let the doctors and nurses know exactly who was in charge of the hospital. They brought a new meaning to the term *control freaks*. Thirty years later, they still hold on to these delusions of grandeur and in the Christmas issue of the BMJ 2012, Professor Sir Brian Jarman[p] pointed out *that the imbalance between the power of managers and doctors, which Griffiths set in train, is harming patients.*

Their apparent *carte blanche* in the disciplining of doctors is the card which they love to play best of all. They can report doctors to the General Medical Council, but doctors cannot report the Stasi to any regulatory professional body, because they don't have one; they wouldn't, would they, because they are not professional?

What they like to do best of all is to suspend a doctor from his job.

This is completely unlawful, because the only two bodies who can legally deprive a person of his livelihood in the UK is either a professional body (in this case the GMC) or the judiciary (at least a magistrate), but it seems that the Stasi have ridden roughshod over this point of law for years.

The Stasi of the North Devon Healthcare Trust suspended me a few years ago in 2007. I had been expecting it to happen at some time, because I had been a painful thorn in their side for ages and ages.

---

[p] *Professor Sir Brian Jarman OBE, PhD, FRCP, FRCGP, FFPH, FMedSci is the past president of the British Medical Association and Emeritus Professor of the Faculty of Medicine at Imperial College, London.*

GIVE A DOG A BAD NAME AND HANG HIM
Revenge is a dish which is best served cold.
Pashtoo Proverb (15th century)

It all started in the late afternoon of a summer's day in June 2007. I had had a very busy day with an outpatient clinic in the morning and an operating list in the afternoon. It had been a difficult list where one of the cases was a big tumour in a young man's neck. It had not been easy to remove because it had been sitting on the nerve to his tongue; I had to dissect it meticulously off the lingual nerve so that he would still be able to move his tongue after the operation. After the list was all over, I went to the ward and waited for the young chap with the poorly neck to come round from his anaesthetic and come back to his bed. Then I could ask him to stick his tongue out and see if his nerve had been damaged by my operation. It is important to do this check as soon after the operation as possible; if the tongue moves when the patient wakes up, but doesn't work the following morning, then you know you haven't cut the nerve and the paralysis is due to swelling. I sat in the office and chatted to the nurses. One of them had just come back from South Africa, where she had been to attend a funeral of her husband's relative. I had better say from the outset that she and her husband were both white.

We talked about racial problems and I told them about my brother, who was a retired senior police officer and had been Community Relations Officer for South Yorkshire. He had told me the main problem that the British police have with respect to racial squabbles is not between the white and the black communities, but between different ethic groups, such as blacks and Asians or the black Africans and the black Caribbeans. Evidently, the West Indians have never forgiven the African tribal chiefs who sold them into slavery. Although they were well aware that it was the white slavers who acted as the traders, the main villains all those years ago were clearly the rival tribal chiefs who acted as the vendors. It would seem that some West Indians still bear a bit of a grudge about this and therefore sometimes pejoratively call their African cousins

Jungle Bunnies, whilst the blacks from Africa, rather unkindly use the jibe *slaves* against the Caribbeans.

My patient suddenly returned from the Recovery Ward and I was summoned to see him. The nurse from South Africa came with me. He had a bed near the window and after I had made him put out his tongue, checked his vital signs (temperature, pulse and blood pressure) and the surgical drain hanging from his neck, I then noticed from the light of the window just how sun-tanned the staff nurse was. She had a swarthy Cornish complexion anyway, but her fortnight in the African sun had tanned her and made her quite dark. I told her that she looked like a real African now, but added (apropos of our conversation in the sister's office) that I didn't think anyone would take her for a Jungle Bunny, saying (in my best Jamaican accent), *"Your lovely blue eyes are a dead giveaway!"*[16]

That is when things started to go terribly wrong.

The nurse laughed. My patient in the bed said afterwards that he hadn't heard what was said, but a visitor on the ward, who had just evidently heard only two words of our conversation (I will leave my perspicacious readers to guess exactly which *two words*) sprang up like a genie out of Aladdin's lamp and accused both the nurse and I of being racists. He said that I should not *under any circumstances* have used those two words and the poor nurse should certainly not have laughed. We both said that although we were having a private conversation, we apologised unreservedly for any offence that we might have given and that he might have taken. It was certainly not enough and he seemed to get more and more troubled. He then said that his son had been *brain-damaged by racism.* I and the nurse repeated our apology to him, but he told me that I did not sound sorry enough. I assumed that his son had been the victim of some awful racist street attack. What I did not know is that he believed his child had been born brain-damaged because his black wife had been neglected during labour, because of her ethnicity and that an official complaint had been brought by him against another nearby hospital (which was evidently still on-going).

(His West Indian wife later told me that he had been really affected by the incident with me and had difficulty getting to sleep that night because of it.)

I did not think any more of it. Then five days later I was summoned to an emergency meeting by the Stasi. This was instead of doing an Outpatient Clinic, which a locum had been paid an enormous sum to do at the last minute. I asked for an agenda for this meeting but was told it would be immediately obvious and no agenda was necessary. I insisted on an agenda, but they were so cagey that I suspected possible suspension, although I did not immediately think back to the somewhat trivial event which had happened on the ward after the neck operation.

On the following morning, before I went to see the Stasi, I sought out the South African staff nurse and my suspicions were confirmed. The personnel department had already taken a statement from her about the incident. I thought it would probably be very useful for both of us to talk to each other before I was actually suspended. When I went to the meeting, they had chosen two old adversaries, neither of whom I trusted. How smug they looked. Even though I was reasonably sure that I had nothing to fear, I thought that I had at that moment had enough of the *NewSchool* NHS.

Amazingly, they told me that they could not give me a definite reason why I had been suspended, but that it would all become apparent in the fullness of time. How patronising could they get? This would not be appropriate behaviour with any adult, let alone one of the senior consultant surgeons at the hospital. They seemed surprised that I had the affront to demand a reason. With reticence they admitted it was because there had been a complaint about racism. They asked me if I had any more questions. I remained as deadpan as I could, looked the Quisling straight in the eye and asked, "*Will I get counselling?*" It was an undoubted flash of inspiration which completely flummoxed them. They clearly did not know whether I was being serious or taking the Mickey.[q]

---

[q] At the time the London docks were being built (and rhyming slang was being devised) one of the foreign labourers was an Irishman, called

They then told me that I must leave the hospital by the quickest possible route and that I must not take anything with me. I did not say that I had previously been to my office and also sorted things out with the nurse. In addition to this I was instructed that I must not (unless I myself was ill) enter any NHS premises. It was a definite case of "*Go to jail; go directly to jail; do not pass GO; do not collect £200!*" I cannot express how angry it made me feel. What made matters much worse is that they then sent a uniformed policeman to my consulting room to escort me to the hospital door.

That is what I would never forgive them for.

As I approached the door, we met an 80-year-old man, a Burma-Star veteran who was an old patient of mine. I thought he would attack the policeman, when he heard what had happened. "*This man saved my life!*" he protested to the embarrassed bobby. I then replied to him, "*When I go out through that hospital door, I have absolutely no intention of ever coming back here again.*" "*Don't give in, Colonel!*" the old chap replied. "*Don't let those bastards upstairs win!*" The old soldier's words stayed with me.

Then I met a young man at the petrol station on my way home. I had operated on him when he was around eleven-years-old. He told me almost exactly the same thing. His mother had evidently told him that the paediatricians had given him up, but that I had saved his life by draining an abscess in his sinus, which had been dangerously close to his brain. Later he had joined the army and when he left the service, he became a member of the local TA unit under my command and I had got to know him quite well. "*I can't believe you are going to give in as easily as that, Colonel!*

Mickey Bliss who was well-known in East London for being a bit of a hell-raiser, and his name was on everyone's lips. As for the term, *taking the piss* from which this is all derived it has been suggested that this has nothing to do with urine but comes from the Anglo-Norman, *pistake (cf.* Latin word *pisittacus,* which means *parrot*). As the parrot taunts with strange speech, so does someone who is taking the piss. Who's taking the Mickey now?

The military were ganging up on me.

The Stasi had told me that I must not talk to anyone – especially not the media. They told the switchboard to tell any callers that I was on holiday! I did not trust the Stasi so I sent an e-mail to the world and his wife saying: *The Hospital Administrators have suspended me on full pay for an indefinite period pending a full investigation on the grounds of my alleged racism. I thought that I had better let everybody know to prevent Rumour Control giving the wrong message. I am anxious that my true colleagues do not think that my enforced absence from the hospital is because of any medical negligence or sexual impropriety by me and I am sending this communication to prevent any false rumours developing about the cause of my suspension. Yours ever, John Riddington Young.*

They were furious about this and demanded to know how I had gained access to the hospital computer during my exclusion from the premises. They got even more cross when a patient I met in the street wrote to the local paper. It was front page headline news.[17] The next thing was when the television and national papers picked it up.

My one great consolation was that I knew they really hadn't got anything on me, even though they were convinced that they had. The Interim Chief Executive (Mrs Jacqueline Kelly) was exultant. The following morning she crowed to one of my consultant anaesthetist colleagues, "*I've got him now!*"[18]

The medical director also thought that they had *got me.* Evidently my colleagues were *outraged at the level of response to my alleged misdemeanour*[19] and the Quisling (medical director) had told one of my friends and colleagues who protested to him that the management had no alternative, because "*JRY has broken the law!*"[20] Obviously he had not heard of the basic premise of British law about one being innocent until proven guilty.

So they both thought they had got me.

But they certainly had not.

My lawyer told me to make careful notes of all that was said by everybody. He also reassured me that I had absolutely nothing to worry about with respect to my conduct even with the new amendment to the Race Relations Law. I was further comforted when a judge, whom I knew socially rang me to say that there was no legal case to answer and that the whole thing would be laughable if it wasn't costing the NHS so much. Interestingly my brother (the retired police officer, whose fault it all was) thought it all highly amusing and told me that I had no worries at all of having broken the law. When I went to the police station in Barnstaple to make my statement about the alleged incident, the police officer actually said that he thought that "*someone at the hospital had it in for me*." I told him that I could see why he was a detective and we both laughed. But I wrote it down.

Next to investigate the matter was the Race Relations Board. Their spokesman had already been on local television, saying how pleased they were that the hospital had not failed to report someone *so senior*. I got the distinct impression that they too were clearly sharpening their knives for the kill. I was told that the RRB team, who visited the hospital, was led by a bossy unpleasant Asian lady, but I have to say that I did not find her so; I never even met her or indeed any of her team. The officious lady got short shrift from my personal secretary, who is married to a Turk and as such has a Turkish surname. Anthea Salihoglu was asked if I had any problems with the fact that my PA did not have an English surname. It's almost unbelievable but that is what she asked her. Anthea quickly retorted that far from having problems with it, I had acted as her husband's sponsor, when he had applied for British citizenship!

In the end, after talking to all the witnesses, they decided that they did not want to interview me because there was clearly no evidence that I had acted in a racist manner or indeed was a racist. What was significant however was the fact that they asked all the females whom I worked with about whether or not I had sexually harassed them. One 65-year-old nurse on the ward was tickled pink by this and said that sadly the doctors had stopped pinching her bottom years ago. I did wonder why they should take it on themselves to try and dig dirt on me in this manner (but I wrote it all down to add to the contemporaneous report, which I send to my lawyer).

Dear reader, you might well consider that having been exonerated by the Devon and Cornwall Constabulary and the Race Relations Board from not only racism, but also sexual harassment at work, that that would be an end of it. I am sure that you would also be forgiven if you thought that any persistence in this campaign against your author must be driven by vindictiveness, spitefulness and malice. That however is precisely what the Stasi did. They continued in their doggedness to discredit me and insisted that I be the subject of a disciplinary tribunal for racism. This however was not to be until November (five months after I had been originally suspended).

Do not forget however that whilst the Stasi Control Freaks are gloating over their nasty few moments of outrageous power, the cost to the taxpayer is enormous. The person suspended is kept on full pay, for which no work is done. His or her work must be done by a locum at an even higher rate of pay and all because of spite. Some poor doctors go into a state of deep depression and quite a few on record find it all too much and commit suicide. The whole business of suspension, which the Stasi prefer to call *exclusion*, is contrary to not only the European Convention but also the United Nations Universal Declaration of Human Rights.[r] Suspended doctors, on the whole, have not challenged this exclusion and there are some terrible stories of how this tyranny has affected some very vulnerable colleagues. An extreme example was the case of a doctor who (presumably because of all the stress of his suspension) was himself admitted to the intensive care unit of the hospital as a patient. He was told to remove himself *as he was an embarrassment to the hospital*.[21] Another doctor was prevented from visiting his dying wife. In a third case, the wife appealed to the Community Health Council that her husband should have visiting rights in the event of her illness worsening. By the time this permission came, she was dead.

---

[r] For a full exploration of illegality of NHS suspension see YOUNG, JR et al. (2008)

When I was suspended, the hospital press office rushed to point out on the front page of the local newspaper that *suspension is a neutral act,*[22]

Neutral act, my foot!

In 2007, the House of Lords[s] pronounced that suspensions are clearly not a neutral act. In the House of Commons,[t] no less a person than the Secretary of State for Health has also said that suspension is not a neutral act. In fact he went so far as to describe it as "*a deeply hostile act.*"(Milburn 1995)[23] At the time, he was supported in this description by Dr Liam Donaldson,[24] later to become "*Drain Sniffer*" Donaldson, the Chief Medical Officer and as a consequence of this Sir Liam Donaldson.

OUT OF AFRICA

We carry within us the wonders we seek without us:
There is all Africa and her prodigies in us.
Sir Thomas Browne (1643) *Religio Medici.*[u]

Whilst I was on what is generally now called *Gardening Leave,* I was wonderfully gratified by all the support I received from friends and colleagues in North Devon, which actually is quite a parochial area, during what could have been a very stressful time. The telephone never stopped ringing and the postman used to joke about the full mailbag he brought round to the house every day for at least a couple of weeks. The local newspapers had supporting letters for ten consecutive weeks and not one of them condemnatory.[25,26,27]

---

[s] Perhaps any American readers can be forgiven for failing to appreciate that the House of Lords is the Highest Court (Supreme Judiciary) in the United Kingdom of Great Britain and Northern Ireland. Failure to know this cannot however be given as an excuse by the Stasi.

[t] The *House of Commons* is the *Lower house* of the Parliament of the United Kingdom. Parliament also includes the *Sovereign* and the *Upper house,* the *House of Lords*; the House of Commons is at present the dominant branch.

[u] *Religio Medici (The Religion of a Doctor)* is a book by a newly qualified mediaeval physician. It was published without the author's knowledge or consent and in its day, was a European best-seller.

I think the best letter I got was from a surgeon in Africa, asking me to resign and go and work there with him. "*That would make a good local headline!*" he said. The papers were full of sympathetic letters from all over the world. I suppose they all found out about it from stories in the national newspapers. The *Daily Mail* in typical style ran the headline, *Top Surgeon Sent Home in Jungle Bunny Race Row.*[28] They got all their details of the story completely wrong too.

There was also the hate mail, usually from the loony left, but I can't honestly say it ever got to me. I also received quite a lot of congratulatories from the BNP and the extreme right. (Indeed it was about the only time that my dear mother-in-law said anything good about me!) Anyway, I was lucky in that I have a resilient character (and of course, I had had the benefit of counselling!) One wonders what to do with all the spare time. It can go on for years and they specifically tell you that you must not go away. It is a sort of house arrest which they try to impose and some of their more diffident victims might even take notice of it (despite the fact it too is completely unlawful). The longest two cases of doctors being suspended were similar in length. Both were prevented from practicing their profession for over ten years (both without any charges being brought against them, and on full pay).[29] It is perhaps significant that they were both female.

Although I was fully aware of the unfairness of the Stasi tribunal system, I think that the whole of this time I never had any real worries about my eventual reinstatement. The tribunals in my opinion are a complete travesty of justice. They are a sort of hybrid between *Alice in Wonderland*, Gilbert and Sullivan and Kafka. The Stasi fill every rôle in these kangaroo courts[v] except that of the accused. They are the accusers, the investigators, the prosecutors, the judge, the jury and the Court of Appeal. I believe they rigged one of the judges in my case. He was brought in (as a substitute) at the last minute. Of course I complained about him, but he denied he had any

---

[v] To *kangaroo* means *to convict on false evidence.* The term *kangaroo court* became used in early 20th century England when trade unions would unfairly pillory strike-breakers or *blacklegs.*

previous knowledge of me, nothing was done and my lawyer (for whom I had to pay) advised me at this late stage to accept him.

During the period, whilst I was waiting for the sham trial, I am such a racist, that one evening I went to a concert of Nigerian music. It was while I was listening to the African tunes that I got the good idea of acquiring some Nigerian robes to wear for my attendance. Luckily my son lived in Hackney at the time and he was able to procure me just what I wanted from Hackney market. I sent him £25 by post the weekend before the hearing. He said he had cursed me wandering round the market in the rain, but when he saw the colourful photo on the front page of the newspaper, it had definitely all been worthwhile. He particularly liked the caption, *Out of Africa.*[30] Sadly I have a pal, who is a Nigerian lawyer and he really wanted to come with me, but he had another case up north at the time. It was a bit of a pity because he thought it all a wonderful hoot and the plan was for us both to wear brightly coloured bubas and cause a bit of a stir, when we arrived. As it was I arrived wearing my robes, but didn't keep them on all the time because they were rather hot. (My staid English lawyer would not even countenance wearing them himself – and even advised me against it).

The tribunal's findings were that I had not acted in a racist manner, but that I should never have even mentioned those awful words, *'Jungle Bunny'* on NHS premises. (Nay, perish the thought!) The picture on the front page of the paper made me into something of a local folk hero, which was rather nice and I did not have to buy myself a beer when I went into local pubs for many weeks to come. I received umpteen cuddly bunny rabbits and framed pictures of rabbits and hares to put in my consulting room .The general opinion in our little community was that the Stasi had scored a very definite own goal.

As the mock trial (AKA tribunal proceedings) drew to an end, I was told in a patronising and didactic manner that this was now definitely the end of the matter – that I *must forget about it and draw a line underneath it.* That *drawing a line* bit is pure Management Speak. I had no intention however of ever forgiving them, of forgetting about it, or even drawing a metaphorical line. I looked the head of the kangaroo court in the eye and summoned up my best Churchillian voice and answered, *"This is not the end. This is not even the beginning of the end. But it is perhaps the end of the beginning."*[w]

Perhaps this book is the end.

COCK–UP CLUB AND THE GMC

A wise man will learn from another's mistakes;
But a fool never learns from his own.
Motto of the Mackenzie Club, Durrants, London.

There once used to be a very exclusive and rather small club, made up of well-known and highly respected specialist surgeons who met once a year just before Christmas somewhere in Harley Street.[x] It was affectionately known by the members as the *Cock-up Club* and membership was strictly by invitation only. The aim of this élite group was to learn from each other's mistakes.

The club was inspired by a famous surgeon from the Victorian era, Sir Morell Mackenzie, the leading throat specialist of his time, who was involved in a bitter international controversy over the death of the Kaiser, Queen Victoria's grandson (at that time the Crown Prince of Germany) who had been stricken with a serious throat disease in May 1887. So great was Mackenzie's reputation in Europe, that he was specially summoned to attend him. Crown Prince Frederick's illness had been diagnosed by the German specialists as throat cancer and he had been told that the only treatment was surgery. Mackenzie disagreed and insisted that the disease was not demonstrably cancerous and therefore that a dangerous operation was unnecessary. Ironically he had based his opinion absolutely on a biopsy report made by the

---

[w] Sir Winston Churchill said this about the Battle of El Alamein in a speech at the Mansion House on the 10th of November 1942. It was often repeated by my father, who fought at El Alamein.

[x] Harley Street is a street in the City of Westminster in London, England which has been noted since the 19th century for its large number of private specialists in medicine and surgery.

world-renowned German pathologist Rudolf Virchow. It was clearly a difficult case with great political implications. As it was, Morell Mackenzie's opinion was followed: the Crown Prince went to England, under his treatment, and was present at the Jubilee celebrations in June. By November, however, the imperial voice-box had become worse and further examination now confirmed it as cancer. Frederick became Kaiser Frederick III of Germany, but died the following year. A bitter international controversy over his death erupted between Mackenzie and the German doctors.

Whose mistake was it?

All this talk nowadays about evidence-based medicine deals with the interpretation of diagnostic test results. That is just what Mackenzie did. Was the fault therefore the English surgeon's or the German pathologist's? Morell Mackenzie was pilloried for it by the German medical world. They published an account of the illness, vilifying Mackenzie, who promptly replied by writing a best-selling book, entitled *The Fatal Illness of Frederick the Noble* (1888).[y] It was so successful that the publication then earned poor old Sir Morell censure from the Royal College of Surgeons, since in those days it could have been considered as advertising. .

Mackenzie had acted in good faith for his patient, believing the findings of the most eminent pathologist in the world at the time, Professor Rudolf Virchow. Over the years, the *Cock-up Club* became known as the Mackenzie Meeting. Members wore ties with (garish) representations of the unfortunate British physician and solid silver cuff-links, showing the thumbs-down sign.[z]

Most presentations at medical meetings are by physicians and surgeons anxious to let their colleagues know just how

---

[y] This surprisingly interesting and readable book is still available (reproduced Nabu Press 2011; ISBN: 1178639398) There is even a free Google version on the internet! I can wholeheartedly recommend it. The original edition was, somewhat unbelievably a blockbuster and sold thousands of copies (more than James Bond novels!)

[z] It is assumed that "thumbs down" was the signal that a defeated gladiator should be condemned to death; "thumbs up", that he should be spared.

bright they are and how excellent at their art. They often present their own new operations or ideas and go on to show just what an outstanding contribution they have made. These presentations are usually thinly disguised attempts at self-aggrandisement.

Nothing could have possibly been further from the truth with cases presented by the members of the Cock-up Club. Members present the worst case they have had during that year. They give details of their biggest "cock-up" and then tell the other members just how, why and where they went wrong. Usually like Mackenzie they had acted in best faith, but luck had run against them and their judgement had been proven wrong.

Members of this privileged society needed to be extremely carefully selected. One black ball excluded a potential candidate for admission. It would be no good having anyone amongst them who was so egotistical that he couldn't admit to being occasionally infallible: that's the whole point. Like the Order of the Garter, there were only thirteen surgeons allowed to be members at any one time. When one retired, another was admitted.

Even if this club were still in existence, it would be proscribed by the General Medical Council. Doctors do not make mistakes. Perish the very thought! And if they do and one of their colleagues gets to hear about it, he then has an absolute duty, which exceeds his every other duty to report that mistake to the GMC. Now there's a thing!

BACK TO PLASTERS, PILLS AND OINTMENT BOXES[aa]

It is easy to get a thousand prescriptions but hard to get one single remedy.
Chinese Proverb

[aa] This is part of a review in *Blackwoods Edinburgh Magazine*, August 1818 of John Keats's wonderful poem, *Endymion* by the curmudgeonly Scottish critic, John Gibson Lockhart. It alludes to Keats training as a medical student, which he gave up to be a poet. He wrote, *it is a better and wiser thing to be a starved apothecary than a starved poet; so back to the shop, Mr John, back to plasters, pills and ointment boxes.*

When I was a lad, pharmacists[bb] were a separate but honourable profession who were able to make up medicines and drugs as and when required. I now pull the leg of the pharmacy department when I 'phone them by asking if I am through to the grocery department.[cc] A Canadian pal recently upset them by saying, *"A barmaid is just a pharmacist with a limited inventory."*

When I asked the Chief Pharmacist at the hospital where I work, what was the worst aspect of the *NewSchool* changes to his profession, somewhat predictably, he told me the old, old story. In the past you were allowed to get on with your job; you prepared medicines and you enjoyed your work. You (rightly) felt that you were a valued and important part of the team. Now you spend half your time filling in forms to say that you are doing things according to the Standing Operative Pharmacy Procedures and you are positively never allowed to make anything.

He gave me an illustrative example. Only a few years ago some poor little child on the children's ward had a high temperature and needed some medicine to bring her fever down. Aspirin is an exceptionally good drug for doing this and was formerly the treatment of choice. Nowadays it is not used because of a tenuous and unproven[31] link with an exceedingly rare condition called Reye's syndrome. Unfortunately the little girl in question had a sore throat and could neither swallow tablets nor suspension. The pharmacy staff was therefore asked if they could provide aspirin as a suppository.[dd] Of course, they

---

[bb] Although the term *"chemist"* became popular in the 20th century, the name *pharmacy* is much older and is in fact used by Chaucer, in *The Knight's Tale* (written around 1386) when he describes a medical preparation of plants as *"farmacies of herbs"*.

[cc] Apothecaries, who have never been chemists or pharmacists, split from the Guild of Grocers in 1617. Up until then the grocers' trade included crude drugs and prepared medicines. The grocers have had their own guild in the City of London since the 13th century.

[dd] The word *suppository* is from the Latin verb, *supponere, to place underneath*. Interestingly, suppositories are not very popular in UK, in

immediately acceded and rose to the occasion; they ground the aspirin tablets into a powder and then mixed them with a gelatine base to form them into small bullet-shaped[ee] suppositories. These quickly[32] had the required effect and brought the child's temperature back down to normal. The pharmacy team felt rightly pleased that they had been able to help; they felt job satisfaction and knew that their efforts in this simple though valuable task had really helped in the treatment of this sick child. Sadly this could never happen in our wonderful *NewSchool* (*Improved*) hospital. These highly trained professionals would now not be allowed to make a suppository (or anything else).

How does that make them feel? There is little wonder that like everybody else in the hospital, the pharmacists do not feel valued.

This ridiculous situation evidently arose from a knee-jerk reaction to a tragic incident which occurred in Boots Chemist, Runcorn where peppermint gripe water twenty times too strong was dispensed by mistake for a baby who then died.[33]

I can remember old Mr. Wood, the local *OldSchool* pharmacist in Yorkshire, to whom patients would go for medical advice before bothering the doctor. He was actually able to *make* pills and potions from the raw ingredients. When I was a schoolboy, he showed me how he made pills with a very old white tile and a special brass *pill machine*. I remember that he told me *pills* are different to *tablets*, because they are spherical and not cylindrical. He said that pills were much more special than tablets. I don't know what he would have thought to capsules! In the days before Mr Wood's

---

contrast with France, where they are surprisingly well-liked. The reader is left to draw his own conclusions.

[ee] The bullet or torpedo shape of the suppository was investigated in 1991 and it was found somewhat surprisingly that these medications worked more effectively if the blunt end was inserted first, rather than the generally used mode of inserting the tapered end first. This conclusion was reached because blunt end first suppositories were found to travel further up the colon as a *mechanical consequence of the natural actions of the bowel's muscular structure and the rectal configuration.*

"Chemist's Shop," pills were even more special. For the really rich patient, the little balls would then be coated with gold leaf! This didn't really make the tablet more efficacious – in fact quite the reverse; gold is inert in the gut and prevented the absorption of the drug. It did however make the faeces sparkle.

I often wonder why they take such a long time nowadays *making up a prescription*, when all they have to do is reach something down from a shelf and stick a label on it. It is even easier than this at the *NewSchool* hospital, where there is a huge electrically operated revolving set of shelves, so that nobody has to stretch to get a box down. In the past, the place was full of huge coloured glass bottles of medicine, from which smaller blue, brown and green glass bottles were filled with nostrums through different sized glass funnels. *Old School* Pharmacists would be counting out tablets (and sometimes even pills!) in metal counting trays. They would be making ointments and mixing powders into solutions.

Sadly they are no longer trusted to do this!

I am not suggesting for one minute that pharmacology has not improved massively in recent years. Paradoxically, as the number of hugely expensive (and effective) new drugs has increased, many cheaper drugs and effective but simple medications have been lost. Gentian violet, for example is a wonderful treatment for athlete's foot, nappy rash, ringworm and thrush. Acriflavine, Mercurochrome, Whitfield's Ointment and Castellani's Paint are other excellent cures for simple disorders and skin infections. A young man visiting my home (a suitor to one of my daughters) on hearing that I had worked as an army doctor for many years asked if I would look at his foot. It was really foul and stinking; very sore and certainly much worse than any case of athlete's foot I had ever seen in Her Majesty's Land Force. I rooted around and eventually found a dusty old brown bottle with the faded label, *Crystal Violet Paint* (AKA Gentian Violet). The poor lad had been putting expensive creams between his toes for over six months. He had even been taking tablets – all to no effect. In four days, the Gentian violet had cured him! His feet were so dry, pink and healthy again that he went on to marry my youngest daughter.

It was especially good for *impetigo*[ff] – an infectious condition of the skin, which school children would often get. Impetigo looked pretty awful with nasty weeping pustules all over the face. The application of Gentian Violet did not do much to improve the cosmetic appearance; in fact painting all the bright red pimples lurid purple added to the effect of making the poor child appear a bit more like some sort of leper. This gave an added public health benefit of making all the other children avoid the poor wretched sufferer like the plague. This was certainly a good thing because impetigo is highly contagious and spreads through a classroom like wildfire. It has been removed from the British approved drug list, because evidently if it is fed by the kilogram to rats, it eventually gives them colonic cancer. I am told however that it is still used in France to cure babies of oral thrush.

Another excellent nostrum which is now impossible to get hold of is *Ammoniated Tincture of Strychnine and Quinine*. Donald, the *OldSchool* pharmacist next-door to the GP surgery where I once worked used to make it up when I was a GP. It was exceptionally good in the treatment of night cramps and was far more efficacious than ordinary quinine tablets.[gg] The very definite disadvantage is that it took poor old Donald two days (yes, two days!) to prepare.

A GRANNY IN THE GUTTER

Defend me therefore, common sense, say I,
From reveries so airy, from the toil
Of dropping buckets into empty wells
And growing old in drawing nothing up.
William Cowper. *The Task.* III,187. (1785)

What about the case of the poor old grandma in the gutter? Perhaps this tale underlines best how far we have lost our way

---

[ff] In Latin the word simply means *an attack*!

[gg] An old Irish lady, a friend of my Granny, used to say that you would never stop getting the cramps unless you turned your slippers upside down before getting into bed; *To be sure, it stops the Little People from getting into them – and it's them what gives you the cramps!*

from the simple old-fashioned compassion which you could find in any *OldSchool* hospital in the United Kingdom.

It wasn't all that long ago that the St John Ambulance responded to all emergency medical calls and this continued until long after the inception of the NHS. In North Devon it provided this excellent and yeoman service until 1974. I have been a member of the St John since I was a junior doctor and I can remember the old timers reminiscing about when they used to have to attend car crashes, suicides and other gory situations. They used to do all the work the paramedics do now. They were of course excellent first-aiders and did all of this ambulance work on a purely voluntary basis. When I was a little lad and burst my appendix, I can remember the old black and white ambulance with the Maltese Cross on its side and the two St John volunteers in their black uniforms with their white bags. It was a terrible winter and they couldn't get the ambulance to my parents' house. It got stuck in the snow a few hundred yards down the road so they had to leave it there and carry me on a stretcher wrapped in a bright red blankets through deep snow back to the wagon. The dedication and humanity of these two voluntary *OldSchool* ambulance men contrasts bleakly with the story of the poor old lady below.

An 81-year-old old lady slipped and fell over in the rain outside the hospital in Burnley, Lancashire, in the car park just outside the casualty department.[34] She had cuts and bruises on her face and also her legs, shoulder and arms, so that and she could not get up. Her granddaughter, who was accompanying her was heavily pregnant and so could not lift the old girl. She rushed inside to tell the receptionists, but although they brought out an umbrella out to her, the poor old soul was left lying in a puddle in the car park, soaking wet. She still could not get off the ground. They said that no doctors were available to come outside and check on her and that they must dial 999 for an ambulance. They did not think of sending a nurse.

Consequently an ambulance was dispatched from another hospital at Altham seven miles away. It arrived some 30 minutes later, and the paramedics (NB not doctors) merely drove the old lady 300 yards round the corner to the hospital's

A&E unit. Her heavily pregnant granddaughter said, "*You would have thought they would have spared a doctor for two minutes rather than wasting all those resources on sending an ambulance. The paramedic literally drove us to the hospital entrance, which I could easily have walked to. The way she was treated is disgusting.*" Things didn't get much better when she finally got into the hospital. She eventually went home five hours afterwards still wearing her drenching wet clothes.

A couple of years ago my younger son decided to hold the evening shenanigans part of his wedding on a boat in Poole harbour. There was a traditional jazz band on board and it was a very pleasant evening. We went for a sail round the Needles. All went extremely well until we got back to the quay. From the boat, we could see a drunken couple on the dockside and then to our horror, the woman (fully clothed) jumped into the water! Then the man jumped in after her. My other son managed to get the woman out but she was drenching wet, blind drunk, possibly a bit stoned and shivering. I dialed 999 and then had the devil's own job trying to get an ambulance to come to this pathetic lady. Not only was she going into a state of hypothermia, but all cases of attempted suicide should definitely be sent to hospital (before they make a better job of a second attempt). The 999 lady was asking me what seemed like an irrelevant catechism of questions and I managed to keep my sang-froid, until she asked me if the woman who my son had just fished out of the harbour was armed. At this point I asked for the 999 lady's name and told her that I was a consultant surgeon and that I had not made a body search of my patient, but needed to go back to her immediately. She was not best pleased and insisted that I go on answering her seemingly infinite list of questions. I hung up and the ambulance came.

What has happened to common sense and compassion?

Has anything in the NHS actually got better or is it like my father said, *all change is for the worse*?

REFERENCES

[1], WORTH, Jennifer (2002) *Call the Midwife. A True Story of the East End in the 1950s.* Phoenix, London.

[2], MOIR, Jan (2012) *GPs visited at night. Nurses knew your name. Is this why a series about Fifties midwives has struck such a nerve?* Daily Mail. 21st February.

[3]. COOPER, Charlie. *(2013) NHS watchdog covered-up scandal at hospital where eight babies died of neglect.* The Independent 19 June.

[4]. RUSSELL, Vivienne (2013) *CQC apologises for Morecambe Bay failures.*
Public Finance. 19 June.

[5]. COHEN, Tamara; BROWN, Larisa (2013) *Care Home covered up Neglect that Killed five.* Daily Mail. 19 October, p.6.

[6]. DAILY TELEGRAPH (2012) *Reform the regulators.* Leader. Aug 2012.

[7.] SIDDIQUE, Haroon (2013) *NHS regulator 'not fit for purpose' by maternity deaths.* The Guardian. 19th June

[8]. Personal communication (2013) Iain McKenzie.

[9]. BBC 6 o' Clock News 15 Mar 2012.

[10]. DEWAR, HA (1978) *The hospital nurse after Salmon and Briggs.* Jour.Roy.Soc.Med.Vol.71.399.

[11]. *Ibid.*

[12]. LEE POTTER, J. (1997) *A Damn Bad Business.* Gollancz, London. p31.

[13]. Griffiths R. *NHS Management Inquiry Report.* HMSO, 1983.

[14]. JARMAN, Brian (2012) *When Managers Rule.* Brit.Med.J 345. 1.

[15]. *Ibid.*

[16]. Personal communication, (2007) Recorded at the time on my contemporaneous record of events.

[17]. COURTENAY, Catherine (2007) *ENT Surgeon is suspended.*
North Devon Journal. 21st Jun. p. 1

[18]. Personal communication, (2007) Recorded at the time on my contemporaneous record of events (evidently took place on the back stairs outside the Intensive Care Unit).CJC/JRY

[19]. Personal communication, (2007) RAG/JRY/SJE

[20]. Personal communication, (2007) SJE/JRY/SO'K

[21]. YOUNG, JR et al. (2008) *The Hospital Revolution.* Metro. London. Page 190.

[22]. North Devon Journal 21 June 2007 p. 1.

[23]. Milburn, A. (1995) *The Suspension of Dr O'Connell.* Committee of Public Accounts Report No. 40. London. HMSO

[24]. Donaldson, L.J. (1994) *Doctors with problems in an NHS work force.* Brit.Med.J. 308: 1277-1282

[25]. NORTH DEVON JOURNAL (2007) *Respect and Support Riddington Young.*

28 Jun.p38.

[26]. NORTH DEVON JOURNAL (2007) *Support for racism row doctor keeps coming.* 5 Jul. p46.

[27]. NORTH DEVON JOURNAL (2007) *Riddington Young Support floods in.* 12 Jul. p46

[28]. SALKELD, Luke, (2007) *Top Surgeon Sent Home Over Jungle Bunny Slur.*
Daily Mail. 22nd June. page 37.

[29]. YOUNG, JR et al. (2008) *The Hospital Revolution.* Metro. London. Page 185.

[30]. COURTENAY, Catherine (2007) *Surgeon cuts a dash in his African robes at racism complaint hearing.* North Devon Journal. 29th Nov. pp. 1,4,44.

[31]. ORLOWSKI J.P.; HANHAN U.A.; FIALLOS M.R. (2002) *Is Aspirin a Cause of Reye's Syndrome? A Case Against.* Drug Safety, Volume 25, Number 4, , pp. 225-231(7)

[32]. ABD-EL-MAEBOUD, K. H. et al. (1991) *Rectal suppository: commonsense and mode of insertion.* The Lancet 338 (8770): 798–800.

[33]. BBC NEWS (2000) *Chemists fined after baby death.* http://news.bbc.co.uk/1/hi/health/660055.stm. Wednesday, 1 March, 2000

[34]. DAILY MAIL REPORTER (2012) *Grandma in the gutter.* Daily Mail 29 Sep. p 58.

CHAPTER 2

MEDICAL SCHOOL AND BEYOND

Before you learn anything else, learn how to behave properly.

I once saw this written outside the University in Hanoi, elaborately carved above the door.[a] I was told that this aphorism of Confucius is always prominently displayed near the entrance of any Centres of Learning in that country. I struck me then that we have a lot to learn from the inscrutable Orientals.

IN A NUTSHELL; OldSchool vs. NewSchool:
OldSchool **Medical Education:** Medicine was the hardest University course to get onto and the going was very gruelling. This meant that the students felt they had achieved a lot if they finished it. Many fell by the wayside and the attrition rate was high. The first year after qualification was even more challenging and it was commonplace to work over 80 hours a week. Experience of course was the reward for this and at the end, doctors were all fully prepared and fit for purpose. There was a full and marvellous social life in the hospital, which was a much happier place to work and live.
NewSchool **Medical Education:** Medicine is still the hardest course to be accepted onto, but the syllabus has been emasculated and fewer drop out. Owing to the European guidelines for lorry drivers being misinterpreted by the Stasi, housemen (now called F1 doctors) take twice as long to gain experience

---

[a] It was of course in Vietnamese, but unlike everybody else in Indo-China, the Vietnamese use the Roman alphabet (a valuable legacy from the French).

and even then are not as experienced as their predecessors. There is no longer a wonderful social life associated with the hospital and "residents" have to pay £7,000 a year for their hospital flat.

OLD SCHOOL MEDICAL EDUCATION

I hear and I forget.
I see and I remember.
I do and I understand.
Confucius.[b] (fl. 450 BC)

Getting a place at a British medical school used to be extremely difficult. It is still (thankfully for the British public) not too easy. Indeed, it is more difficult to get onto a medical course[c] than any other. It remains the first serious hurdle to overcome for anyone who wishes to become a doctor.[d] This is another one of those self-evident facts that are now often conveniently forgotten by hospital workers without a medical qualification themselves. A far greater stumbling block to obtaining that qualification however, came once you had got in.

The *OldSchool* medical education started with the pre-clinical years. This was the most harrowing part of your preparation to become a doctor. For the majority of students, it lasted for about eighteen months and this was all before you actually went into a hospital. The word *clinical* is from the Greek word *cline* (κλίνη) meaning *bed*. *OldSchool* nursing education was different. Nursing students needed to have a good basic education, but certainly never needed to go to

---

[b] This is from the *Analects of Confucius*; these are a selection of sayings and ideas attributed to the Chinese philosopher Confucius (551 - 479 BC), traditionally believed to have been written by Confucius' followers.

[c] This includes medicine, dentistry and veterinary sciences, but it does NOT include nursing, audiology, chiropody (podiatrics), physiotherapy, radiology, dietetics or electrocardiogaphy.

[d] It used to be more difficult to get into *all* veterinary schools than *most* UK medical schools is a fact often quoted by vets' wives (to doctors' wives), but they conveniently miss out the qualifying adjectives.

university. It was never perceived as an academic vocation by either the *OldSchool* nurses themselves or the laity. To get into a School of Nursing, the requirement was 'O' level (which was the old name for GCSEs) Maths and English (which was the same for cadets to the police force.[e])

Almost all medical schools insisted on a personal interview. This was an excellent idea but it is massively frowned upon by the politically correct *NewSchool* educationalists as élitist. One of the chaps on the interviewing panel might have known your dad – or one of the old goats on the selection board might fancy one of the young girls with the large breasts – or one of them might be from Scotland and appreciate the fact that you too have a Scots accent – or whatever. Of course all this PC claptrap is nowhere near as important as actually being able to talk to someone, who you would then be able to assess their interpersonal skills and ability to communicate in a harrowing situation (after all, an interview is a most difficult predicament to be in). There is no better way to be able to assess a candidate's suitability than by interview. I believe that if they cannot communicate with a member of the interviewing panel they have just met in a fraught situation, then they probably will not be a very good doctor.

The other important aspect, which an interview brought to light was whether or not the candidate was a good all-rounder. I mean by this whether or not one had outside interests other than biochemistry and science. The *OldSchool* medical school candidate was far more likely to be selected in a competitive field if say he was particularly good at sport or music. I don't think it is any exaggeration to say that in the past, most doctors would be able to play a musical instrument and have a reasonable fluency in at least one European language.

The value of a classical education is now disregarded, but there is little doubt from reading a scholarly paper in an old Lancet that the standard and style of written English prose is light years ahead of a stultifying contemporary article in the

---

[e] *NewSchool* now call it police *service. but for some reason the chaps at the airport are called the Border Force.*

British Medical Journal. The *OldSchool* doctors had a much better general knowledge too. Let me give you an example. My friend and colleague, another consultant surgeon (who plays the cornet in a brass band and speaks reasonable French) was talking to a group of twelve medical students from Birmingham Medical School in 2013. He mentioned Vaughan Williams.[f] They looked a bit puzzled and it transpired that not one of the twelve knew who he was. One of them then asked if he was a pharmacognoscist, who had written a review article on antihypertensive drugs.

After you passed the interview and got into medical school, things got even more fraught.

DISSECTION OF THE CADAVER
Anatomy is destiny.
Sigmund Freud, *Collected Writings*. (1924) vol.5.

For the medical students, the *Baptism of Fire*[g] was that unforgettable very first morning, when you went through the doors of the Human Anatomy Dissecting Room and started to learn the anatomy of the body by painstaking and meticulous dissection of the human cadaver. One of the worst things I remember about it was the overwhelming eye-searing fumes of formalin, which were used to preserve the cadavers and prevent them putrefying. They hit you in the face like a shovel. They made a lot of the students start to wheeze. Going into the dissecting room was a little bit like going into the CS gas chamber in the army training course; the fumes just suddenly hit you. They burned your eyes, your nose and your throat and lungs.

Some of the more squeamish girls told me they found it all rather emotionally harrowing. Being suddenly placed in a

[f] For the benefit of any Americans or other colonials still struggling with this book, Ralph Vaughan Williams was the dominant British composer of the 20th century and the founder of the nationalist movement in English music.
[g] Properly this was applied to martyrdom, but the term became used for a soldier's first experience of battle and then any first experience of something particularly harrowing or dangerous.

hostile chemical environment was bad enough, but in addition to this, there were twenty dead naked bodies (most of them male) all lying eerily still on white ceramic tables with tags on their ears (like those worn by cattle). A lot of us had never seen a corpse before and so it came as a bit of a shock to see quite so many all at once. Now that medical students don't attend the anatomy dissecting room from day one, they don't of course have such immediate exposure to cadavers. I could hardly believe my ears the other day when I was told that one of the *NewSchool* medical students at the hospital had asked if he could leave the clinic early because he had to go for a counselling session because he had seen his first dead body! At first I thought that the lad had chosen the wrong profession and that he should be advised to leave medicine immediately. Then I was told that it was not because he personally felt that he needed this psychological support in such a dire situation. It was the *NewSchool* touchy-feely university medical course. After all, how could a student of medicine be expected to foresee that part of the job of being a doctor would include looking at dead bodies?

The dress code in the old Dissecting Room was strict; jeans were absolutely forbidden. The young men wore a collar and tie. This was not just because *OldSchool* doctors should dress and act like *ladies and gentlemen,* but as a very significant mark of respect to those noble fellow members of society who had given their bodies to anatomical science. The girls of course in the sixties wore skirts[h].

I remember that one of the girls in the year fainted (and we all got a view of her knickers). We kept reminding the poor girl of both these facts for the next five years. Another lady medical student became vegetarian for a couple of months. Another lass, who had just left home in London to live in digs in Sheffield, said that when she got back to her lodgings, she had to move her human skull (we all had to purchase a real human skeleton as part of our essential study of the bones) out of her bedroom before she could get to sleep.

---

[h] And one or two were berated (amazingly by male lecturers) for wearing mini-skirts!

Whilst on the ticklish subject of gender, it should be added that (rightly or wrongly), there was a statutory 20% quota of female medical students at Sheffield University Medical School and in 1965, this was considered an enlightened and very high number of ladies. There were 80 students in the year (and therefore 60 men and 20 women). This has now completely reversed and it will not be long (2017) before there are expected to be more female doctors than male.[35]

There is no better way of learning the structure of the body than by painstakingly dissecting it yourself. It must be conceded however that anatomical dissection (even of a dogfish) is a skill which is not quick or easy to learn and if you haven't striven long enough to acquire the knack, you don't get the full benefit from your sessions with the cadaver. Some students seem to have been born with two left hands and no amount of dissection practice seems to make them any better. (Or is it because they have neither the patience nor the motivation?) With the decrease in availability of human cadavers donated to anatomy departments, there has been an increase in the use of *prosection*. This is when students observe an experienced anatomist demonstrate the nerves, blood vessels, nerves and organs, as he expertly lays them open to view. The ideal of course is to watch a prosection and then go away and do it for yourself.

Not only the declining number of people in this country leaving their bodies to medical education, but also the soaring costs of human dissection have made modern medical schools look for an alternative (even though there isn't one). Of course, there are virtual reality anatomy computer games. I remember wasting many a happy hour, when I bought a new PC about fifteen years ago. There was a free Boeing 707 flight simulator complete with joy-stick, so I could land a jumbo-jet over and over again in the comfort and safety of my study. It was great fun, but hardly a substitute for the real thing. Most British anatomy departments do have adjuvant computer-based education, but almost all of them continue to use experience with actual cadavers as the foundation of their teaching. I was particularly saddened to hear that the Peninsula medical school, based in Plymouth became the first modern medical school to carry out its anatomy education without dissection and rely entirely on computer-based education. I had been an Honorary Clinical Teacher there for about ten years but have since resigned.

Aside from computers, wonderful new prosections have now become available thanks to the work of the eccentric and brilliant contemporary anatomist, Professor Dr Gunther von Hagens, who always wears a black fedora in homage to his hero, Dr Tulp. Nicolaes Tulp was the teacher wearing the big pointed black hat in Rembrandt's famous picture of the 17th century Amsterdam anatomy lesson. Von Hagens defected from Soviet Poland, when he was still a medical student. He then worked as an anatomist in Heidelberg, where he developed a groundbreaking new process to preserve human bodies, in which the water and fat are removed and replaced by plastic. He calls it plastination. Instead of *OldSchool* real anatomical specimens, which were leathery, greasy and eye-stinging (from formalin preservative), the *NewSchool* plastinated ones can be handled and manipulated and have the great added advantage of not eventually rotting. I was absolutely amazed when I went to his wonderful travelling exhibition (now officially the most popular touring exhibition in the world ever), when it visited Brick Lane. It is called *Body Worlds* and has not only human dissections, but prosected horses, and even a giraffe. They are undoubted works of art and put me in mind of the collection of beautiful wax anatomy models made in the Florence in the eighteenth century, which are now housed in the Josephinum Museum in Vienna.

Von Hagens performed the first public autopsy in the UK in 170 years, wearing his big black hat. It was in a London theatre to a sell-out audience of 500 people. He had been warned by Her Majesty's Inspector of Anatomy that a public autopsy would be an illegal act in the United Kingdom (in contravention of Section 11 of the 1984 Anatomy Act). The show still went on. Police officers attended, but did not interfere and the full dissection of the body went ahead and was completed. No legal proceedings ever took place and the autopsy was later shown on television, which went on to receive the record number of complaints for any programme.[36]

There has long been a feeling among doctors though, that the dissection of the human cadaver is about more than just learning anatomy. I believe that it goes far beyond this. You work on the same body every day for a year, entering every part of it. You look in the very centre of the brain and push your fingers through heart valves and into the chambers of the heart. You develop a strange highly intimate relationship with it. That cadaver, on which you do so much painstaking work, is as it were, your first patient. He or she (usually he) teaches you about respect and humanity. He helps you to come to terms not only with disease and your relationship with future patients, but helps you to keep the right distance away from them and from disease. I think it even starts you developing a healthy philosophy about the inevitability of your own mortality.

I am very sure that a computer will never be able to do this.

LONG HARD GRAFT

A man's grasp should exceed his reach.
Robert Browning (1855) *Andrea del Sarto.*

Long is the way and hard,
That out of Hell leads up to Light.
John Milton. (1667) *Paradise Lost.* (2, 432)

It was not only that anatomy is such a massive and difficult subject, but also that it was an important crisis time in one's life, when one had just made that life changing wrench in one's existence and cut the umbilical cord with home and one's family to come and live a new independent life, either in digs or university college or hall of residence.

And it was not just anatomy; biochemistry was particularly complex and then there were also physiology, bacteriology, psychology, pharmacology and pathology. These were all pure sciences. There was no room for interpretation or discussion. The origin and insertion of the biceps muscle was not a topic open for debate; it is a finite fact. You either knew where it was inserted or you didn't. And of course, you were far more likely to remember it if you had actually painstakingly dissected it out and traced it to the tuberosity on the top end of the forearm bone called the radius[i]. One needed an encyclopaedic brain to "download" all these facts (and in those days you didn't download anyway; computers were in the future; you learned them – committed them to memory).

Every morning for over a year was spent in the Dissecting Room. Dissection is not that easy. It requires a certain manual dexterity which has to be learned and is only acquired by time, diligence and industry. It soon became apparent that the high IQ necessary to get you into medical school is nowhere near enough to get you through it. Much more important than that is the capacity for sheer hard work – late on into the night - and not just one night per week. This ability to *graft* is the real key to becoming a doctor. Added to that is the fact which becomes rapidly apparent – that the vast majority of all this work is quite tediously boring. It is the capability to keep at it, which will get you eventually through. You might happen to be in the top 3% of the community, but you certainly do not need to be of *exceptionally* high intelligence to become a doctor, but you do have to be a hard worker. You will have noticed that I have the greatest of respect for the sayings of Confucius, but I think he got it wrong when he said, '*Choose a job you love, and you will never have to work a day in your life.*' I think I understand the philosophy behind what he says, but this is one occasion where I emphatically disagree with him. Although I love my job and would never be happy doing anything else, I worked exceptionally hard from my first day at medical school until well near my retirement nearly fifty years later.

Stephen Hawking,[j] although considered to be one of the brightest men on the planet could certainly not have made it

---

[i] *Radius* is Latin for the *spoke of a wheel*, which (with the eye of faith) that bone resembles.

[j] Stephen William Hawking, CH, CBE, FRS, FRSA (born 8 January 1942) is a British theoretical physicist and author of *A Brief History of Time*. His significant scientific works to date have been on the Big Bang, the framework of general relativity, and the theoretical prediction that black holes should emit radiation, often called Hawking radiation.

through the nose-grinding medical curriculum; he openly admits to an innate laziness at university.

DEDICATION

Talent is cheap; dedication is expensive. It will cost you your life.
Irving Stone, *The Agony and the Ecstasy.*

The only tyrant I accept in this world is the 'still small voice' within me.
Mahatma Ghandi.[k]

The other requirement is dedication. As quite a senior member of the profession, I am often asked by young people about medicine as a career. I always tell them that there is no greater occupation, but that if they could possibly be content doing absolutely anything else, then it were better that they do not take medicine any further and do whatever else it is that would make them happy. It is such a long stony road to becoming a doctor, that if there is any acceptable alternative for them, they should take it. Both my wife and I are medically qualified and we have five children. Not one of them has followed us into medicine and although we are a bit disappointed, we would never have pushed them into it, because that dedication was not there. They did not have that *burning need* to become doctors, which we both had at their age. The poet, John Keats (who was once a surgical dresser at Guy's Hospital) once said that if it *'comes not as naturally as the Leaves to a tree it had better not come at all.* [l]

---

[k] Ghandi visited UK in August 1931 and at that time shook hands with my grandmother, Lily Young who was a keen member of the Women's Co-operative Party. She described the experience to me as, "*like getting hold of a kipper.*"

[l] John Keats the poet (1795-1821) did say this in a letter to John Taylor in February 1818, but he was referring to poetry rather than surgery. Keats would have almost certainly agreed with the concept however, since it was one day when he was operating on some old lady's head that he realised he was thinking more about a line in a poem he was writing, than the surgical job in hand. He resolved to give up surgery as a profession there and then.

A few years ago, a neighbour came round to my house one evening to ask my advice. He said that he had always wanted to be a doctor, but had *gone into design technology* instead. I listened. He asked how he should best go about becoming a doctor. I knew that he would never really get any further. If he had come to ask me which medical schools were best, or whether or not to try for Oxford or Cambridge, that would have been different. But if he had been really motivated, he would not have needed to come to ask a neighbour how to get into a medical school. Nonetheless, I gave him all the encouragement I could muster and told him that medicine is the noblest of all avocations and that the best medical school was at Sheffield University and that he should write there and ask for an application form. Ten years later, he is still *in design technology (and still lives in a more expensive house than me!)*. He had evidently never written to the medical schools.

Too often nowadays, it is "dedication by proxy" when the motivation comes from the parents rather than the child and a half-hearted student is pushed into a medical career merely so that he can bring status to the family and get a lucrative living. I was once told a joke (by a Jewish fellow medical student) about the young Jewish mother, who was pushing twins in a pram down Golders Green High Street.[m] When an old lady enquired about the health of the twin babies, she was thanked for asking and told that "the lawyer" had a bit of a cold, but that "the doctor" had not yet caught it.[n]

In some countries and cultures where arranged marriages outnumber marriage by love match, a medical degree is seen as a definite advantage in the nuptial stakes. Once the girl is qualified, she doesn't even have to practice; why get her hands dirty? As the United Kingdom becomes more culturally

---

[m] Golders Green is an area in Barnet, London, which is so well known for its high Jewish population, that it is nicknamed *Goldberg's Green* (Cassell's Dictionary of Slang).

[n] In the same vein, a famous Jewish comedian (Henny Youngman) told the joke, *"There is a big controversy on the Jewish view of when life begins. In Jewish tradition, the foetus is not considered viable until it graduates from law school."*

diverse, the percentage of qualified doctors who do not actually practice is getting higher and higher.

Many colleagues (both hospital and GP) have told me quite plainly that they have actively dissuaded their offspring from following in their medical footsteps, because they now feel that the Stasi have made it all so unpleasant and de-professionalised medicine to such an extent that it is no longer the noble vocation, which it once was.

SEE ONE, DO ONE, TEACH ONE

I will respect the hard-won gains of those physicians in whose steps I walk, and gladly share such knowledge as is mine with those who are to follow.[o]
Hippocratic Oath.

When I was a medical student, the process of teaching surgeons was a sort of apprenticeship. It was based on the famous Hippocratic Oath, quoted above (although strictly speaking the original Greek oath was opposed to surgery "*the knife*"). If the surgeon you were working with took a shine to you and thought that you might "have a good pair of hands," he would teach you how to perform surgery. Historically an apprentice was *bound to a master craftsman in order to learn a trade* and this is what used to happen in surgery. One of my bosses at a non-teaching hospital was absolutely wonderful to me. He would spend hours painstakingly teaching me how to do things properly. He had taught me how to take an appendix out and allowed me to get on with eighteen operations, before I even took my final doctors' exams. I was not especially unusual in this respect; any young surgical dresser[p] who showed an interest in the art of surgery was helped in this way.

This is certainly not the case now and I can tell from the look of absolute incredulity that *NewSchool* doctors don't actually believe me when I tell them that I was actively encouraged to perform surgical operations as a medical

---

[o] Hippocratic Oath
[p] a *dresser* is the name formerly given to a medical student during his surgical training.

student. It is not as though I wasn't meticulously supervised. As for the legal aspects, there weren't really any more problems than there are now. The boss was always responsible for his apprentice, whether he was qualified or not. He still is and that is why so many *NewSchool* consultants are suspended by their vindictive Stasi managers, who it appears to me just cannot wait to try and humiliate their betters by suspending them, when one of the juniors makes an occasional (inevitable) mistake.

The problem now for the *NewSchool* trainee surgeons is that they do not get anywhere near enough surgical experience. The fact is of course that this has also become a problem for the public. Their attending surgeon will not have had a fraction of the experience which an *OldSchool* sawbones used to get. I was recently on a shooting holiday in Scotland with a professor of surgery from the London area. He was terribly concerned about this and asked me which year I qualified. When I told him that I became a houseman in 1970, he sighed frustratedly and told me that he had just been on a committee to appoint a new consultant (abdominal) surgeon to a district general hospital in the South West and that he was fairly sure that I (as an ear, nose and throat surgeon) had probably taken out far more appendices[q] through a traditional incision in the lower abdomen than the young man he had just appointed! I have to admit that I developed a feeling of profound unease, when I realised that this is the new generation of surgeons into whose hands I might well fall, when I become old and decrepit and might need a surgical operation.

It is not just the noble art of surgery but the whole of medicine, which has been weakened by this lack of *hands on* experience. As I have become older, I realise the truth of the words of my old professor of medicine. He told us a story about Thomas Sydenham, hailed as the English Hippocrates. He had become known as the best teacher of medicine in England and had eschewed all the old unproven dogma, which had held sway for so many years. He was evidently a

---

[q] *Appendices* is the correct plural word for *appendix,* a Latin word for *something that hangs on.*

wonderful clinical teacher and accepted nothing on face value, unless it could be proved. One of his disciples asked him what he would recommend as the best textbook of medicine. Hitherto the only books were those which had been copied again and again since the time of the ancient Greek father of medicine, Hippocrates who had flourished four hundred years before the birth of Christ and whose dogma were still held to be unassailable. Sydenham[r] smiled and told them they might as well read Cervantes (*Don Quixote*) and that the only real textbook of medicine is *the patient*. The art of medicine was to be properly learned only from its practice; surgery is only likely to be learned from a proper apprenticeship.

I have always been so proud of my Alma Mater, Sheffield Medical School, where the emphasis was always on learning from patients. When I look back at what I have learned in over forty years of medicine, everything is based on clinical practice with actual patients and personal experiences with disease and poorly folk. If I think of tuberculosis or syphilis (now happily both fairly uncommon maladies), I remember actual patients, whom I have examined. I can usually recall their faces and sometimes even their names. This was the basis of how we were taught our skills. I don't really remember things I have read in books. The truth of the matter is that I hardly ever looked at books. What did I need them for? There was an absolute wealth of clinical material in the hospitals. There were brilliant clinical teachers who were so adept at pointing things out so that it would always stay with us. I also remember that when medical students and newly qualified doctors from London medical schools came to Sheffield, they inevitably said how much more exposure to patients we got there than they did in the metropolis. I was recently at a reunion with some colleagues who were in the same year and we were all reminiscing on how lucky we had been to have had such a wonderful and privileged training, which involved so much contact with patients.

---

[r] Interestingly Sydenham was the only great 17th century physician to support Cromwell – the other great medical thinkers, including the medical genius William Harvey, had all been staunch Royalists.

I was so saddened therefore to see in the alumni magazine how the Sheffield Medical School was actually *boasting* about a new Clinical Skills Centre attached to a hospital (which is presumably packed full of real-life patients), where students pretend with a model in a TV studio. It would be funny if it wasn't so soul-destroyingly pathetic. Why are students now denied that essential contact with patients which has been allowed to all their predecessors – from Ancient Greece to just a few years ago? Why have they started to go so badly wrong? They are not allowed to dissect real bodies, they no longer get to see autopsies and now – worse of all – they are being denied access to real human patients!

I recently Googled Peninsula Medical School principally to see if they had mentioned any justification for their anatomy teaching, but also to try and learn about *NewSchool* changes in the training of doctors at medical school. I was absolutely amazed. You had better Google it yourself, because I do not think you will believe me, after my high-minded *OldSchool* ideas above about the dedication and professionalism of medical students. The downloaded brochure didn't even mention the medical course (let alone the innovation of cadaver-free anatomy) but it did boast of *Luxury Student Accomodation* and made particular mention on the first page of *122 Double Beds and one Single Bed!* I could hardly believe it; it went on *En-Suite Showers* and *Free high speed Broadband in every bedroom* and *Flat Screen TV.* There was a map showing how close the (apparently appropriately named) *Jack Rabbit* Pub is to the dental/medical School (their choice of order) and also the proximity of Macdonalds, KFC, Pizza Hut and also Derriford Teaching Hospital.

PROFESSIONALISM
All professions are conspiracies against the laity.
George Bernard Shaw. (1911) *Doctor's Dilemma.*

More than thirty years ago, when I first took on my consultant post at a district general hospital in the South West, I was lumbered with the post of Post-Graduate Tutor for the hospital. It was a bit of a "Muggins[s]" job, which was foisted on the most recently appointed member of the hospital staff, which just happened to be me. It was completely unpaid; the word generally used for this type of post was *honorary*. There were whispers that you might get brownie points towards a Merit Award, although to be fair, this was strenuously refuted by the previous incumbent. The appointment consisted of arranging all the lectures and courses which would keep the other consultants *up to scratch[t]* with recent new medical developments. Each month, I would try to persuade a lecturer from a teaching hospital to travel to the wilds of Devon and give us an educational talk on some medical topic. There would always be a three course dinner to follow the presentation and the whole thing would be completely free and totally subsidised by the pharmaceutical industry, who would have a promotional stand outside the lecture theatre. A drug firm representative would be on hand to speak to the doctors attending[u] the talk and give information about their latest drugs, which certainly to me as a surgeon was an extremely useful way of keeping up with developments in medicine. Twice a year, there would be a Dining Out Night, which would be a black-tie dinner at a nearby hotel or restaurant also accompanied of course by a lecture.

When I first took on the job in 1981, these lectures were well attended. The lecture theatre would always be quite full. If I had been able to cajole a well-known top level speaker to come, there might even be a waiting list for the dinner! There

---

[s] In the 19th century, this was sometimes called "*Joe Muggins*"; usually self-deprecatory, when one has been duped or fooled. It also meant a local politician (e.g. councillor)or in US, bourbon whiskey!

[t] Under the 1839 London Prize Ring Rules, which preceded the Marquis of Queensberry Boxing Rules, a round in a Boxing Match ended when one of the Prize Fighters was knocked down. After a 30 second interval, the fallen fighter was allowed a count of eight, during which time he must stand upright on a mark scratched in the middle of the ring. Failure to *come up to scratch* would lead to his being declared as the loser of the contest.

[u] Believe it or not, I have recently heard folk who attend a meeting referred to as *attendees*, though I cannot understand why this suffix implying passivity needs to be used at all. Why not *attenders*?

was always one talk per month and I remember it was really difficult to keep on getting enough good speakers. That was thirty years ago. Now there is just one lecture every year and I still have the dubious privilege of organizing it. There is still a black-tie dinner afterwards. The big difference however is that nowadays there are so few people attend that we could almost hold the entire affair in a telephone kiosk!

Each October I always have to send an embarrassing letter to all my colleagues in the hospital pointing out how cringeworthy it will look if nobody turns up. They merely suggest that I should stop arranging them. I remember one year, when we once had Sir Terence English come to talk to us. He was the first surgeon ever to perform a successful heart transplant in the United Kingdom (in 1979) and I had somehow inveigled this highly eminent Professor of Surgery from Cambridge to travel all the way to Barnstaple to talk. Quarter of an hour before the lecture, there were so few people sitting in the lecture theatre that I 'phoned the Head Porter asking him to get as many people as he could to just come to the lecture theatre and make the place look a bit more full! A handful of doctors as well as a few well-educated porters and nurses then enjoyed a masterly lecture from an absolutely brilliant speaker. Presumably some of my *really professional* consultant colleagues were sitting at home watching *Coronation Street* on the telly. I was reliably informed by one of the ward sisters who dutifully replied to a summons to come down to make up the numbers, that the times did in fact clash.

The doctors who did continuously come to the lecture year in and year out were always *OldSchool* and indeed often retired! Our younger colleagues on the staff at the hospital simply will not go to anything, which they are not compelled to attend or worse – for which they get paid. Eventually in 2013, I arranged the one eponymous lecture of the year. I had somehow managed to cajole a world famous lecturer to come all the way to North Devon from London to give a talk on a Monday evening. I knew that if I arranged it for any other night there would be a poor turnout. There was to be a black-tie dinner after the lecture at a prestigious hotel, the price of which had been heavily subsidised. Only one person put their name down and the whole thing had to be (somewhat embarrassingly) cancelled. When I met my colleagues in the hospital corridor and asked them why they did not want to come, they would look at me as though I had just tried to get a Royal Marine to go and watch the all-male performance of *Swan Lake*. *NewSchool* doctors evidently have better things to do. It is all very depressing.

It shows a lack of dedication and a deficiency of *OldSchool* professionalism. Being a doctor was never a job like any other. It really was considered a privilege. One was often accused by one's spouse that one was married to the profession rather than to them and that one's first love was medicine. Perhaps there was a bit of truth in this. I remember many years ago being told by a Portuguese girlfriend that love was different for a woman to what it was for a man. She said that for a woman, it was her whole life and existence, but a man also had his work!^v

It is a sad reflection on our country that this lack of professionalism and dedication doesn't extend to the continent of Europe. I was amazed to be asked recently to give a lecture in the medical school in Malta on a Saturday morning. I thought that I must have misheard the date, but no, the organizers had hoped that I would be able to talk in Valetta at half past ten on a Saturday morning. What is more, the whole half day course was excellently well attended (so much so that the main lecture theatre was completely packed and TV monitors were set up in *two* annexing rooms). This would never have happened in the UK. Hardly anyone would have attended.

EUROPEAN WORKING TIME DIRECTIVE
The French make them,
The Germans read them,
The Italians ignore them
And the British actually obey them.
EU LAWS, Anonymous

---

^v If a man had ever said this (however unlikely), I am sure it would be considered sexist.

The European Working Time Directive (EWTD) was *an EU initiative designed to prevent employers requiring their workforce to work excessively long hours, with implications for health and safety.*[37] It was one of those ideas dreamed up by Europeans in Brussels and then totally misinterpreted by the British. It was initially meant to protect exploitation of PSV[w] and lorry drivers (and other road users) but of course the interfering hospital administrators (who would all be actually better employed if they stayed at home and did *nothing*) decided to extend it to junior doctors. They averred self-protection as a motive rather than any humanitarian caring for the overworked trainees, saying that if a mistake was made by a junior who could show that he had been working over and above his maximum 58 hours, then the Stasi could be taken to task and ultimately to court.

This curtailment of junior doctors' hours has been perhaps the single biggest problem in the deterioration of standards of hospital medicine in recent years.

Why has this heinous state of affairs been allowed to develop and is the fault entirely that of the Stasi? I honestly think that the profession itself must shoulder quite a lot of the blame and nobody more so than the Royal Colleges of Surgeons and Physicians and the British Medical Association – precisely the bodies who should be the main bastions of maintaining the highest possible standards of training, which this country has hitherto enjoyed. Instead of citing trainee doctors as a "special case" (which, with their support would have almost certainly have sailed through), the BMA and colleges gave it their full support.

They went even further than that and cut the hours to a mere 56 (per week) in 2007 and a paltry 48 hours in 2009. A colleague recently returned from the Republic of Ireland and said how much better the training of junior doctors was there because they had diplomatically ignored the EWTD saying that medical training was a special case. Not only the Irish, but I think the rest of the world have completely ignored the

---

[w] Public Service Vehicles (buses).

directive and batted on regardless, considering the job itself to be a privilege and just getting on with it,

Not too long ago, when an *OldSchool* doctor qualified, but before he was let loose on the community, he would do his house jobs. There would be one six-month period doing a surgical job under the careful supervision and guidance of a consultant surgeon and if this all went satisfactorily, there would be a further six months but this time working with a physician.

There are two fundamentally different types of hospital doctors: surgeons, who perform surgical operations and physicians, who don't. They are not just different types of doctors; they are different types of people. They have dissimilar personalities and their outlook on life is often poles apart. It was once said that it was possible to divine at medical school which students would become surgeons and which would be physicians. The physician (archetypically the more intellectual of the two) would be struggling with the *Times* crossword, while the surgeon (the practical one) would be lying underneath an old car trying to get the engine to work. Although as Dickens once said, "*All generalisations are dangerous, even this one*", there is quite a lot of truth in this.

Up to and including the end of this twelve month period, the doctor would not be registered with the General Medical Council, but at its completion (assuming that he had performed satisfactorily – and almost everyone did) , his name would be entered on the General Medcial Register. It was accepted that he was then fully trained and safe to practice on his own. During this wonderful but hectic year, the houseman would have worked like a Trojan and got an amazing amount of practical experience, not from books but from patients. He would have learnt his personal skills and would be *fit for purpose*.

With the limited work hours imposed by the EWTD, however even the Stasi realised that this was no longer the case. Because the essential experience with patients has been so drastically curtailed, the poor young doctor now has to wait a further year before he can be fully registered and set loose on the public. Instead of the *OldSchool* system of one year's pre-registration housejobs, the *NewSchool* houseman now has to complete two pre-registration or *Foundation* Years. They are known as F1 and F2 (a bit like hybrid sweet peas[x]).

And even then he doesn't get as much experience. It has recently been reckoned that in the past, it took about 30,000 hours to train an *OldSchool* consultant surgeon, which interestingly is just the same amount of training hours to prepare a concert pianist. The present number of training hours is estimated at 10,000 hours.

Let us just hark back to less than a generation ago. I was working as a houseman in the Doncaster Royal Infirmary, where I worked up to and including an 84 hour week. In still earlier times, they used to send little children up chimneys and down coalmines: in the opinion of some of my colleagues, both of these would have been preferable to working as a house surgeon at the Doncaster Royal Infirmary! The socialist government of the day was quite politically radical and appeared to be hell bent on restructuring British society and in particular the class system. This included a plan to remove the élitist social status of doctors. The way they achieved this was quite brilliant.

The Health Minister, a Lancastrian redhead called Mrs Barbara Castle[y] ostensibly fought the corner of the overworked underpaid hospital doctors in training, who worked so many hours in the hospital and sometimes even slept on the ward

---

[x] In sweet pea propagation, *F1* stands for the *first filial generation* rather than the *first Foundation Year.*

[y] Although she did *act* as Minister of Health, her Labour predecessor Crossman (who took over the post after the Labour general election victory of 1968) had for some reason changed the title to 'Secretary of State for Social Services'. One of your authors, who is from Sheffield, remembers a tale about this Lancastrian redhead. A new pub had been built in Sheffield on the site of an older one called '*The Castle*'. Because of Sheffield's long association with the Labour Party (hence its nickname 'The People's Republic of South Yorkshire') it was thought that it would be a nice gesture to ask the titian-haired Minister to open it. The story that went around at the time was that, when invited to perform the opening ceremony she asked for a fee, and, as a result, the idea was abandoned. Whatever the facts, the pub was not renamed '*The Castle*', but '*The Red Cow*'. They have an odd sense of humour in Sheffield!

when they were on call (I did!) This of course was so that they would be available to patients. It also gave the most invaluable experience in learning the practice of medicine. Mrs. Castle instituted the revolutionary new 84 hour week, with mandatory alternate weekday nights off. This then meant that in order to provide the same service, twice as many doctors would be needed.

Needless to say, not all our chiefs were in favour of these "namby-pamby[z] milk-sop reforms": they had had to work hard during their own apprenticeships to gain essential experience and they didn't see how anybody could learn their trade unless they saw enough cases, nor, perhaps more importantly, how youngsters who had prolonged their self-centred adolescence through five or six years in medical school, could learn to subordinate their interests to those of their patients without a some degree of sacrifice (and there was certainly a degree of truth in their views – anachronistic as they may seem in today's society).[aa]

I can quite clearly remember an *OldSchool* surgeon gathering everybody together and saying very definitely that nobody need bother filling in the forms to say how many actual hours they had been working, because they would *certainly not* be signed! Your author hastens to add that this surgeon was a caring, dedicated man who was himself willing to work every hour that God sent, and didn't see why fellow professionals should start to fill in *overtime slips* (like factory workers) for learning to practise a vocation which should be considered a privilege in itself.

It was a seminal moment in the slippery slope away from *OldSchool* professionalism. We were no longer high-minded members of a noble profession with philanthropic Hippocratic ideals, dedicated to the patient whose needs were paramount, with pay of secondary importance (in some hospitals it was

---

[z] Initially Namby-pamby was the nickname given by the dramatist, Henry Carey to Ambrose Philips, an awful 18th century poet who dedicated most of his *"artless art"* to little babies.

[aa] For a full examination of these reforms see YOUNG et al (2006) *Hospital Revolution (op.cit)* Ch.1.

called a *stipend* – the salary paid to a clergyman). We had begun to lower our ethical standards and our commitment to those of a garage mechanic.[bb] It could justifiably be argued on etymological grounds that we had started to prostitute ourselves.[cc]

He would have been horrified by the *NewSchool* doctors, who might well have told him during a surgical operation that they were about to scrub out of the operation, which they were both doing and knock off because the time was fast approaching five o'clock.

This state of affairs is now not at all unusual.

So much for *NewSchool* professionalism.

If he had then mentioned the fact that he considered this to be highly unprofessional of them, they might well have regarded this as bullying and reported him to the Stasi. In fact the definition of bullying is that the recipient perceives it as such (even if nobody else does). Hippocrates, the father of medicine once made this the opening statement in a medical text, *"The physician must not only be prepared to do what is right himself, but also to make the patient, the attendants, and externals cooperate."* The execrable Stasi would clearly not agree. They would be delighted to make the *NewSchool* doctors as unprofessional as they are themselves.

At least a few other colleagues share my views. I was interested to read the blog of a fellow *OldSchool* Professor[38] of thirty years' experience at a teaching hospital. He had got so fed up with *NewSchool* medical students that he had decided to jack it in altogether. He described them as *increasingly rude, unprofessional and in-your-face* and no longer of the same calibre as when he was a student with regard to *their lack of professionalism, clinical skills, demeanour or general knowledge.* I know precisely what he means. Like me, he is finding it is no longer a joy to teach and that things, oh so sadly, are getting even worse.

[bb] Your author does not, of course, include his own mechanics in this! He has the utmost respect for their competence and professional manner.

[cc] The word *prostitute* is derived from the Latin words *pro* and *statuo* meaning *to place before* - one's profit before one's principles.

HOSPITAL AT NIGHT
.....golden care!
That keep'st the ports of slumber open wide
To many a watchful night.
Shakespeare, (1597) *Henry IV (2) IV,5,23.*

It was not only humanitarian considerations which the *OldSchool* bosses were concerned about. They had a real and justifiable concern that if you were only there for one night a week, rather than three or four, that you would not get enough experience. This is such an obvious result that it has been accepted and junior doctors now expect to work for two years rather than the one, which I as an *OldSchool* drudge was expected to endure. The doctors themselves of course were never consulted. Would they have rather got it over with in one single year (like we all did in the *OldSchool* days) or are they such namby-pambies and milksops that it would all have been too much for them and they couldn't really hack it. The poor darlings might have got so tired that they could not possibly think straight.

That of course, is what the litigation-obsessed Stasi were afraid of. If the housemen had, after all, been considered a special case and allowed to get on with the work in the time honoured way, but something had then gone wrong (which is eventually inevitable), whether indeed they were at the beginning or end of a shift what did it matter, the NHS is always held responsible. They were scared shitless about possible litigation. They saw spectres of lawyers pointing out that the poor doctor was exhausted.

Of course *OldSchool* doctors never worked a night shift as such; they got an occasional night off or worked all day and as long as necessary into the night until all their patients had been seen. That was when the consultant had propriety over his patients. They used to be his patients and he and his firm would look after them. Since that ownership has been forcibly removed by the Control Freak Stasi, the poor patient might not see the houseman who clerked him in (and who in the *OldSchool* days would have looked after him throughout his stay) ever again. An important relationship, which was certainly to the benefit of the patient usually developed not only between that junior doctor, but her consultant and all his firm. The consultant's name was written high up above the bed. Through thick and thin, they would all know every detail of their patient. When he got better, he would remember them and thank them all before he left the hospital. If on the other hand, all did not go well and he died, the whole firm would attend the post-mortem (and often learn important lessons, which had not been apparent during life). These of course would be an essential learning experience and benefit future patients.

The junior doctors no longer are indoctrinated with that sense of propriety. The consultant's name is still above the bed, but it doesn't really stand for much. When my own wife (a specialist herself) was seriously ill in hospital, the consultant's houseman never spoke to her in three weeks! My wife said she never even said, "*Good Morning.*" Remember what it says outside Vietnamese universities: *Before you learn anything else, learn how to behave properly.*

Now that patient propriety (and it would seem propriety in general) has gone, a potty new controversial system has evolved which, for some reason involves a "Senior Nurse" who co-ordinates the doctors called *Hospital@Night* (always written like that with the commercial *at*). The trendy newspeak name itself speaks volumes. Evidently the *nurse co-ordinator allocates jobs out to the doctors according to their seniority and at some sites a nurse practitioner / support worker based on his / her assessment of the requirement of that task.* The question which immediately comes to an *OldSchool* mind is, "*Which lunatic doctors ever agreed to have anything to do with such a system?*" It is both unfair to the "Senior Nurse" and to the doctors, demeaning them both.

Details of this potty system beggar belief. Remember that this is all about seriously ill hospital patients in the middle of the night (when one's statistical chance of dying is at its highest.) On the ENT ward in a large South Devon hospital, the specialists who are called at night to ENT, gynaecology and orthopaedics are all interchangeable. So if you have had a gynaecological operation (e g a hysterectomy or a prolapse repair) during that day and you develop a post-operative problem that same night, you might well get a throat specialist or a bone and joint specialist come to see you.[39]

Tasks also come with an allocation of red / amber / green status indicating their required timescale for completing (instant / 1 hour and wherever respectively). The concept is it stops the doctors being bleeped every 30 seconds, and allows them to get on with the clinical priorities.

There are even plans afoot to institute a similar system during the day. The idea is that the doctors sit in a sort of rest room near the A&E department (comparable perhaps to those which firemen[dd] use whilst waiting for a fire to fight) and as different emergent situations arise in the hospital, they take it in strict rotation to attend the ward. This does still mean that a gynaecology houseman might well get called to an ear, nose and throat emergency. This has not yet been considered – or perhaps it has and it is seen as an opportunity to garner a wider experience of different branches of our ever widening profession. I cannot really see it working since when it was implemented many years ago in closely related specialties (e.g. ENT and facio-maxillary surgery) it gave rise to a lot of problems and was discontinued. It certainly is not in the best interests of the poor patient.

Hardly surprisingly, these batty changes have not been met with a lot of enthusiasm. In a poll of junior doctors, the majority thought that it *"de-skilled"* them. I would have thought the word *de-skilled* falsely assumes they have already had time to develop some skills in the first place.

In response to an article in the *Lancet*[ee] in 2012, suggesting that Medical Education was being systematically eroded, 85% of doctors responded to a BMA poll saying that they thought it certainly was.[40]

[dd] The *NewSpeak* non-genderist word is *firefighters.*

[ee] *The Lancet,* founded in 1823 is one of the world's best known, oldest, and most respected non-specialist medical journals.

WHAT A MESS!
Everything revolved around the Mess.
O'Leary, Capt. M.M. [ff]

During the 1950s, Chairman Mao closed the tea houses in China. This was a bit like Killjoy Cromwell closing taverns in England. Mao thought they were a threat to his Cultural Revolution and would encourage sedition. They were not appropriate to the revolutionary spirit. In exactly the same way, the Stasi have shut down doctors' messes and hospital social clubs

This made a very significant change to the whole ethos of the hospital. When I was "on the house," I used to live in the *OldSchool* hospital doctors' mess; it was in effect my home. I not only used to sleep there (when I was not sleeping on the ward), but because one had to spend up to 84 hours a week on call, I would spend many of my waking hours there too. There were of course newspapers and a television in the mess and indeed I once lived in a large mess, where there were two television rooms – to prevent any disharmony about which station was on (there were then only two). I remember I was a houseman, when the decimal currency was instituted in 1971 and one of the house surgeons at the Sheffield Royal Infirmary (a young lady) had been stuck in the mess for four or five days working. When she eventually escaped and got on a bus, she was evidently mocked by the bus conductor for apparently having no idea about the new coinage, which had been introduced the previous week.

Most old hospitals were built near the centre of a town and therefore usually had their own local "hospital pub", which was either adjacent to or within spitting distance of the main hospital door, where all the doctors would go whilst they were on call. I can remember when, if the switchboard wanted somebody in the evening, they would usually call the pub first before trying the bleep.

[ff] This is taken from the 1998 Canadian Army Staff Course handout (*"The Making of a Warrior"*).

There was a far more relaxed view towards alcohol in hospitals in the past.

The prissy puritanical Stasi have not only tried to stop doctors having alcoholic refreshment, but have recently suggested that the poor patients are not allowed a drink either. Relatives are now forbidden from bringing alcoholic presents in to their sick loved ones! I can remember when I was newly qualified, the houseman's evening ward round. Patients on the medical ward, where I worked at the Barnsley General Hospital were actively encouraged to have a nightcap. Beer and stout was thought to be a better bowel regulariser than stronger laxatives and it was thought that a small dose of alcohol would be preferable to chemical soporifics. I also remember two *OldSchool* consultant physicians who considered *and prescribed* a glass of sherry as an appetite stimulant and aperitif before both lunch and dinner (in Barnsley, these were called *dinner* and *tea*). The only complaints from the old ladies who were the usual recipients of this medication was about the quality of the Cyprus EMVA Cream Sherry.

There was always a bar in the hospital too, but it did not usually open until about half an hour after the nearest pub to the hospital had closed: and then it usually stayed open until about two or three o'clock in the morning, when everybody got tired of waiting for emergencies to materialise and went off to bed with a nurse.

During these short opening hours, the mess bar was always full. There were inevitably plenty of nurses of all grades there (students, staff nurses and even sisters) often, if they had just come off late duty, in those wonderfully sexy old uniforms they used to wear. The mess bar wasn't just run for junior doctors: consultants also used it, as the UK licensing hours were more draconian in those days and it was a means of getting a drink after all the pubs in town had shut at half past ten! It was always buzzing with life. In those days, hardly any of the young doctors were married and during the swinging sixties (and seventies), there did seem to be a much more permissive moral attitude, but having said that, I can honestly say that I was never aware of any drug abuse[gg] other than tobacco and alcohol.

The mess bar was usually properly licensed. I was the licence holder for three messes, during my period as a junior doctor and that meant I occasionally had to go to the magistrates' court to renew the licence at the Brewster Sessions. Although it was often difficult to get time off during the day, the boss never quibbled about this important extramural duty. Some of the bigger city teaching hospitals even had a dedicated licensee. At district general hospitals, the license holder would sometimes be the mess president. This democratically-elected post was usually given to the most senior consultant at the hospital. (The junior doctor who actually ran the mess would be the *vice*-president.) It was always a bit of an honour to be mess president. It also meant that when there was any problem with the Stasi, and even in those days there might be little niggles, that the representative of the doctors' mess was the most important person in the hospital.

There was an occasion at the old Northern General Hospital in Sheffield, when the story had leaked to the management board that the junior doctors were going to have a stripper come to dance for them after their next mess dinner. There had been a story in the *News of the World*[hh] that some hospital in the Midlands had recently had some similar erotic after dinner entertainment. I was the vice-president of the mess at the time and the mess president, a very senior and well respected consultant physician asked me if the rumours were true. Evidently the Board had approached him to say that they had heard a whisper and thought it would be *totally inappropriate.* I think he was a bit disappointed to learn that in fact the mess had booked a conjuror (I remember he wore a fez

---

[gg] Drug abuse is now often (and I blame those masters of incorrect English, the Americans) referred to as *recreational use.* How absurd is this?

[hh] The *News of the World* was a national red top newspaper published in the UK from 1843 to 2011. It was at one time the biggest selling English language newspaper in the world and was known for somewhat salacious lurid stories and exposés.

and went under the name, *Ali Ben Ali, the Twister from the East*). The old physician pointed out that the mess was our home and as such, what we did there was absolutely nothing at all to do with anybody else. If we wanted to get a stripper to come and entertain us, we had every right to do just that (and would we let him know if we did). In fact we never did have an *erotic dancer* come to the Northern General Hospital, although a good few years later, I do remember that a certain *Miss Crystal* from Newton Abbott was engaged to provide entertainment after a mess dinner at the North Devon District Hospital in Barnstaple. This of course would never happen in a boring *NewSchool* on-call alcohol-free doctors' mess and if it did, the housemen (mainly now young ladies) would want Chippendale-style male strippers anyway.

I remember that once as a final year medical student, I did a locum for a house surgeon who was off on his annual leave. This was an excellent way for me to get real experience and I considered myself very fortunate to be asked to do the job. The post was not entirely voluntary. The Hospital Management Committee paid me £1 a week *honorarium*. This might seem difficult to believe, and even in those days it wasn't very much, but I never even got the full *one pound*. I had to pay National Insurance at 13 shillings and fourpence (which was exactly two thirds of a pound, i.e. 67p) and I was also charged graduated pension – but I was exempted paying tax. I finished up with the princely sum of 2 shillings and tenpence (which in new money is 14 pence). I have still got that cheque for my first week's NHS work (as a doctor). I got very little sleep, no time at all off and certainly worked well over 84 hours, but I got to do three operations myself and the ward experience was fabulous.

In addition to the pittance, the boss also said that I could have as much to drink as I wanted on his bar bill (when I was either on or off duty). That, if I remember correctly, came to substantially more than fourteen pence!

In one place where I worked (the now long defunct Manchester Ear Hospital), you got a free pint bottle of beer with your lunch every day, courtesy of the nearby Boddington's Brewery. The "Ear Hole" cook said that the brewery had sent six dozen bottles a week, since one of the family had had an ear problem before the (Great) War. I loved going to work there. As you arrived in the morning, the cook not only asked if you would be staying for lunch (which was a rhetorical question, because you always did) but what you would like! She offered to pop out and buy you a lamb chop if you fancied one. She made steak and kidney puddings to die for and I usually had one of these. This was probably the acme of *OldSchool* hospital doctors' dining rooms.

Other factors have been very important in altering the mess. There have been concomitant changes, which have taken place in society over the last twenty years. When I was a houseman in the early seventies, it was very unusual for any for the mess members to be married. For one thing, they got so very little money that they couldn't afford to get wed. This made a huge (and obvious) difference to the nature of the place. On nights off, one did not have to rush back to the little woman (and indeed there were lots of little, big and medium-sized women who visited the mess anyway, who appeared to have just one thing in mind!). One of my older colleagues called the sixties and seventies the *Pre-AIDS, post-contraceptive pill generation* and it appears to me now that the sexual mores were much more free and liberal then than they are today.

Another factor has been the massive influx of Commonwealth doctors into British medicine (originally at the request of one of the best Ministers of Health this country has ever had – the Right Honourable J. Enoch Powell). Quite a lot of these ethnically diverse immigrants are Muslims and do not drink alcohol. This of course did not prevent them from wanting to go and engage in social intercourse with their colleagues. When I ran the bar in Doncaster thirty years ago, a healthy proportion of the bar profits came from soft drinks.

Of course, hospital rooms were never very palatial, but at least they were always warm and not usually too far away from the wards and the nurses' home. The first time I ever lived in a doctors' mess was over forty years ago. I was a medical student but I was doing a locum for a houseman. The second most memorable thing about living in the mess which I remember, was being awakened by the maid, who said, "*Good morning, Doctor; do you have sugar in your tea?*" (I did in those days.) It was the first time I had ever been called "*Doctor*" and of course I wasn't: but it did sound incredibly good. Junior doctors in those days didn't get much money; . as I said, I was given £1 which then had tax and insurance deducted!

So much for the privileged élitist life of the junior doctor, getting tea (and goodness knows what else) in a free hospital bedroom. In the summer of 2008, the embittered Stasi stepped in and stopped this complimentary accommodation for newly qualified doctors.[ii] A spokesman for the NHS said (with undisguised jealousy and spite), "*Gone are the days when junior doctors were required to be available all hours of the day and night. There is now absolutely no need for junior doctors to be contractually resident… it is entirely appropriate that they are treated in exactly the same way as other NHS staff.*"[41] (except of course, the totally unqualified six figure salary managers).

The BMA made a token remonstration calling it *disgraceful, inequitable and unacceptable,*[6] but that is about all they did. They complained at a conference that the free accommodation had been removed without any compensatory pay rise and pointed out that *NewSchool* housemen would have to face bills of up to £7,000 a year (equivalent to a 20 per cent pay cut) to live in the hospital grounds. It was reckoned that the so-called trusts would make £35million from charging their first year junior doctors for their tiny little rooms. The BMA do not seem to really put themselves out very much unless changes are to the detriment of their darling GPs. The medical students made a bit more of a protest against what they saw as a cut in their first year's salary by sleeping in tents near London's Regent Park.[42]

Nothing at all happened and first year doctors still have to to live in cramped hospital flats and pay several thousand pounds a year for the privilege.

[ii] This did not obtain in the Principality of Wales.

REFERENCES

[35]. MANDAL, Ananya (2011) *More Female Doctors than Male – Gender equality or Feminization of the Profession.* Healthcare News. 30 November.

[36]. DEANS, Jason (2003) *ITC defends C4's live autopsy* The Guardian. 27 Jan.

[37]. ROYAL COLLEGE OF SURGEONS OF ENGLAND (2012) www.rcseng.ac.uk/fds/nacpde/eea-qualified/ewtd

[38]. ODYSSEUS (2012) doc2doc BMA blog 8 Nov.

[39]. PERSONAL COMMUNICATION (2013) JRY/SH

[40]. THE LANCET, (2012) Volume 379, Issue 9823, Page 1273, 7 April.

[41]. SMITH, Rebecca: (2008) Hospital trusts ripping off junior doctors by charging for accommodation. Daily Telegraph 8th July.

[42]. DAVIS, Anna(2008) *Medics sleep in tents for housing protest.* Evening Standard. 8th June

CHAPTER 3

THE FINAL CUT

Indagandis Sedibus et Causis Morborum[a]
Carved (and still plainly visible in 2014) above the main door of the Rokitansky Institute in Vienna.

IN A NUTSHELL; OldSchool vs. NewSchool:

OldSchool: Post-mortem examinations on deaths occurring in teaching hospitals were routine and clinical medical students attended the PM room every day. This important experience was one of the most important cornerstones of the medical school curriculum in learning the subject of pathology.

NewSchool: Owing to cost and potty governmental directives, PMs have become more and more uncommon to such an extent that some *NewSchool* doctors have never even seen one!

A STUDY OF THE DEAD

Much can be learned about the living from a study of the dead.
Royal College of Pathologists, *The Autopsy and Audit* (1991) [b]

Until the 1960s the autopsy was at the heart of modern medicine, crucial to the discovery, characterization and understanding of disease. It was at the centre of medical research, education and professional development.[43]

Even as late as 1977, some hospitals had a post-mortem rate of 80%.[44]

---

[a] To Investigate the Basis and Causes of Disease

[b] The Joint Working Party of the Royal Colleges of Pathologists, Physicians (London) and Surgeons (England) *"The Autopsy and Audit"* 1991.

We saw in a previous chapter how medical students are now (almost unbelievably) deprived of the invaluable experience of learning human anatomy by dissecting cadavers. They are nowadays also denied the similar experience of daily visits to the post-mortem room (Morbid Anatomy Department) to watch post-mortem examination of recently deceased patients take place. Admittedly one or two of the less robust students initially passed out or had an attack of the vapours on their "first time" and in this respect, it could be viewed as a rite of passage.

Anatomy and pathology are the two great pillars of medicine and surgery and clearly the very best way to learn them is from the dead body itself.

We have already paid tribute to Sydenham's great truism: *the patient is the only real textbook of medicine.*

It is one thing to pore over a chapter in a book or sit and listen to a lecturer drone on. Facts obtained in this way are quickly and easily forgotten. It is quite another to stand, as I once did, and watch a patient who has just died from mumps have her abdominal cavity cut open and see a soapy-looking fluid with globules of fat swilling about inside. It is called fat necrosis and is a rare complication of the disease. I will never forget it.

I will also never forget witnessing the pathologist's sharp knife slice through the brain of the young butcher who had had an epileptic fit whilst serving in his shop. He had never regained consciousness and died in hospital. The soft blancmange-like tissue contained a large secondary cancer, spread by the blood from the butcher's lung: he was a heavy smoker and had given himself a lung cancer.

Another PM engraved in my memory is the poor 43-year old lady, who had tried to kill herself by hanging herself with her husband's belt. She died a few days later in hospital and post-mortem revealed an undiagnosed pregnant uterus. The best "textbook" of medicine is undoubtedly the patient. Alive or dead - there is no substitute for it and never can be. It is Confucius who is attributed with the aphorism, "*I hear and I forget. I see and I remember. I do and I understand.*" And it is undeniably true.

When I was a lad, after the morning ward rounds, medical students would invariably go to the PM room, usually with the boss leading the way with his whole firm in close pursuit. Of course, the opposing firms would also be there and a healthy rivalry almost hung in the air. Names of the recently deceased were chalked up on a board, and an order of play had usually been decided. The consultant surgeon or physician in charge of the case would first present the history to the pathologist, who would then open the body (with a huge "Dan to Beersheba" incision) and then meticulously expose the truth for all to see. There were almost always surprises (like the pregnancy above). The PM Room was often nicknamed the "Department of Truth." There were never actual league tables, but inevitably there was healthy leg-pulling between firms about missed diagnoses. Things were hardly ever what they had seemed.

This still happens, but nowadays of course it does not always come to light.

In a research study performed in the UK in 2008, at least a third of autopsies revealed a cause of death which had not been known before the patient died. In routine natural deaths, 34.7% of the time the process that was believed to be the cause of death prior to autopsy was completely wrong.[45] In America that same year, an eminent pathologist[46] said, *"Consistent with my own life experience, more than a quarter of autopsies reveal a major surprise other than the cause of death"*.

These daily visits to watch post-mortems, (when taken in the context of a continuum of seeing and caring for the patient when alive) were certainly one of the best learning experiences of my medical education. What I do not think I ever realized at the time was that "serving" in the PM Room also helped me to confront the essential fallibility inherent in my profession and started me off on my lifelong conflict with the inescapable uncertainty and error. I am sure this is what old Hippocrates meant (400 years ago) when he said[47],

"Life is Short, but the Art (i.e. medicine) *is Long: The Crisis fleeting; Experience perilous, and Decision difficult*[c].

---

[c] What he actually said (being an ancient Greek) was, "Ὁ βίος βραχύς, ἡ δὲ τέχνη μακρή, ὁ δὲ καιρὸς ὀξύς, ἡ δὲ πεῖρα σφαλερή, ἡ δὲ κρίσις

POST MORTEM, AUTOPSY AND NECROPSY

Death rejoices to help those who live.
Above Post-Mortem Room Door.

The truth now is that amazingly fewer and fewer PMs are being done with every passing year. This is not just in UK but the whole of the world. In Germany, the rate fell from 10% in 1980 to a mere 3% by 1999[48]. In the United States, there has still been a major decline from 67% to 26% between 1989 and 2003. *Post mortem* means "*after death*" (*cf. ante mortem* which means "*before death*"). Americans have always preferred the term *autopsy,* which was defined in my old English Medical Dictionary[49] as "a term *curiously* applied to a post-mortem examination" (my italics). It seems that they have now started to use the much more pedestrian term *necropsy,* which just means "*looking at the dead*".[d] When we realise that autopsy in Greek literally means "*seeing with one's own eyes*"[e], we can perhaps forgive our transatlantic colleagues, since this is precisely what a PM was; the moment of truth: one was not just taking a jumbled history from a confused old patient or feeling the skin of an abdomen or examining an X-ray, but looking at (and perhaps even handling) the knobbly surface of a cirrhotic liver. But it was much more than this: it was the liver, which you had just seen cut out of poor old jaundiced[f] Mrs Smith, the lady in the side ward, to whom you had talked and who had offered you one of her biscuits 48 hours before. It was a valuable learning experience which you would probably never forget.

I will always remember seeing the liver of a 12 year old girl, which appeared to have changed into the colour and

---

χαλεπή. A shortened Latin version of this is often given as, *Ars longa, vita brevis* (Motto of my old alma mater – Sheffield University Medical School) or as Chaucer said in the Parliament of Fowles, "*The lyf so shorte, the crafte so longe to lerne*".

[d] Νεκρός (necros) *dead.*

[e] Αὐτοψία (autopsia) from αὐτός (autos) *one's self* and ὄπτομαι (optome) *to see.*

[f] Jaundice means yellow-skinned (from the French *jaune,* yellow)

consistency of a car-sponge, because her mother had given her paracetamol tablets for a childhood fever (and only about a dozen over the space of 12 hours). I have personally neither used, nor prescribed paracetamol ever since!

When my wife was a houseman, she worked for a boss who was an excellent chest specialist and also had a qualification as a pathologist. After many years caring for a poor old lady with a rare respiratory disease, she remembers him in the PM room carrying a bucket, containing that poor old dear's lungs. Now at last, although he could no longer keep her alive, at least he could examine the organs microscopically and take them to pieces macroscopically (naked eye). Doctor and patient had both held a great affection for each other and now that he could do no more for her, at least she could help him in death. His mood was one of scientific curiosity and a satisfaction that he would now be able to learn the truth and perhaps share it with his colleagues. His careful examination might just even help others. Some pathology departments used to sport over their entrance the motto, written in Latin,[g]

"This is the place where death rejoices to help those who live."

A joint report from the English[h] Royal Colleges of Surgeons, Physicians and Pathologists in 1991 stated that, '*Many undergraduates and junior doctors have never attended a necropsy and therefore have little insight into its value in investigating disease.*'[50] To an *OldSchool* practitioner like me, that is somewhat alarming. If it was true at the end of the last century, it has certainly not changed for the educational better since then. The sad truth that quite a lot of *NewSchool* doctors do not really know what a post-mortem entails was brought home to me recently.

Although I recently retired from all clinical practice, I still have a retirement job as medical referee to the local crematorium. In this rôle I am required to check all the

---

[g] *Hic locus est ubi mors gaudet succurrere vitae.*

[h] There are also eminent Royal Colleges in the Republic of Ireland (despite the fact, which you might have noticed, it has no Royal Family!) and in Scotland.

Application for Cremation forms to ensure that all the necessary paperwork has been completed. In particular I must verify that at least two properly registered British doctors have examined the body after death. This is for two (I would have thought) fairly obvious reasons: firstly to make sure that the body is definitely dead and secondly to exclude cases of concealed homicide. In 2013, I was checking a form and was astounded to find that the signatory doctor had written in the box asking the date of examination of the body, "*body not examined*". I could barely believe my eyes and so immediately rang him up to find out why on earth he had signed the form but failed to look at the body. It all became abundantly obvious. He had rung the Coroner's Officer about the death and she had told him that "no post-mortem examination would be necessary in this case". This poor *NewSchool* doctor had taken her at her word and not bothered even to do an external bodily examination, confirming death and excluding ligature marks, stab wounds, hypodermic needle punctures, etc. etc. He had not made an examination at all after death (or post-mortem). He got quite shirty when I told him he had a statutory duty to go to the undertakers and perform this obligation before I was able to make the necessary authorisation for cremation to take place. Because he had never been to an *autopsy*, he did not realise that it is the same as a *post-mortem*.

He was following the instruction of the Coroner's Officer literally.

NewSchool doctors, because they have never attended one, have no perception of what they are really about.

ET TU BRUTE[i]
Which death is preferable to every other? The unexpected.

---

[i] Julius Caesar's alleged last words, when his adopted son, Brutus joined in the other senators in stabbing the old Emperor, whom they thought had started to abuse his absolute power. Caesar initially resisted, but when he saw Brutus amongst the conspirators said "καὶ σὺ τέκνον" (even you, my child?) and resigned himself to his fate. The Latin version, "et tu Brute" (you too Brutus?) was immortalized in Shakespeare's play and is now traditionally used to address treacherous friends. (Cultured Romans all spoke Greek)

Ironically, one of the few quotations attributed directly to Julius Caesar is the one quoted above.

Not only was his own death unanticipated, but many accounts relate (apocryphally) that then, as now, this unexpected death merited an Ancient Roman *autopsia cadaverum*. Some reports go further and state that the physician Antistius performed the first ever post-mortem on the Emperor in 44AD. They even go so far as to argue as to whether it was the second or the last stab wound (of 23) that killed Caesar, but Antistius[51] said it was definitely a wound to the chest that finished him off.[j] The business about it being the first ever autopsy is just not true: we must assume that Erasistratus (310 – 250 BC) had done post-mortems much earlier, since he states that the liver of a man dying from dropsy was as hard as stone and compared this to the soft liver of a man who has died from a snake bite.[52] There is much argument as to whether the Romans did PMs at all. In 1953 a fourth century fresco was found in a catacomb in Rome, which showed two men pointing at a hole in the abdomen of a third man lying on the floor. It might or might not have been a post-mortem, but certainly gave rise to great debate on the subject.[53]

There is of course, no doubt that dissection of the cadaver (both normal and diseased) has been the only way that medicine and anatomy could possibly advance the progress of medical science. It is often thought that post-mortems were not performed during the Renaissance period, because the Catholic Church stopped them, but nothing could be further from the truth. Antonio Benivieni was a great pioneer of the autopsy in fifteenth century Florence, where PMs were so common that in his book, *The Hidden Causes of Disease*[k] (1507), he commented about a rare case in which a post-mortem was refused, and he was so indignant about this that he wrote, '*The*

---

[j] Gaius Suetonius Tranquillus, commonly known as Suetonius (ca. 69/75 – after 130), was a Roman historian, who wrote a history of the Caesars and included this story about Antistius. (Jul. Caes.82)

[k] *De abditis nonnullis ac mirandis morborum et sanationum causis*

autopsy was refused because of some superstition on the part of the family!'

THE RESURRECTION MEN
By man came also the resurrection of the dead.
I Corinthians, ch.15. v21.

Rembrandt painted his famous portrait of the citizens of Amsterdam (only two of whom were physicians) observing the *Anatomy Lesson of Dr Nicholaes Tulp* in 1632. These public anatomies however, were only performed twice a year in Holland. In England, when the Lumleian public anatomy demonstrations started in 1582, they were held on a weekly basis.

During the eighteenth century in Britain, however things took a "grave" turn for the worse, because of the bumbling intrusion of government into medicine. This was the era of grave robbers and "Resurrection Men", when dissection and post-mortems became completely deregulated.

Laws were introduced which only permitted the bodies of executed criminals to be used for medical science. This was at the height of the so-called Scientific Enlightenment: medicine had just started to blossom, but had been suddenly and needlessly stultified by the intrusion of idiotic government agencies who had no concept of the practical scientific realities. (What's new?) It is conservatively estimated that around that time the teaching hospitals required about 500 bodies each year. With only about 50 executions being carried out in London every year, demand far outstripped supply. Medical education had to either grind to a standstill or make its own (unlawful but necessary) arrangements with grave robbers. Then as now, the more intelligent doctors quietly ignored the officious intervention of Whitehall. Unfortunately their only alternative to obtain a continuing source of cadavers was from the body snatchers. In the absence of any refrigeration facilities, these would generally be fresh corpses from new graves. Relatives (presumably hoping that their loved ones should be allowed to *rest in peace)* would mount guard on fresh family graves, only to be thwarted by body-snatchers digging tunnels![54]

The law did not do a lot to deter the Resurrection Men . Because a body was not strictly speaking *property*, stealing a corpse was only a misdemeanour at common law, rather than a felony.[1] The grave robbers were careful therefore to strip the body, even of its shroud and leave these chattels in the coffin. If they were caught and it could be shown that they had stolen clothes or jewels, they would be subject to execution or transportation.

The scale of the problem was vast. In 1776, two years after the stupid law came into force, London's newspapers reported the grisly discovery of the remains of more than 100 naked bodies in a shed on Tottenham Court Road, where they had been stored pending delivery to surgeons and medical schools.[55] It appears that if a surgeon was interested to find out the actual cause of death of one of his patients, he would have had little difficulty in obtaining the body after death (for a price) to perform an autopsy.

It perhaps should be reiterated in these present day UK constraints of the Human Tissues Act, that there is little doubt that their grim work was crucial to the historical development not only of anatomical knowledge, but of pathology and surgical expertise, particularly during their heyday, from the 1780s to 1832. It was not until the Anatomy Act was passed in this year that common sense once again prevailed and changed the legal requirements for the provision of corpses.

Von ROKITANSKY AND VIRCHOW
Veritas Omnia Vincit [m]
Cicero.

---

[1] Offences against the person in English law have never been regarded as seriously as offences against property and the worst of all of course are offences against the State. That's why in the UK, you still get a custodial sentence of several years in HM's prisons for forgery, but a suspended sentence for kicking an old age pensioner into unconsciousness.

[m] *Veritas Omnia Vincit* ("The Truth will Out" or literally *Truth Conquers All*) was sometimes a motto depicted in ceramic tiles on PM room walls.

In the nineteenth-century the two great pathologists, Baron Karl von Rokitansky in Vienna[n] and Rudolf Virchow in Berlin laid the foundation for modern post-mortem science and practice, not only in Europe, but the whole world. They demonstrated to their colleagues fairly conclusively that pathological conditions found in dead bodies bore a constant and definite relationship to signs and symptoms of the illnesses, which had occurred in that patient before death. They pushed forward the frontiers of our medical knowledge by painstakingly examining every body after death. The Vienna Krankenhaus was the biggest hospital in the world and Rokitansky performed an estimated (and colossal) 60,000 autopsies in 47 years.[56] Medical progress, certainly during the first part of the last century was dependent on both the bedside and the PM room. If the post-mortem did not confirm what the doctor had believed during life, then he would have found out where he went wrong and learn from it. It became the norm until the end of the last century for most hospital deaths to have a PM (even if there was no ante-mortem doubt about the cause of death).

Doctors who did not order PMs were viewed with suspicion: were they trying to cover a mistake up, which would be exposed by the pathologist? There is no better rebuttal to the old adage, "*Doctors bury their mistakes*" than regular post-mortem examinations. The PM was the "ultimate audit." *The autopsy also served as an unrivalled education instrument at all levels from the beginning student to the august professor.*[57]

Although of course the main goal in the practice (and art) of medicine is to cure the patient and win the battle against disease, a very definite secondary aim is to make a diagnosis.[o] It is always an intellectual challenge. Of course, it is difficult

---

[n] Rokitansky worked in Vienna but was born in Königraz in Bohemia in 1804. At the time of writing his great, grandson is a surgeon in Vienna.

[o] The one branch of medicine where this does not happen would seem to be psychiatry. Alienists seem to be very averse to "labelling their service users" (ie *diagnosing patients*). Perhaps that is because, as my old professor of psychiatry used to say, "*The specialty has the great disadvantage of being at the same stage as cardiology before William Harvey discovered the circulation of the blood.*"

to treat and heal your patient if you do not know what pathological process is going on, but it is far from impossible. There are some cases in which cure is not possible, but diagnosis still helps and is satisfying for the physician to make. Indeed, it is like solving a difficult conundrum or crossword, the more difficult the diagnosis, the greater the reward.

Experience of a previous similar patient is usually the key, which allows one doctor to appear smarter than his colleagues and get the answer right. There are however always cases which one cannot work out. The reason is because one does not have enough data. That missing information almost always becomes available at post-mortem. That is where the final pieces in the puzzle are lurking. Here there might well be facts not hitherto suspected. This is precisely why the recognition of discrepancies between clinical and post mortem diagnoses not only led to self-improvement, but also furthered the science of medicine. It is reckoned that the aetiology of over eighty diseases has been brought to light since 1950 as a result of autopsy.[58]

DECLINE IN NUMBERS OF POST-MORTEMS
... the dread of something after death
The undiscovered country from whose bourn
No traveller returns puzzles the will
And makes us rather bear those ills we have
Than fly to others we know not of?
William Shakespeare (1601) *Hamlet, Prince of Denmark.* III,1,78.

I was very surprised to learn that this drop in the rate of post-mortems is even occurring in America. I would have imagined that with their obsession with litigation, they would have kept up a high rate of autopsies, since after all there is no better argument against malpractice than a favourable autopsy report. Conversely if the relatives are genuinely suspicious that the doctor has been negligent, they can have no better evidence than the pathological facts.

There is no satisfactory answer to why there has been this decline in numbers. Some believe that it reflects the changing patterns of health care. Twenty years ago, it would have been the same junior doctor, whom the relatives had seen and got to know (and trust) during grandma's final illness. In the old days, by the end of the week, you were just about a friend of the family, but now sadly that has all long gone. Now it's sometimes a different doctor (who probably doesn't even "look like" a doctor) every eight hours. Whichever houseman is on the shift when a death takes place, which might well be in the middle of the night, might have a reluctance to ask the family. It should be perhaps stated that it is necessary for a doctor to receive legal informed consent from the next of kin before a post-mortem can be performed.

Not only have the *NewSchool* doctors had little experience in asking this rather sensitive question, but they feel that they don't really know the family well enough to say, "*Can we do a post-mortem, please?*' As an *OldSchool* houseman in the seventies, I frequently had to ask for consent to PMs. Most concerns were not superstitious ones, but real fears by relatives that their loved one would be mutilated or disfigured for the "open-coffin" part of the funeral service (usually held at the home before the coffin lid was screwed down). Since a modern PM never shows any visible sign of obvious intervention, these questions were much easier to talk about than, "*Don't you think that he has suffered enough already?*" The best and possibly most honest approach was to point out that a post-mortem would be the only way of eliciting the *real* cause of death and suffering of their loved one. Recently an eminent pathologist with, he estimates, more than one thousand autopsies to his credit, has said that, "*In over three decades, I have never known a family to be sorry they got an autopsy on a loved one. I have known many who refused to allow an autopsy who were very, very sorry afterwards.*"[59] He went on to say that, "*Giving families the explanations they want is one of the most satisfying things that I do.*"

In Atul Gawande's excellent book, *Complications*,[60] the American surgeon says somewhat enigmatically that he thinks that the reason for a decline in numbers is because nowadays we "*are riding too high in the saddle*". Greater reliance on special diagnostic investigations done before death, such as magnetic imaging scans (MRI) and Computer Assisted

Tomography (CT scans) and biopsies done through fine needles under local anaesthesia are probably the most frequently cited cause for this decline. The only study to be done in fact showed the precise opposite! The lowest rate of discrepancy was with old fashioned X-rays and the highest with CT, isotope and ultrasound scans.[61]

Another Australian study from a hospital where Post-Mortem Computed Tomography is routine concluded that the *concept of "radiological" autopsy is flawed* and that CT can supplement but not replace autopsy.[62]

Other reasons[63] cited are: unwillingness to dwell on failures; fear of malpractice suits[64]; difficulty in obtaining permission and the fact that holding a post-mortem might slow up the funeral proceedings. This last reason could be a consideration with the increasing numbers of non-Christians in the country. None of the published explanations dare to mention what glares out to a cynic like me: pressure from the administration to save the expense of a costly autopsy!

Neither orthodox Jews nor Muslims allow of cremation and furthermore both these religions prefer to inter the dead body within 24 hours of death if possible, although this haste in Hebrew burial is waived to avoid interment ever taking place on a Saturday. If a Jew needs to be examined post-mortem, a rabbi should strictly speaking be present at the autopsy. With respect to cremation, if a Jewish family defy the rabbi and have a body cremated, they are advised when interring the ashes to let them come in contact with the earth rather than be contained in an urn. When it comes to post-mortem, there would appear to be no hard and fast rules. A mob of orthodox Jews in Jerusalem recently[p] rioted and threw stones at the police in a violent protest, when a rabbi's wife was the subject of a forensic autopsy to ascertain the cause of her murder.[65]

Historically, Arabs were performing dissection and conducting autopsies, centuries before European physicians and in many ways were far more advanced in anatomy and physiology. Indeed there is evidence that the Arab physician,

---

[p] 3rd July 2008

Ibn al Nafis had discovered the circulation of blood three hundred years before William Harvey! There are usually no objections by Muslims to PM when the death is suspicious in nature. Interestingly, there have also been recent Muslim legal opinions (i.e. *fatwa*), stating that post-mortems are *halal* (*i.e.* acceptable) because they benefit the living.[66] Some Islamic fundamentalists evidently believe that it is possible for the deceased to feel pain even in death and will therefore oppose routine PM (not that these now ever exist) and would certainly not permit autopsy for research purposes.

Far from wishing for a hasty interment, the Buddhist faith only allows PM after the soul has made its transition (Mahayana Buddhists prefer for the body to be left untouched for up to eight hours, while Tibetan Buddhists usually wish it to be undisturbed for a full three days). Cremation is common in Buddhism, although many Chinese Buddhists prefer burial.

CORONERS[q] AND CERTIFICATION OF DEATH
Simplify me when I'm dead.
Keith Douglas (1941) poem.

Coroners (and the *coronial system*) were introduced by the monarchy after the Norman invasion and occupation of England. During these early days, it was found that quite a lot of Norman noblemen kept being found dead with bashed-in skulls and none of the Saxons evidently knew anything about it! Principally to raise money by imposing fines for such untimely deaths, King John decided that it might be a good idea to have inquests for suspicious and "accidental" deaths.[r] Because the Norman invasion never got as far as Scotland, they do not have coroners there and in the northern province, the *Procurator Fiscal* takes on these responsibilities.[s]

---

[q] The word *coroner* derives from the Latin *corona* or *crown*. King John first appointed a coroner in 1197 to *keep the pleas of the crown (custos placitorum coronas)*. They were formerly known as "crowners."
[r] Coroners were also made responsible for the finding of treasure.
[s] In fact, coroners only exist in English speaking (Old Empire) countries. Some states of the USA have kept the old system, but others have *Medical Examiners*, who fulfil the same rôle.

Registration of deaths began in 1837[t]. These first death certificates listed when and where a person died. No cause of death needed to be given until 1879, when a doctor's signature became necessary on a death certificate.[u]

The first purpose of a death certificate according to the Office for National Statistics' (ONS) Death Certification Advisory Group (who presumably should know if anyone should) is to *enable the deceased's family to register the death*.[67] They go on to say that it *also provides a permanent legal record of the fact of death and enables the family to arrange disposal of the body,* The ONS give other reasons. Secondarily, *it is a safeguard against the disposal of bodies without professional scrutiny of the need for further investigation*; so far, so good; as a third reason they advise us that *it is the main source of the national mortality statistics which are important for public health and health care.* Indeed it is the only source.

Certification of death is the duty of the doctor who attends the patient during their last illness. He must attest to the best of his knowledge and belief what the cause (or causes) of death was. It is also the doctor's duty to then deliver the MCCD (Medical Certificate of Cause of Death) to the Register Office. This is hardly ever done by the GP and is usually undertaken by the relatives. The Registrar (and not the doctor) has a legal obligation to refer certain deaths to Her Majesty's Coroner (HMC). This hardly ever happens in practice and it is almost always the attending physician who contacts HMC. Having said this, legally it is the duty of every person who is "about

---

[t] It was a wee bit later in Scotland (1855). Scottish Certificates have always been rather more detailed than in England and Wales. For example, the maiden surname has always been needed for females; this has only been requested information more recently in England and Wales. Additionally, the Scottish death certificates detail the dead person's father's name and mother's maiden name.

[u] Although the certification (*i.e.* filling in and issuing of the death certificate) remains the duty of a registered doctor, nowadays nurses and in some circumstances, even paramedics are delegated to pronounce death (see erosion of professionalism Ch.1).

the body" (which usually includes the doctor anyway) to notify the coroner of unnatural deaths. In these cases either the coroner himself will either issue an MCCD or grant the doctor permission to write one.

Deaths occurring after a surgical operation (or before recovery from the anaesthetic) or when there is any type of accident or injury, or indeed any unexpected, unnatural or violent death (including suicide) or when the patient has not been seen by a doctor for over a fortnight, should all be referred to Her Majesty's Coroner,[v] who might or might not consider that an inquest should be held.

In 1996 at the height of the AIDS scare, there was a controversy in the British Medical Journal about a London[w] coroner's view that, *death from AIDS, as a direct consequence of anal intercourse, is – on the balance of probability – 'unnatural', according to the current values of our society and is proper to put to a jury.*[68] Since the term 'unnatural' had not been defined legally at that time, it was the subject of a ruling by the Court of Appeal,[69] and the Head of the Coroners' Section at the Home Office decided that a death from AIDS should be viewed as a death from natural causes.[70] For some reason, this put me in mind of the cartoon many years ago on the front of Private Eye, where the Prime Minister (it was Harold Wilson) is being asked "*What should we do about the Homosexual Bill, Prime Minister?*" and he replies, "*Pay it.*"

HMC also has the absolute right to demand that a post-mortem examination of the body be performed, and in this case has no obligation to obtain written consent from the relatives. It is however inconceivable that the coroner would not discuss the matter with the family beforehand. Once again however, coroner's post-mortems are becoming increasingly rare. So

---

[v] There are other cases, which HMC would wish to know about, which include: death resulting from an industrial disease, drug overdoses and alcoholism. The post-operative period following surgery extends to twelve months and the coroner defines an operation as any procedure requiring an incision or a general anaesthetic. Deaths occurring in HM's prisons or in police custody or when the deceased is in receipt of a service disability pension should also be reported.

[w] From Poplar.

much so that in the last couple of years, they no longer take place in some hospitals. In the past, arrival at an absolutely definite and cast-iron certainty for the cause of death was thought to be the ideal goal to aim for. This is undoubtedly no longer the case. It is almost as though, this appears nowadays to be an actual bonus. I have little doubt that the coroner's main concern is to exclude concealed homicide; then he or she will be happy. Whether this noticeable reticence to learn the factual cause is driven by considerations of cost is unclear, but ascertaining the real pathology definitely seems to be much less of a consideration than excluding foul play.

MEDICAL REFEREES

The doctors found, when she was dead,
Her last disorder mortal.
Oliver Goldsmith, (1759) *Elegy on Mrs Mary Blaize.*

The relatives of the deceased have every right to request an autopsy, but this too is in fact seldom done. The Home Office[x] Medical Referee, who is responsible for authorisation of cremations also has the right to order a post-mortem if he has concerns about the certified cause of death before he allows a cremation to take place. Just as the coroner has the responsibility for the death certificate, the medical referee is legally accountable for the cremation forms and has a duty to withhold the authority for a cremation to take place, if he is not satisfied with the investigations done by two independent doctors and their medical opinions.

As I said earlier in this chapter, I am in fact a medical referee for the local North Devon Crematorium and have held this post for thirty years. Sadly, the filling in of cremation forms has deteriorated beyond belief in recent years. In 2012, I was becoming so disillusioned with the *NewSchool* doctors' sloppy attempts at completing cremation forms that I decided to audit them. My hope was that if I could actually quantify how awful the accuracy was and show this to the local doctors,

[x] The *NewSchool* name for the Home Office is now the Ministry of Justice.

that they would be so ashamed that they would improve. Let me tell you what happened.

I looked at 300 consecutive random cremation forms at the North Devon Crematorium, where I work and checked them for mistakes. This was a tedious exercise, but the result made it worthwhile. I had not expected the findings to be so dire. Out of three hundred forms, only 21 (7%) had been properly filled in. The average number of errors and omissions in 300 forms was 2.84 mistakes per completed cremation form. You might be forgiven for thinking that most of the forms would at least show the full name of the deceased. One could hardly disagree that on this statutory legal document, this is highly important. The name had only been properly recorded in 38% of the forms. The most common error was omitting to enter the middle name of the dead person. If the doctor completing the form had only entered an initial (e.g. John B. Smith), it was counted as an omission. What flabbergasted me was that in 10% of cases, the doctor had not even bothered to fill in her or his own full name correctly.

In 2008, the fee for filling in the forms was increased from £34 to a very generous £76. This had been prompted by the Shipman Enquiry (see below). In suspected cases of foul play and without any possibility of exhuming an interred corpse, once the body of the deceased had been committed to the fire, all the hard proof was gone and testamentary evidence was all that remained. The new forms were intended to ensure that all the appropriate persons should be easily contactable. There was a box on the new "crem forms" asking for "Full name and Address Details of Persons Present at Death" and also similar information about persons nursing the deceased during the final illness. In my audit less than half (38%) were properly completed.

For "Full name and Address Details of Persons Present at Death" a common answer was merely "family". Similarly vague answers were given for the full name and address details of nurses such as "Nursing Staff NDDH". The results were so depressing that I harangued my colleagues in a letter to both GPs and hospital staff using such phrases such as *shameful* and *lack of professionalism.* I also issued what I hoped would be useful guidelines. I then did a further audit a few months later. (In audit jargon, this is known as *closing the audit loop*.)

I suppose in audit jargon, my work would have been considered a great success. The percentage of properly filled in forms jumped from 7% to 21% (There were 104 out of 500 this time). I will try to console myself that this is a good result. I do however think that as a profession, we can do better than this. I think our patients deserve better too. GPs admit that the findings are disgraceful, but say that they *have so many forms to fill in nowadays etc. etc.* I somehow cannot believe that they would completely omit their own middle name when filling a passport application. They don't get paid £76 for doing this either.

I am afraid there can be no valid excuse for this sloppiness, which is further evidence of a decrease in standards by the *NewSchool* doctors.

CORONER'S OFFICERS

Here's a corpse in the case with a sad swelled face
And a 'Crowner's quest' is a queer sort of thing.
Thomas Ingoldsby, *Ingoldsby Legends.* (1840)

Up until 1977, *OldSchool* coroner's officers were almost exclusively very experienced retired police officers,[71] but nowadays this very satisfactory tried and tested old system appears to have been replaced. In some areas of England and Wales *NewSchool* coroner's officers are still serving police officers; in others, they are civilians employed by the police. In certain areas, they may be employed by the local authority and have no direct link with the constabulary.[y] When I was a young doctor, I knew that I could get hold of the coroners' officer at any time of day or night. This is no longer the case.

Round about the turn of the Millennium, a government review decided that the rôle of the coroner and in fact the whole certification system was *obsolete.*[72] Certain events had given rise to this review. Reviews are the typical government

---

[y] Teesside University, Middlesbrough, Tees Valley does a two week course.

"knee-jerk" reaction to try to convince the commonalty that "things are being done" as the result of some disaster. In fact there was more than one disaster and more than one knee-jerk, but the main instigator was to Dr Harold ("Freddie") Shipman, the GP mass murderer from Hyde who had been quietly bumping off his patients for years.[z] The majority of his cases, that he is thought to have unlawfully killed were cremated and this led to yet another knee-jerk, with regard for cremation certification. I have not yet knowingly met one doctor (i.e. one who actually treats patients) who thinks that legislation would ever catch out or prevent another Shipman, but the Government feels that they have to be seen to be "doing something".

In addition to the Shipman case, there were two other events cited in the Government review. Nurse Beverley Allitt (convicted in 1993) was dubbed the *"Angel of Death"* by the media. She was a state enrolled paediatric nurse in Lincolnshire, who murdered four children and injured nine others. Her method of murder was to covertly inject her child victim with potassium chloride (to cause cardiac arrest), or with insulin (to induce lethal hypoglycemia). Allitt was condemned to thirteen concurrent terms of life imprisonment, which was one of the longest minimum custodial sentences ever imposed by the British judiciary. She was labelled as suffering from the *Munchausen Syndrome by Proxy*, which, the alienists[aa] tell us is a form of attention seeking device.

The review also said that the Alder Hey organs scandal had thrown the whole coronial system into disrepute. Alder Hey hospital in Liverpool had retained huge numbers of organs (hearts and even heads) from children, without their parents' knowledge, let alone consent.[bb]

---

[z] Shipman is the only British doctor found guilty of murdering his patients: he is among the most prolific serial killers in recorded history with 218 murders (by lethal injection) being positively ascribed to him, although the real number is likely to be higher than this.

[aa] Psychiatrists.

[bb] More than 2,000 pots were found in the hospital cellars, containing body parts from around 850 infants.

Unfortunately the review suggested an even greater cut in the rate of post-mortems performed in *England*. Their reasons are predictably somewhat flawed. The principal motive is because the English figures are higher than those in Scotland, Ireland, Canada, New Zealand or Australia. The authors of the report fail to mention that post-mortems would indubitably improve the quality and accuracy of death certification. It is merely because our figures are higher than the figures from the former colonies! The other reason, even more predictably of course, is the cost implication. Both are hardly admissible in such an important matter.

Although, there is hardly any chance whatever that changes in legislation will ever prevent a highly intelligent psychopath like "Freddie" Shipman, there is however still a great need anyway to improve and reform the British death certification process. If, for the sake of argument, post-mortem examination had been performed on everybody in Hyde, Shipman would never have got away with killing more than a handful of poor old grannies. Routine autopsy would be the ultimate deterrent to "concealed homicide".

OLD AGE AND NATURAL CAUSES
He died in a good old age, full of days, riches and honour.
I Chronicles, ch. 29; v. 28.

The ONS have said that a final but nonetheless very important function of proper death certification is that MCCDs provide the main input to the national statistics on mortality. An analysis of these causes is regularly published by the Office for National Statistics. As just about the only record of the cause of death, they should be an important archive and a means of monitoring British health trends.

For this to be in any way valid however, the cause of death as recorded has to be accurate.

In the past, when post-mortems were the norm and almost every hospital death had an autopsy, the statistics provided by MCCDs would indeed be a valid and accurate record of why a person had actually died. If a post-mortem had taken place, there would clearly be no need for the attending physician to *best guess* what to write down on the death certificate.

Nowadays, it is by no means rare to see the cause of death recorded as *"Metastatic Cancer, Primary Site Unknown"*. (*Metastatic* is a medical term meaning that the cancer has already spread round the body from its original or primary site.) Obviously it is much more useful for the Public Health doctors to keep an eye on whether or not some specific type of cancer is on the increase (or decline) if they know where it arose. Thirty years ago, it was almost unheard of, particularly if a death had taken place in hospital, to record *"Primary Site unknown"*. A post-mortem would almost certainly have been performed and no stone would be left unturned in the quest to find the primary site and origin of the tumour.

At least however, it does state a pathological cause, however vague. Clearly "old age" as such is not a pathological entity. It is a physical description in the same way as "blue eyes" or perhaps "grey hair".[cc] It does not even imply any infirmity; you can be chronologically old but still have good health. The World Health Organisation has made a massive list, which is supposed to contain and categorise all the diseases recognised by medicine. It is called (rather unimaginatively) the International Classification of Diseases; or ICD 10 for short. The "10" is because the WHO keep revising it, as new diseases are found and the most recent one is the tenth. On none of these ten lists is "old age" to be found.[dd]

Why, then oh why, did the Chief Medical Statistician advise, in 1985, that in certain circumstances, *old age* or *senility* would be accepted as the sole cause of death on British death certificates? In 1985, he recommended that this could only be used if there was a lower age limit of 70 years, but nowadays (although unbelievably), the Registrar General is still happy to accept this solecism as a cause of death, the age at which one can die for no other reason has been increased to

---

[cc] US "gray hair"

[dd] *Senescence* is the nearest thing, which is a fancy term of course, for *old age*.

80. *Old age* however, cannot be used when the death has occurred in hospital or if the patient has not been personally cared for by the signatory physician for "*a long period of years or months*". Since none of these makes "*old age*" a pathological entity or an actual cause of death, it might leave the lay reader wondering why the Chief Medical Statistician allows it at all. (It certainly does me!)

The truth of the matter is that *Old Age* is an absolute cop out. It is often used when the physician in charge does not really know why the person died and is not willing to make an informed guess, based on the clinical facts, his experience as a doctor and the balance of probabilities.

I was once a principal in general practice and I cannot deny that every now and again, there were deaths which occurred in my practice in very old people, who just seemed to get weaker and frailer and then take to their beds, eating less and less food and drinking fewer and fewer fluids and then one day, they were found dead in bed. They didn't so much die as "fade away". There was clearly no foul play. Neither could you say that they had died from heart disease or indeed any other specific disease. You did not really know why they had died and might well write "old age" on the MCCD, rather than the truth, which was that the cause of death was unknown. It would of course have been infinitely better to write "senile decay" or "senile decrepitude," which would have had the great advantage of being more accurate and precise English. This way, you would avoid the expense (and upset) of a post-mortem. In cases such as these, even if a post-mortem is performed, it might well not reveal any pathological process. In these circumstances, it is quite acceptable for the cause of death to be registered as "unascertained."

In the past, the term "natural causes" was admissible, but now this is not acceptable. The expression "natural causes" was really meant to imply that undiscovered homicide (an unnatural cause) had been ruled out. It is interesting to observe at this point that the absolute opposite state of affairs exists in the United States of America. Over there, doctors are not allowed to write "old age" on the death certificate, but it's quite acceptable to put "natural causes". It was George

Bernard Shaw[ee] who wrote that England and America are two countries separated by a common language.

When a cremation is requested by the relatives, cremation forms have to be completed in addition to the ordinary death certificates. Clearly, if the mortal remains are about to be totally destroyed by fire, there is an added requirement from the physicians involved to ascertain that all the available evidence has been accurately documented. In the notorious Shipman case, it is unlikely that a conviction would ever have been obtained if all his victims had been consumed by fire in the crematorium. The main evidence gleaned from post-mortem examinations of the exhumed bodies of his victims was paramount in his successful prosecution. At the Shipman Inquiry, it was queried how Shipman was able to certify the cause of death as "old age" in so many cases,[ff] without being questioned further. In keeping with the trend in society, the majority of the old ladies he murdered were cremated.

Although coroners have no alternative but to accept "old age" in certain limited circumstances, this is only for death certificates. This constraint does not apply to the medical referee with respect to the cremation certification. Although there is a difference from area to area, there are certainly a few referees who will not accept it under any circumstances, when the body is to be cremated. There then could exist the absurd situation, where the certifying doctor has to think again for a more considered cause of death, which would then differ on the second certificate. What of course happens in these areas is that the GPs are aware of the local rules and write a more logical actual cause of death in the first place.

This excellent state of affairs is what probably existed prior to 1985!

[ee] George Bernard Shaw (1856 - 1950) Irish dramatist and wit.

[ff] Richard Lissack QC, leading counsel at the inquiry opened on behalf of many of the relatives by stating that "it is a sobering thought that the systems in place at the time that Harold Shipman murdered remain in place today effectively unchanged". Mr Lissack queried how Shipman was able to certify the cause of death as "old age" in numerous cases, without being questioned further.

ALOIS ALZHEIMER et al.

...Last scene of all
That ends this strange eventful history,
Is second childishness and mere oblivion,
Sans teeth, sans eyes, sans taste, sans everything.
William Shakespeare. *As You Like It.* (1599) act 2, l. 63.

In 1907, Professor Alois Alzheimer[gg] described a case of a
51 year old lady behaving like an 80 year old with senile
dementia.[73] Then in 1911, he published another detailed
description of a 56 year old man with a similar condition.[74]
Dementia in extremely old people had, of course, been well
understood for years, and Shakespeare refers above to *second*
childishness and mere oblivion.[75] Alzheimer's contribution
was to describe the disease when it occurred in someone, who
was not otherwise old enough to be considered senile.[76] This
was otherwise known as *presenile* dementia (rather than *senile*
dementia) and was all the more poignant and pathetic for it.
My old medical school notes say that it should be reserved for
patients under the age of 65. Today however, the term is used
indiscriminately for any old personage who has demented.
Perhaps it is part of the euphemistic general trend: after all it
does not sound as insensitive to say to a relative, "*I am afraid*
that Grandma has got Alzheimer's disease; after all she is
eighty" than "*I am afraid that your mother has senile*
dementia." I suppose in the same way, it is less harsh to tell the
relatives that Grandma died of old age rather than senile decay
or decrepitude, even if the latter two terms are more correct.

It is very common to see *Alzheimer's disease* cited as a
cause of death on a death certificate nowadays and almost all
of them refer to patients above the age of 75, let alone 65.
Indeed, the term is being (mis)used so frequently that were it
not a specific medical term, the continued novel but incorrect
usage in our accommodating English language would have

[gg] Aloysius "Alois" Alzheimer, Professor of Psychiatry in Breslau,
Germany (1864 – 1915) described an unusual form of dementia,
occurring in younger patients. He described pre-senile changes in 51 year
old Frau Auguste Deter and a 56 year old Herr Johann F.

certainly by now have given rise to a new meaning for the word and a new entry into the Oxford English Dictionary. The fact remains however that, whatever some *NewSchool* revisionists might have us believe,[77] the disease which Alzheimer described was not senile dementia, but presenile dementia.

Another anomaly, which one wonders might be another euphemism, from a profession previously thought of as a bit more robust, is the expression "*cerebrovascular event*". This cumbersome medical term is becoming increasingly common on death certificates. It could almost always (and according to the Registrar General *should* always) be replaced by the simple word *stroke*. The term *cerebrovascular* comes from the two words, *cerebral* meaning *brain* and *vascular* which means *blood vessel*. The (lay) dictionary definition of *stroke* is,

'a sudden serious illness when a blood vessel in the brain bursts or is blocked, which can cause death or the loss of the ability to move or to speak clearly.'

What is all this business about cerebrovascular event then? Well, when I was a lad, my old professor of medicine thought it was perfectly acceptable for him to insist that medical students and doctors got things absolutely right. He believed that we all had a duty to try to achieve the same high standards that he demanded from himself. You will notice in the layman's definition of stroke given above that it says the blood vessel, *bursts or is blocked;* well, we were expected to diagnose which one of these two options had happened. Had it burst or had it blocked? If we considered that it had burst, we would call it a cerebral haemorrhage or if we thought the evidence pointed towards a blockage, we would say that a cerebral thrombosis had occurred. Of course (like a lot of the art of diagnosis), it was not always easy. Then for those dummies, who either could not work out the more likely eventuality, or did not wish to commit themselves (for fear of opprobrium or ridicule from a cleverer physician) the term *Cerebrovascular Accident* (CVA) crept in. You could be very sure that whether or not it had burst or got[hh] blocked, it was

---

[hh] US *gotten*

certainly unintentional and so this new name fitted the bill nicely. It was happily used for decades and I was surprised about five years ago to notice the new term *cerebrovascular event* being used by *NewSchool* doctors, unwilling to commit themselves to a block or a burst. It was still non-committal but sounded medical. I was then horrified to learn that its inception was purely and exclusively to allay any suspicions by the relatives that negligence might have occurred! It was considered unwise to use a word like "accident" in these litigious times and CVE sounded more professional than *stroke*. The Office for National Statistics in fact specifically pleads against any term using the vague word *cerebrovascular*, very clearly preferring the name, *stroke*. *NewSchool* doctors appear to be studiously ignoring this advice.

ALL WE CAN BE SURE OF IS OUR LACK OF CERTAINTY

Then I, however, showed again, by action,
Not in word only, that I did not care a whit for death.[ii]
Socrates. (fl. 480 BC) *Plato. Apology 32d.*

The British Medical Association has a blog,[ji] which is called *doc2doc*. This somewhat naff name is a clue to the sort of issues which are discussed. I am slightly embarrassed to write about how crass my colleagues have become with respect to this.

Doc2doc regularly has polls for BMA members, which leave me fearful for the future of what was once a noble profession. In March 2012, doctors were polled "*Is it acceptable for a student to prostitute themselves to pay for medical school?*" I have purposely left the bad use of English grammar unchanged in this question. Perhaps more interesting than the actual result was that some colleagues bothered to actually vote in this poll. Evidently 67.3% of voters thought

---

[ii] On being ordered by the Thirty Commissioners to take part in the liquidation of Leon of Salamis.
[ji] I didn't know either. A blog is evidently a contraction (or a portmanteau) of the term *web log* and is a discussion site published on the World Wide Web and consisting of many discrete entries ("posts").

that it was not a good idea for students to sell their genitalia in this manner.

Since the blog is only open to members of the British Medical Association and one has to be medically qualified to join the BMA, one has to presume that the polls are designed by doctors, but the choice of answer does make one wonder. In 2012, doctors were invited to vote on the indications for autopsy, but the only choices for when should an autopsy be performed were: (a) Never; (b) At the request of the family; and (c) For forensic reasons. They were the only three options to vote for. What I find quite alarming is that 11% of BMA members voted "Never"! One wonders whether these *NewSchool* doctors, who voted for the abolition of all autopsies, hang a black chicken's head and a white chicken's head at the foot of the patient's bed.

In 2005, senior pathologists at the famous Christie Hospital in Manchester clearly very concerned about the future implications of the falling post mortem rates, reviewed over 11,000 published cases and analyzed them looking at the diagnosis before death and the results of microscopic examination of autopsy material obtained at post-mortem.[78] They concluded that, "At *least a third of death certificates are likely to be incorrect and 50% of autopsies produce findings unsuspected before death.*"

After reading their study I was left with two rather worrying thoughts. Seven of the articles[79] they had looked at, quite definitely stated that there was a significant number of patients who had potentially treatable conditions, which had not been diagnosed during life and which only came to light at post-mortem. Had they not had an autopsy, this information would have gone to the grave unknown. This is of course, not to say that there was any negligence or malpractice in these cases. What it does certainly state loud and clear is that, the attendant physicians and surgeons would have learned a very useful lesson, which would almost definitely serve them well in the future. Remember the motto above the old mortuary door, "*This is the place where death rejoices to help those who live*".

This major pathological review went even further than this. It looked at the value of taking specimens of tissue during a post-mortem (autopsy histology) and examining these under the microscope. The Royal College had already recommended that if and when autopsy is performed, tissues are removed from all the major organs and scrutinised microscopically. It was found that failure to do this led to discrepant results in as many as 28% of cases.[80] Bronchopneumonia is one of the commonest recorded causes of death in the UK. When patients diagnosed as having died of bronchopneumonia however, were subjected to microscopic examination at PM, almost a third of them (31%) were found to be wrong.

This means that there is little doubt that post-mortem histology is essential to confirm (or refute) clinical ante-mortem diagnoses.

It would appear then and it certainly comes as no great surprise, (or as they say nowadays, "It's not rocket science!") that although the numbers continue to decline, post-mortems and particularly autopsy histology are still the most accurate method of determining the cause of death.

REFERENCES

[43]. ROULSTONE, J; BENBOW, EW; HASLETON, PS; (2005) *Discrepancies between Clinical and Autopsy Diagnosis and the Value of Post Mortem Histology; a Meta-Analysis and Review.* Histopathology (47) 551-559.

[44]. ALAFUZOFF, I; VERSS, B; (1993) *The Selection for Post Mortem Examination.* Qual. Assurance Health Care (5) 345-349.

[45]. BIGGS, MJP; BROWN, IJR; RUTTY, GN, (2008) *Can the Cause of Death be Predicted from the Pre-Necropsy Information Provided in Coroners'Cases?*
J. Clin. Path. 61: 124.

[46]. TAVORA, F; CROWDER, CD; CHEN-CHI, S; BURKE, AP: (2008) *Discrepancies between Clinical and Autopsy Diagnoses* Am.J.Clin.Path. 129: 102.

[47]. HIPPOCRATES: Aphorisms 1:1. (400BC) trans. Sprengell, Sir Conrad (1735) Nice original leather bound volumes are certainly a joy to own, but paperbacks are now available on Amazon.co.uk!

[48]. aspergillusblog.blogspot.com13 Mar 2009 *decline in autopsy rate leads to underdiagnosis of fungal disease.*

[49]. HOBLYN, Richard D. (1887), *A Dictionary of Terms Used in Medicine.*

Whittaker and Co. London.

[50]. LAUDER, I (1991)*Learning from Surprises* Brit.Med. J.: 303 1214-5

[51]. RIVES, James (2007), *The Twelve Caesars*, New York, New York: Penguin Classics, ISBN 9780140455168

[52]. KING, L and MEEHAN, M (1983) *A History of the Autopsy.* Am.J.Pathol. 73(2): 514–544.

[53]. PROSKAUER, C. (1938) *The Significance to Medical History of the Newly Discovered Fourth Century Roman Fresco.* Bull.N.Y.Acad.Med.: 34, 672-688

[54]. The Lancet (1896)147 (3777): 185–7.

[55]. The Independent *(2009) 27 March.*

[56]. ROKITANSKY, Alexander (2013) Personal Communication. Friday 13 September during Lecture in Josephinum, Vienna entitled *Aspects of the Life of Karel Rokitansky.* 7th Working Meeting International Society of History of ORL.

[57]. KING, L and MEEHAN, M (1983) *op.cit* (n. 10) p.537.

[58]. HILL, RB; ANDERSON, RE: (1900) *The Autopsy – Medical Practice and Public Policy.* Butterworth Publishers, Stoneham.

[59]. FRIEDLANDER ER is the Associate Professor and Chairman, Dept. of Pathology, Kansas City University of Medicine and Bioscience (formerly University of Health Sciences), Kansas City, Missouri (2010) http://www.pathguy.com/autopsy.htm

[60]. GAWANDE, Atul (2002) *Complications, A Surgeon's Notes on an Imperfect Science.* Profile Books, London.

[61]. GOLDMAN, L;SAYSON, R;ROBBINS, S;COHN, LH;BETTMAN, M;WEISBERG, M;(1980) *The value of autopsy in three medical eras.* New Engl.J.Med. (308) 1000.

[62]. O'DONNELL, Christopher et al. (2011) *Can supplement but not replace autopsy.* BMJ. 342: 69. (c7415)

[63]. The following are cited as causes in FINKBEINER, W.E. et al. (2009) *Autopsy Pathology*, Saunders. Phil.: GOODALE, F. (1978): *Future of Autopsy* Am.J.Clin.Path. (69): 260-2: KAPLAN, R.A.: (1978) *The Autopsy-to be or not to be* Hum.Path. (9):127-9; WHEELER, M.S. (1982): *One Resident's View of the Autopsy* Arch.Path.Lab.Med. (106):311-3

[64]. ROULSTONE, J; BENBOW, EW; HASLETON, PS; (2005) *op.cit.*(n.1), p. 551

[65]. UPI-1-20080703-17444300-bc-israel-autopsy.xml

[66]. RISPLER-CHAIM, V. (1993) *The Ethics of Postmortem Examinations in Contemporary Islam.* J.Med.Ethics; (19):164-168.

[67]. OFFICE OF NATIONAL STATISTICS; *Death Certification Advisory Group, (rev. 2008) Guidance for doctors completing Medical Certificates of Cause of Death in England and Wales.*

[68]. Anon. (1996) *HIV Deaths 'Violent and Unnatural'* BMA News 21 Feb 1996, p22.

[69]. QB610 (1993) R. v. HMC Poplar *ex parte* Thomas

[70]. OFFICE OF NATIONAL STATISTICS (1996) *AIDS Related Death*. Letter to Doctors. 1st July 1996

[71]. CLEMENTS, Police Constable Bob (1984) *A Coroner's Officer's Lot is not a Happy One*. North Devon Medical Gazette. Vol.I, 1, 11.

[72]. HMSO (2003) *Death Certification and Investigation in England, Wales and Northern Ireland. The Report of a Fundamental Review. Cm 5831* page 16 para. 3; page 41. para 6.

[73]. ALZHEIMER, A; (1907) *Über eine eingenartige Erkrankung der Hirnrinde.*

Allg. Z.Psychiatr. Psychol.-Gerichtl. Med. (64). 146.

[74]. ALZHEIMER, A; (1911) *Über eingenartige Krankheitsfälle des späteren Altes.* Zbl.ges.Neurol. Psych. (4) 356.

[75]. SHAKESPEARE, William. *As You Like It* Act 2, scene 7, 166.

[76]. GRAEBER, MB et al.(1997) *Rediscovery of the Case described by Alois Alzheimer in 1911: Historical, Histological and Molecular Genetic Analysis.* Neurogenetics.1 (1): 73–80.

[77]. ROSES, AD (1996); *The Alzheimer Diseases.* Curr. Opinion Neurobiol. (6):664.

[78]. ROULSTONE, J; BENBOW, EW; HASLETON, PS; (2005) *op. cit.* (n.1)

[79]. STEVANOVICH, G et al. (1986) *A Retrospective Study of 2145 Autopsies.* Hum.Pathol. (17) 1225; SHANKS, JH et al. (1990) *Value of Necropsy.* J.Clin.Pathol. (43) 193: MOSQUERA, DA et al. (1993) *Surgical Audit without Autopsy.* Ann.Roy.Coll.Surg.Engl. (75) 115; MERCER, J; TALBOT, JC; (1985) *Clinical Diagnosis: a post mortem assessment.* Postgrad.Med.J. (61) 713; CAMERON, HM; McGOOGAN, E; *A Prospective Study of 1152Hospital Autopsies* (1981) (113) 237,285; BARENDREGT, WB et al (1992) *Autopsy Analysis.* Hum.Pathol. ((23) 178; BERNICKER, EH et al (1996) *Unanticipated Diagnoses* Am.J.Med.Sci. (311) 215.

[80]. NATIONAL CONFIDENTIAL ENQUIRY INTO PATIENT OUTCOME AND DEATH (2001) *Changing the Way We Operate.* London, HMSO.

CHAPTER 4

THOU SHALT BRING FORTH THY CHILD IN PAIN[a]

In India, a man whose wife is having a difficult labour, might wash his big toe and give her the water to drink. The big toe was traditionally the seat of a man's strength and this was considered a way of transferring some of it to his ailing wife.[81]

IN A NUTSHELL; OldSchool vs. NewSchool:
OldSchool **(called "having a baby"):** Doctors diagnosed pregnancy on clinical grounds and sometimes (but not always) confirmed it with chemical testing. GPs provided ante-natal care and sent women to hospital to see a consultant obstetrician, who would examine them at least once. Most women were admitted into hospital when they went into labour under the care of this named specialist, who would be assisted by hospital midwives. Usually nobody else (other than medical staff) attended the birth. Whilst in hospital, the consultant obstetrician would have responsibility for their care and doctors would visit and examine their patients on a daily basis. After the birth, the baby would be seen by a medically qualified paediatrician before discharge and the woman would attend **a hospital specialist or** her GP for a post-natal check-up.

---

[a] Genesis 3, 16. *I will greatly increase your pangs in childbearing; in pain you shall bring forth children, yet your desire shall be for your husband, and he shall rule over you.*

NewSchool (now called "birthing") When a woman thinks she might be pregnant, she goes to the pharmacist for a home pregnancy test. If it is positive, she rings the GP who does not see her, but sends her to a midwife. She might never see a doctor and have her baby either in hospital or at a "Birthing Unit" under the exclusive care of midwives. A doula, the husband and Uncle Tom Cobley and all attend the birth (some with video cameras!) This sometimes involves so-called natural innovations, such as birthing pools, (which are of course totally unnatural). Other *NewSchool* potty "natural" ideas include eating the placenta or even worse leaving it attached to the child until it drops off! She is sent home as quickly as possible without seeing a medically qualified paediatrician to examine and check the newborn baby. The GP might not even see her then.

THE FIRST FEW MOMENTS

It is as natural to die as to be born, and to a little infant, perhaps, the one is as painful as the other
Francis Bacon (1625) *Essays, 'Of Death.'*

There was a large poster in the GP surgery where I used to work in the small mining village in South Yorkshire, which was an attempt at health education to induce women attending the GP ante-natal clinics to go promptly into hospital when they went into labour. It said "*The first few moments of Life can be Crucial.*" Underneath some wag had scrawled, "*The last few moments aren't much fun either!*"

In the past, the *OldSchool* ante-natal care was often done by the GP and the delivery was preferably done in hospital under the principal care of a medically qualified consultant obstetrician. When a girl became pregnant, the *OldSchool* GP would refer her to a specialist of his choice at the local hospital. In a shabby effort to save money, the money grubbing Stasi have handed over complete control of the care of pregnant women to non-medically qualified midwives. In the past, expectant mothers always saw a consultant specialist in obstetrics at least once and indeed, he would be in nominal charge of their antenatal and for that matter postnatal care. Now, without any discussion with the patients, the Stasi have changed this system, which had always worked very well. Now the *NewSchool* obstetric care has been completely relegated to midwives, whether the patients like it or not.

My readers are left to draw their own conclusions as to which is the safer and better system and indeed which they themselves would prefer for this crucial and important part of their life.

PHYSICIANS, SURGEONS AND MAN-MIDWIVES

The midwife laid her hand on his Thick Skull,
With this Prophetick blessing, "Be thou Dull."
John Dryden, *Absolom and Achitophel.* (1681)

Most doctors in Britain have the basic (post nominal) medical qualification, *MB, ChB.* Although this entitles the graduate to call himself "Doctor" and practise medicine, it is not really a "doctorate" at all; it is in effect a courtesy title and stands for *Bachelor of Medicine* and *Bachelor of Surgery*[b]. In 1995 the General Dental Council allowed dentists also to use of the courtesy title 'Doctor,' but added the proviso that they must certainly not use it in such a way as to mislead patients or public into thinking that they were "anything other than dentists." (Why, perish the very thought!) As a surgeon, I always called myself Mr Young[c] rather than Dr Young and never had a problem with it.

---

[b] Actually it stands for *Medicinae Baccalaureus, Baccalaureus Chirurgiae*, but nowadays of course less than 1% of the *NewSchool* Doctors would have any knowledge at all of Latin.

[c] Surgeons of course, are also qualified doctors. After quite a few years of postgraduate training (as an apprentice, as it were) they might well get admitted to the Royal College of Surgeons. They then traditionally drop the title, "Dr" and become known as "Mr" (or Mrs) again. This is because surgeons are the lineal descendents of the Guild of Barber-Surgeons and are evidently proud of this heritage.

When I was a student, I yearned to have a brass plate, which proclaimed that I was a "Physician and Surgeon." There was an eccentric Northern Irish GP, whose surgery was not too far from my parents' house, who had a highly polished "shingle" (i.e. brass plaque) outside his surgery which pronounced him to be not only a physician and surgeon, but also a "*Man-midwife.*" This intrigued me for years. Then many years later, I asked one of my colleagues (another Ulsterman) what his post nominal letters, *BAO* stood for. He had qualified in Belfast and said they were for *Bachelor of the Art of Obstetrics.*[d] This degree is peculiar to Irish medical schools, and both Northern Ireland and the Free State still award the BAO, but sadly it is no longer recognised by the General Medical Council.

The word *midwife* is usually considered to be a female noun. The etymology however would refute this. The term is derived from Middle English: *mid* means *with* (similar to the German, *mit* and Dutch, *met*) and *wyf* is *woman* (not a *wife*, but any woman). Hence *midwyf* literally means the person *with the woman* or *attending the woman* (whether that person is male or female).

In the 1960s the *OldSchool* medical student certainly was expected to qualify, having had quite a lot of hands-on obstetric experience. Indeed during the 19th century, the legislation at the time insisted that medical schools had a final examination in obstetrics. I found my old obstetric case diary recently, in which I had meticulously written records of the twenty normal deliveries, personally performed by me and five abnormal ones, which I attended, including such things as twins, forceps and breech deliveries.

When I became a GP a couple of years later, almost all babies were still delivered in hospital, but I did finish up delivering a premature baby on the sofa in a coal miner's cottage and I felt that I had been well prepared to do this by my excellent *OldSchool* medical training.

I was absolutely horrified to find when talking to one of my junior colleagues, now a *NewSchool* anaesthetist and

---

[d] *Baccalaureus in Arte Obstetricia*

114

giving a perfect general anaesthetic for one of my patients, that when he qualified a few years ago, he had never actually delivered a baby into the world. I don't think he believed me when I told him that we could not qualify until we had filled our own personal obstetric log book with at least 20 normal deliveries, which we had performed ourselves and been duly certified by the obstetrician or Sister Midwife.

He told me that the biggest problem for the male medical student nowadays, which he considered had prevented him personally from delivering babies, was the midwives. Most big teaching hospitals are in big cities and quite often near the centre of that city. "Inner city" areas in UK are ethnically diverse with not only different races, but different religions, one of which is alleged to have gender issues. The difficulty for medical students to get practice in delivering babies I am informed by my junior colleague, is ethnic. The midwives ask the mothers if they have any objections to a man medical student delivering their baby, rather than a female pupil midwife and point out that the mother has every right to refuse. My readers will be allowed to work out for themselves why so few male doctors qualify with any experience in the art of midwifery.

I went back to my obstetric logbook, because I thought I remembered a 33 year old Pakistani lady and indeed I delivered her of her sixth child, a healthy 6lb baby girl. The mother was sterilised and kept in hospital for four days because of "*overcrowding of home.*" The only difficulty in this labour had been a "total lack of English." Things have changed since then.

I then wondered what happens in the huge world beyond the United Kingdom. I asked a dear friend and colleague from Iraq about his training and he told me that in Baghdad when he qualified, he had to deliver thirty babies and was dismayed at the story from the anaesthetist from London. He went on to tell me a tale about one night when he was working in the Baghdad Casualty Department, a man brought his wife (and her mother) to the hospital. She was evidently bleeding from her vagina during advanced pregnancy (this is known medically as a *threatened abortion*). The man specifically said that he did not want a male doctor to touch his wife. My pal said that he could arrange to send for a lady doctor to come. This was perfectly feasible, but might take some time. Thus assured, the husband then abandoned the situation and went home leaving his wife alone with her mother in the casualty department. As soon as he was out of the door, both the wife and her mother told my Iraqi colleague to get on and start sorting her out. He made a token protest, but the women said the husband was an old fool and they did not wish for valuable time (and blood) to be wasted in sorting her problem out. The two women clearly had more common sense.

I had just seen an excellent film on female circumcision in Burkina Faso,[e] and this dreadful mutilation of little girls (with a horrific 15% death rate[82]) was also shown to be driven mainly by the male members of the society.

DIVIDE AND CONQUER
And if a house be divided against itself, that house cannot stand.
St Mark, III, 25.

...they should declare the causes which impel them to the separation.
Thomas Jefferson (4th July 1776) *Declaration of Independence.*

In the preparation of this book, I asked colleagues in different specialties, what they considered to be the biggest single deterioration in their field in recent years. A couple of my friends in obstetrics and gynaecology quite quickly agreed that the worst thing which had happened was the separation imposed on them by managers between obstetrics (childbirth) and gynaecology (diseases of the female genital organs).[f] Our old professor of gynaecological pathology always used to say that gynaecology could be defined as, "*diseases peculiar to women*" and always added, "*and by God, they're peculiar!*"

---

[e] *Moolaadé* ("magical protection") is a 2004 film by the Senegalese writer and director Ousmane Sembène.
[f] *Obstetrix* in Latin means *midwife* or more literally *one who stands in front. Gyne* (γυνή) simply means *woman* in Greek.

In the same way that there is a Royal College of Surgeons in London and a separate one for physicians, there is also a Royal College of Obstetricians *and* Gynaecologists. If you ask a specialist in the United Kingdom what his specialty is, he will usually say, *"I'm a gynaecologist"* and not bother to mention obstetrics. American gynaecologists somewhat confusingly say, *"O.B.G.Y.N."* (thus including it, albeit enigmatically). One wonders if this is why some impressionable young British gynaecologists have started to use the term "O and G".

A few years ago the Stasi decided to irritate the obstetricians and gynaecologists by trying to separate the two parts of the specialty and in some part they succeeded (in both irritating them and separating the two groups of patients). The managers do not know the first thing about either subject and wanted for logistic reasons to put the gynae patients in the same ward as the general surgical ones, rather than have them on a ward to themselves in the maternity block (or as it is now so sickeningly called the Women's Block.[g]

There has been a recent problem in recruitment and training in this/these specialties and when *NewSchool* junior doctors were asked in 2006 about whether or not they would like to see their specialty divided, 77% said that they would. Unfortunately the feckless reason which was given by all the trainees who wished to do gynaecology alone (and leave childbirth to the obstetricians) was that they were less likely to get called out in the middle of the night![83] One cannot help but wonder if they might have been better off working as school dinner ladies than going into medicine!

In a separate enquiry into the reasons why doctors are not going into "Obs and Gynae" cited by the trainees themselves, was the *poor working and professional relationships between junior doctors and midwives*. The study found that midwives were *disrespectful to and argumentative with junior doctors*. A startling 69% said that the midwives did not give them a chance to examine patients on the labour wards. I can

---

[g] They were completely fazed when I asked them if that meant that the other was the Men's Block.

remember many years ago in the late 1960s that this was a problem even then. But in those days it was the midwives versus the *medical students* rather than midwives versus *junior doctors*. The powerful ward sisters wanted their protégées pupil midwives to get experience in the art of delivering babies and since they were *on the spot* as it were, when a lady went into labour, it was the pupil midwife who would get the chance to examine the patient and perform the delivery. I can imagine that things are even worse now that the midwives have been told that they are professionals *in their own right* (see below). The junior doctors felt that their bosses, the consultant obstetricians were more respectful and courteous towards them when compared with midwives and the majority felt that there was a serious communication difficulty between doctors and midwives.[84]

PROFESSIONALS IN THEIR OWN RIGHT

All professions are conspiracies against the laity.
George Bernard Shaw, (1911) *The Doctor's Dilemma*[h]

...though
We are not now that strength which in old days
Moved heaven and earth, that which we are, we are;
Alfred, Lord Tennyson (1842) *Ulysses*

The word *profession* (like indeed most English words) has changed over the ages. Those *OldSchool* doctors with a classical education might recall that a professional person was one who professed as a calling one of the learned or liberal vocations, as opposed to a trade or business. This limited a gentleman's professions to the Church, the Law and the Army.[i] This of course leaves medicine firmly out of the frame. Physicians and more especially surgeons, who after all, were only glorified barbers, were tradesmen - and even as late as the nineteenth century relegated to the tradesmen's entrance. In

---

[h] Shaw's brilliantly witty play is a belligerent but passionate view of the mercenary early 20th century doctors.
[i] The term *lay* person also originally only applied to those not attached to the church.

such a polite book as this, your author certainly would not wish to dwell on the profession (sometimes indeed known as *the most ancient profession in the world*[j]) left open to "ladies" in those unenlightened times. Suffice it to say that as the world has become more free-thinking, more and more vocations are being entered by the fairer sex. As we have observed the meanings of English words are continually changing (the basis of so-called *political correctness*).

I am reliably informed (by the Royal College of Midwives) that midwives have been *autonomous professionals in their own right* since 1902 in England and from 1915 in Scotland. It is only fairly recently, however that they have proclaimed this fact to the whole world. It was certainly not apparent to a couple of retired obstetricians, whom I asked; they said that they thought it had only come about very recently in the last ten years. When teachers, footballers and journalists also claim nowadays to be professionals, they cannot understand why I raise a sceptical eyebrow. If one accepts journalists as professionals, then indeed why not midwives?

According to the RCM, one of the reasons why the doctors and patients might not have realised about the midwives' autonomy was that until the early eighties, hospital systems required a named consultant to be in nominal charge of all hospital patients (which I have to admit does seem a very reasonable idea). Evidently newer hospital *systems though do enable a woman to be "booked" as under the care of a named midwife, midwifery team or simply under midwife care.*[85]

The big problem is (to use a *NewSchool* phrase) their *knowledge base.* I will give a couple of examples of what I mean. When one of my daughters told her midwife about previous surgery to her urinary tract, she had to spell out the name of the operation to the girl, who had never heard of it before (and indeed why should she have heard of a *persistent urachal duct*) but I am sure that all consultant obstetricians would have known what one was. On a much commoner tack, the midwives (God bless 'em) do not really know much about

---

[j] Rudyard Kipling (1881) *In Black and White.* On the City Wall

diabetes or epilepsy (and indeed why should they?). They should perhaps not give out misinformation and learn that there is no loss of face to admit they do not know everything. It would be better to say nothing than to tell a young mother absurd stories such as that teething in a child is caused by the teeth moving backwards and forwards underneath the gums, or worse still, that pregnant women should not eat shellfish or peanuts. One of my daughters, during her second pregnancy was rather alarmed when the midwife told her that the baby's head does not engage (i.e. drop down into the pelvis) in second pregnancies, when my wife and I had assured her that it most certainly did. Could the girl really have believed this or was she just trying to allay anxicty?

OldSchool midwives were robustly practical women, who weren't too worried about their knowledge base. A grand old lass of 82 (a retired midwife who must have brought thousands of babies into the world) told me that she loved every minute of her work, but that she certainly never wanted to go to university and finds the whole new business, "*Crass!*"

I have to say that I am inclined to agree with her.

HOME DELIVERIES
Pregnancy is more dangerous than jumping out of a plane or riding a bicycle without a helmet.
Susan Bewley (2012) Professor of Complex Obstetrics, Kings College London

In the very *OldSchool,* and before the advent of the NHS, most babies were delivered at home, usually by the GP if he got there in time, but often as not by the district midwife. Both I and my brother were born at home. Some fifty-odd years afterwards, when our house was featured on television *as a 1930s timewarp*, the ancient mahogany bed, on which we were both delivered by old Dr Billington, (together with its matching wardrobe and dressing table) achieved celebrity status[k] and was seen by millions.

Home delivery was the norm in the forties, but at a high price of increased perinatal mortality. This is a very important index and is defined as the rate of *foetal deaths after 24 completed weeks of gestation and death before seven completed days.*[86] This figure went down considerably with the inception of the National Health Service, when hospital births became the rule rather than the exception.

As it continued to drop and in the sixties, I can remember what I was told by my professor as a medical student: that it had reached such a low level that there was not much chance of it getting any less, because it was at rock bottom. The reason why it had hit these excellent levels was due entirely to the fact that almost all deliveries, except the occasional emergency, now took place in hospital and the only way it could possibly be brought down any further was to ensure that all births took place in hospital.

According to the Office for National Statistics, *the level of infant mortality of a country is seen as a key indicator of the health of a nation.* This became a cause for national alarm in the Netherlands, when a Dutch journal in 2010 published the disturbing figures that Holland has one of the highest perinatal death rates in Europe and also an alarmingly high (and rising) rate of maternal mortality too. In neighbouring Flanders (part of Belgium), which is very similar to the Netherlands in many ways (linguistically, socio-democratically and economically), the perinatal death rate has been a startling two-thirds of that in the Netherlands for at least 10 years. The Dutch became so worried by these terrible figures that the government commissioned researchers at the world famous Erasmus Medical Centre in Rotterdam to ascertain the cause.

Their investigation found that *one of the main reasons for the high death rate in Holland was the midwife care system.*[87] It must be said that this fairly damning indictment refers to the

---

[k] Not, I hasten to add because it was the birthplace of your author, but because the house had remained almost totally unchanged since the last war. There was even an Anderson air raid shelter in the rose garden!

Dutch home birth rates, which were cited as *the highest in the world* (30%, but down considerably and falling every year) and the unfortunate midwives are the mainstay of this home delivery system. *They supervise the birth of any woman who does not require the care of a doctor* (i.e. in their view).[88]

It looks like my old professor of midwifery was right.

In an article written round about the same time, the Professor of Obstetrics in Leeds, James Walker said that there had been pressure from the British health ministers to adopt the Dutch system of midwife care. He pointed out that *we should be cautious about moving our pattern of care towards theirs without careful consideration of a potentially adverse effect on maternal and perinatal mortality and morbidity.* He concluded by saying that so far, we had a safe system for mothers and babies in Britain and that *care should be taken not to undo these changes by striving for political correctness.*[89]

Whilst on holiday in Australia in July 2013, I saw on Ozzie TV, a bluff obstetric colleague tell the ladies in the Antipodes (one refrains from using the term, *down under* in a chapter on gynaecology) that it is a definitely proven fact that although the death rate during any childbirth is extremely low, that it has been shown to be significantly higher in home births. He then drawled, *"Well, it's not exactly rocket science."* Evidently there had been a recent court case, where two deaths had been reported to the coroner. Quite a few vociferous (what the Australians refer to as) *Whole-Earth-Mother* types[1] had spoken out in favour of the midwife. The obstetrician wanted to set the record straight that the facts are irrefutable. He quoted the British Medical Journal. *Fifty babies had died in 7,002 planned home births and there is therefore no doubt that home deliveries carried a higher death rate.*[90]

Thank God the UK perinatal death rate does not seem to be increasing, even with the *NewSchool* innovations.

So much for the quantity – but what about the quality? What is definitely increasing is the rate of cerebral palsy in children. This could in part be directly attributable to the

---

[1] Who, the Australians aver often *weave their own knickers on a hand loom.*

change, which has taken place in perinatal care, but we will examine this in due course.

Another alarming statistic is the soaring maternal mortality[m] in London. Susan Bewley, Professor of Complex Obstetrics, Kings College London pointed out in an article in the *The Lancet* that maternal mortality was a sensitive measure of the quality of health in a community. Although the figures throughout the world have dropped from more than 500,000 a year in 1980 to 343,000 a year in 2008, the figures in the UK have remained exactly the same with just as many women are dying in pregnancy and childbirth as they were 20 years ago,[91] leaving Britain trailing behind countries like Albania, Poland and Slovakia, as well as the wealthier nations of Europe.[92] Professor Bewley was particularly concerned that the death rate in London had not only remained the same, but had soared from 9.1 per 100,000 maternities in 2005-6 to 21.6 per 100,000 in 2010-11.

More than 100 mothers have died in childbirth in London during these five years, twice the rate in the rest of the country.

Cathy Warwick, the President of the Royal College of Midwives, blamed it on a shortage of midwives. In a contemporary alarmist report in the *Independent*, readers were told that *In the 21st century we should not have mothers and babies dying on hospital wards* and told a sad tale about an *intelligent and glamorous young woman, slim as a reed*, aged only 27, who was admitted into Queen's Hospital at Romford and left to suffer *unbearable pain* whilst unattended for more than two hours. By the time, she was eventually seen, *she had suffered a cardiac arrest and a ruptured womb and they were forced to perform an emergency Caesarean. Her baby was stillborn and the mother died five days later.*[93] This is a good (but terribly tragic) example of what is meant by UK Maternal Mortality.

---

[m] Maternal mortality is the death of a woman while pregnant or within 42 days of termination of pregnancy, irrespective of the duration and site of the pregnancy. The Maternal Mortality Ratio (MMR) is the number of maternal deaths per 100,000 live births. (World Health Organisation definition)

BACK TO NATURE

Naturam expelles furca,
Tamen usque recurret.
You can drive out Nature with a pitchfork, but she keeps coming back.
Horace, (fl. 10 BC) *Epistles, 1.*

The "Whole-Earth-Mothers" eschew hospital maternity departments (who might after all encourage unnatural interventions such as Caesarian sections and epidural analgesia). Their mantra is *Birth is as safe as life gets, birth is normal, and that babies know how to be born and moms know how to give birth.*[94] This of course is not true: Professor Bewley, quoted above reckons that *pregnancy is more dangerous than jumping out of a plane or riding a bicycle without a helmet.*[95]

The back to nature brigade have invented a whole new vocabulary. The first essential is to have a *doula.* One wonders if the originator of this term realised that it is the classical Greek name for a female slave (δούλη).[n] She is a sort of experienced birth companion who *assists a woman before, during, or after delivery, as well as her partner and family, by providing information, physical assistance, and emotional support,*[96] but for this support there is a charge of around £20 an hour. It was fairly predictable, nay inevitable that *turf wars* would break out in delivery suites between doulas and obstetricians. And of course they did.[97] By definition they have absolutely no medical knowledge at all and at worst are likely to instil potty ideas into vulnerable frightened young girls. At best I suppose, they might be useful in providing company and emotional support to those same frightened young women.

---

[n] The term *doula* was first used in a 1969 by Dana Raphael. She suggested it was a common practice in diverse human cultures for a family member or friend to be present before, during and after childbirth (and that their presence contributed to successful long-term breastfeeding). Raphael's derivation of the term is far from clear; she only says that it as comes from *Aristotle's time* (which of course it did).

When I was a student, the *OldSchool* sister midwives would seldom allow anybody in the labour suite, other than doctors and nurses. The father was hardly ever allowed in. I never held my wife's hand in any of her five deliveries. It would have been impossible in the first two of them, since we were living and working in Manchester and I had sent her back across the Pennines to Yorkshire, so that the babies would be born in that hallowed county. Actually, she certainly didn't want me to be around. She considered having a baby to be rather an undignified natural human act and felt that she should be allowed to get on with it without my support. There are of course other natural human acts, which she does not wish me to witness too, but this might come into the *too much information* category.

I believe that quite a lot of modern men have undue pressure put upon them by *NewSchool* hospital staff to attend the delivery, when they do not really wish to do so. They are made to feel it is a *duty* and that their wife needs their *support* and that they should *be there for her,* whether they want to or not. If they choose to go to the pub opposite the maternity hospital, they will be in some way letting *her down at this crucial moment in her life.* I can quite understand the curiosity aspect; this is perhaps the only opportunity they will get after all to witness the wonder of a human birth and they do not want to miss it. In the hospital where I worked before my retirement, two *birthing partners* are allowed in the labour suite. As I said above, I had personally delivered over a score of babies and so the inquisitiveness aspect didn't really apply to me.

Far worse than doulas are some of the potty ideas, which they promulgate. Perhaps the very worst of these is lotus birthing. In fact it is not part of the birth process, but the doulas like to use the word "birthing" rather than "birth." The lotus name is evidently derived from the preciousness of the lotus flower in the Hindu and Buddhist faiths. The Yogis who advocate it, believe that, like the beautiful lotus flower, the placenta (afterbirth) is precious too and suggest that it is not cut off, but carried around with the newborn baby. That's right; they suggest that this repulsive piece of putrefying tissue is left attached to the poor child for up to ten days. This once essential life line for the foetus dies quickly after it has been separated from the mother (i.e. the "birthing") and provides an excellent culture medium for even the most sensitive and fussy germs and bacteria. This could be a potent and perilous source of infection for the child. Advocates of lotus births say that the placenta belongs to the baby who has been touching it in utero, that it is *a very comforting and familiar thing...With lotus birthing you are letting the baby decide when it's ready to break that bond.*[98] I didn't make this up; a yoga instructor mother actually said it.

Instead of making a didactic statement to educate the laity of how dangerous and absurd this practice undoubtedly is, the Royal College of Obstetricians and Gynaecologists *strongly recommended* (in typically mealy-mouthed manner) that any baby that undergoes lotus birthing be monitored closely for infection.

Most other mammals (even herbivores) eat the placenta. It has been suggested that this had a selective advantage because it hid any trace of childbirth from any predators in the area. Your author thinks that the simpler explanation that after labour, the animal is exhausted and hungry and just gets on and eats it up, as well as giving its new offspring a thoroughly good licking. Humans are among the few creatures which don't. The others are whales, dolphins, seals and interestingly the notable exception of the camel. Although the placenta is revered in many diverse cultures, there is no evidence that it is routinely eaten.[99] It would actually make more sense to eat it than to leave it attached to the newborn like a ghastly decomposing security rag.

Before lotussing became the current "birthing" fad, some American mothers actually ate their placenta, claiming of course that it was the *natural* thing to do. This must have been reasonably commonplace in (surprise, surprise) California, because in San Francisco hospitals, you have to sign an informed consent form to take it home with you in a special "placenta bag." When you get it back to the house, there are several options. There are recipes on the Internet for lasagne, stew, stroganoff, curry and many other delicious options.

There is even a book for placentophagia enthusiasts entitled "25 Placenta Recipes".[o] Of course if you are willing to share the delicacy around with your friends, it provides the rare opportunity to throw a "Placenta Party". Failing this, you can have it dried and made into capsules! It is not only rich in iron (a sort of natural black pudding) but contains high levels of important chemicals called prostaglandin and oxytocin. These are two naturally occurring biochemically active substances. Prostaglandins will make the uterus involute or shrink to its original size and oxytocin is a hormone known to assist in breast milk production. There is not much reliable evidence that this happens when taken by mouth however, or after it has been cooked. There have also been (unsubstantiated) suggestions that it might help those mothers with Rhesus problems.[100]

If the new mother eats the placenta, the Whole-Earth-Mothers would have us believe that she will have a reduced risk of post-natal depression and quote some scant evidence from across the Atlantic to support this. In a questionable survey from Florida, where there was a fashion for eating afterbirths, it was found that 75% of new mothers found that if they ate their own placentas (steamed, dehydrated or raw), they had *improved mood, increased energy,* and *improved lactation.*[101]

Another feature of the *OldSchool* childbirth experience (the cringeworthy touchy-feely *NewSchool* term would be the *Patient's Birthing Journey* – I haven't made this up; that is what they actually call it) is the paediatric check up on the child. When I worked as a junior doctor in the Jenny Lind[p] Children's Hospital in Norwich, no new born child delivered

---

[o] *25 Placenta Recipes* by Robin Cook (not the former British Foreign Secretary) *Easy and delicious Recipes for Cooking with Placenta.* 2013. Available on Amazon.

[p] Jenny Lind, (Johanna Maria Lind 1820 – 1887), was one of the most highly regarded opera singers of the 19th century. She was known as the "Swedish Nightingale" and left a huge endowment with which a paediatric hospital was built in Norwich in 1853. This was later pulled down, but rose like a phoenix as the children's wing of the new hospital.

in the Norfolk and Norwich Hospital was allowed home until it had been examined by a medically qualified paediatrician.

In almost all NHS hospitals, this is no longer the case and children are now examined by a midwife! They are not even all seen by the GP when they do get home.

It goes without saying that the diagnosis of any congenital abnormalities as soon as possible is *a good thing*. Listening to a newborn baby's heart is not even easy for experienced doctors. Picking up even large heart defects is notoriously difficult. It is quite unfair and absurd to expect a midwife to be lumbered with this heavy and onerous responsibility and the suggestion that they should go on a one day cardiology course is possibly the acme of the Stasi's stupid suggestions to save money whilst humiliating doctors.

ALICE, MARY, ANNIE, LORNA AND LAURA
Like as a father pitieth his children,
Psalm 103.

My wife Elizabeth is a paediatrician and like me, is a doctor of the *OldSchool*. We met at Sheffield Medical School in 1965 and both qualified in 1970 (although we did not get together until a few years afterwards). We have been blessed by five children and happily all of them have gone on to do their bit for mankind and have had children themselves. When my wife was pregnant with our first child, she was seen by an experienced obstetrician (who indeed had taught both of us the art of obstetrics). He also saw my wife during her second pregnancy and in addition to all the ante-natal and post-natal care; he personally delivered both our first daughters.

I then moved with my work to Manchester. My wife became pregnant again and once again was referred to an obstetric colleague, who looked after her throughout her next two pregnancies and personally delivered our third daughter and eighteen months after that, our first son. My work then took me to Devon and when Liz was blessed with a fifth pregnancy, exactly the same standard of care was given to us by an obstetric colleague down there, who has become a good friend. This personal care was not just because we were both doctors (although the Hippocratic Oath suggests we do look after each other's families): neither was any of this care in the private sector. It was all provided by the NHS. In those halcyon days, which were not that long ago, everyone who was pregnant got to see a medically qualified consultant *at least once*.

This is no longer the case.

In contrast, let me outline what happened to our daughters?

The first to get married and pregnant was living and working over two hundred miles away. She did her own pregnancy test[q] and confirmed her gravid state. She rang her GP, who did not even see her, but his receptionist gave her the telephone number to ring a midwife herself. She did not see a consultant obstetrician then or at any other time during her three pregnancies. The midwife was doubtless a very nice lady, who I am very sure did her best for my daughter. I told Annie (who is a doctor, but not a medical one) that she had the right to see an obstetrician and suggested that the birth of her first child was such an important event that she should ask for this. She did not take my advice however and thought that I was an old fusspot.

She did not want to cause any bother.

I am informed by the Department of Health that since Lansley's unintelligible Health and Social Care Bill which was introduced in 2011 that this is no longer the case anyway and you have to see a midwife whether you want to or not.[102] (So much for patient choice!)

Eventually Annie went into labour. Labour is divided into three stages . The first stage (which might last for a long time, particularly during the first pregnancy) is from when the contractions start and the second stage begins when the cervix becomes fully dilated (it should not go on for more than a couple of hours); the third stage is the actual birth. Annie is not very stoical. She admits to *histrionic screaming in pain* and asking for analgesia. Because it is generally assumed (by the

---

[q] Purchased from the dispensing chemist and sometimes referred to as "Mother Scare" kits.

majority of both men and women) that the Biblical admonition at the beginning of this chapter[r] is nowadays perhaps somewhat outdated and further that there should not be any pain whatsoever during childbirth, she was given an epidural[103],[s] (this was actually done by a medically qualified person, albeit a junior) and then she was left in peace. Her first stage lasted nine hours. Then her cervix was fully dilated (onset of second stage) and she was told to start pushing.

Some two and a half hours later, Anne was getting a bit exhausted and there was no sign of progress. She was a bit fazed too about the midwife who kept leaving the room because she had a migraine. She had gone into labour at midnight and now it was coming up to midday. This delay in the second stage is considered *a bad thing*. It can be a very bad thing for the baby, who in Annie's case was showing signs of definite distress on the monitor. The migrainous midwife then sent for another junior doctor to come and have a look at her. He put one hand on her tummy and told them that because she had a full bladder, the baby could not get past and that she should be catheterised. As soon as this was done, three litres of urine were drawn from her bladder and the labour progressed like night follows day. Emma was born within five minutes. The epidural numbs sensation below the waist and the overwhelming urge to pass water under normal circumstances is abolished. Unfortunately it also decreases the urge and ability to push and increases the likelihood of needing forceps. Indeed, when I was a lad, an epidural invariably led on to a forceps delivery.

The reason why delay in the second stage is not considered to be a good thing is that during this period of labour, the blood supply to the child's brain might well be reduced because of the pressure round the child's neck and the squashing of the umbilical cord. Muscle cells can go without

---

[r] To save you turning back, it said, *Thou shalt bring forth thy children in pain.*

[s] This is an anaesthetic or analgesic by which a drug is introduced into the spine to relieve pain during labour. The rate of permanent paralysis of the legs following this is 1:250,000. Strictly speaking an analgesic removes pain but an anaesthetic takes away sensation as well as pain.

oxygen for hours but brain cells are not very good at this and can never be replaced if they die off. I think that even hospital administrators might realise that this is not such a good thing. Whether or not they would be concerned about it however, is open to conjecture. Sadly my oldest granddaughter who is a sweet little girl has minimal cerebral palsy (according to my paediatrician wife) as a result of this delay.

Annie however, went on to have two more little girls (again she did the Mother Scare pregnancy test, which she bought from the pharmacy herself) and once again never saw a specialist. She says that on the last two occasions, she never even saw the GP. Now that she was better informed, (albeit not by the midwife), when she went into labour, she refused to have the epidural. She of course experienced some pain, but says that she thought that it was far preferable being in control of the whole situation, rather than having no feelings at all below her waist.

Her second and third confinements both went quickly and satisfactorily.

The third child was sent home without seeing a paediatrician. There was no question of lotus birthing or anything else unorthodox, but the umbilical stump did seem rather long to Annie and it stank. Annie and the sisters all kept thinking that the baby's nappy was full. Annie 'phoned her mother who told her to tell the midwife the very next day. She did and the midwife cheerily told her, "*Gorgonzola, that's normal!*" Annie's mother was duly summoned and soon confirmed that the stinking baby smelled of the rank stench of putrefaction from an infected umbilical stump. Minor surgery and an antibiotic soon cured it but not in time to stop Annie from getting mastitis and in turn a pulmonary embolus. Happily these were seen and treated by doctors and mother and baby are now well.

This obsession with saving money by sending mothers home as soon as possible, but not necessarily as safe as possible was criticised in a recent (2014) report from the Royal College of Midwives. It admitted that 40% of mothers thought that they had been sent home too early (some claiming that they were discharged from hospital two hours after the birth!)

and the midwives blamed the Stasi, saying *"women are discharged inadequately prepared from the ward because the hospital is grossly understaffed."*[104]

BIRTHING IN CHELTENHAM

If the cock goes crowing to bed,
He's sure to rise with a watery head[†]
Proverb (1846) Denham.

Two months after my first grandchild was born, my second daughter had her first baby (2008). She too (against my fatherly advice) never saw a consultant gynaecologist.

Unlike her younger sister, she is lucky enough to have an *OldSchool* GP who believes he has a duty of care to examine his patients (how novel is that?). After having seen her and confirming her pregnancy, he then sent her to see the midwives. She lives in Cheltenham, where they had just refurbished a brand spanking new maternity block (St Paul's Wing). Unfortunately however, the crass hospital administrators did not have enough midwives to staff it adequately and it has since been closed! They had clearly not followed the old axiom that people are more important than places.

Part of the touchy-feely duties of the modern midwife are to provide the pregnant ladies (especially those in their first pregnancies and not knowing what to expect) with a series of ante-natal classes. These are sometimes unkindly called "*Play School*" and are really meant for terrified young girls who have no idea what is going to happen. The lasses are given four or five tutorials about things like the stages of labour and breastfeeding to prepare them for their delivery. My daughter, who is a lawyer, did not really fit into this category, but I am sure that there were many who did. Because they were so grievously short of staff, they gave her one short talk and showed her the new labour ward instead.

When Mary then went into labour, at least she knew where to go. In those days (thank God!) St Paul's Wing was attached

---

[†] If the cock crows in the evening, it will rain the following day.

to a proper general hospital with obstetric specialist doctors and paediatricians. She did not have an epidural and initially the labour (albeit a first one) progressed quickly. Then things almost came to a standstill and there was clearly delay in the second stage (which you will remember is *not a good thing*). It was eventually found that the umbilical cord was wrapped twice around the baby's neck and so every time that my daughter pushed the head down, it was pulled back up by the cord. As soon as the cord was clamped and divided, my granddaughter was born, although somewhat blue and with a long pointed head (known as "moulding"). Mother and child went home the next day.

My paediatrician wife was then urgently summoned to see the babe who was choking on all the mucus she had swallowed and inhaled during parturition. The good doctor slapped little Darcey on the back. She stopped choking and Mary was reassured. In the past this would not have happened, because the babies were not sent home until they had passed urine, filled their first nappy, coughed out all the ingested mucus, etc. etc.

A few years later, with her second baby, the local Stasi had had a change of heart and moved all proper hospital obstetric facilities to Gloucester. The St Paul's Wing had become the Cheltenham *Birthing Centre* in 2011. My cultured, educated readers might experience a mild revulsion at the use of the word "*birthing*." Try to indulge it. Clearly some people can't pronounce the word, parturition. Birthing is not yet an official word in the 2013 Cambridge English Dictionary,^u but has been in the Oxford one for at least ten years. Evidently all you have to do to get a word in the Oxford English Dictionary is to use it often enough. It certainly does not exist in any of the three *OldSchool* dictionaries in my own personal library, but then they are all over thirty years old or more. I had to ask, "*were our children birthed or born?*" Be consoled that at least the word is not quite as bad as "*gifting*".

---

^u The Cambridge Dictionary does however contain *berthing* which means *tying up a boat securely.*

The opening of the *Birthing Centre* coincided with a new £29 million *Women's Centre* in Gloucester. Officially this *is to cater for women needing medical or anaesthetic help during labour.* For any *OldSchool* readers still struggling with this PC gobbledegook, I think this must be the new term for maternity wing. Just to confuse us all further we are told that the philosophy of the *Birthing Centre* is going *to be totally women-centred* and have *very much a family atmosphere.*[105] Mary went back to the midwife-run unit in Cheltenham (which was less than half a mile from where she lived) and found that she was in exactly the same room as for her first confinement, *but now they had painted the wall purple and put in a couple of lava lamps and a sofa.* She had her second child in a birthing pool. This pool is definitely a *NewSchool* innovation. (I think we unwittingly used to have one outside in our garden, until the bulldog tore the side out of it.)

I am not quite sure how this idea of having babies underwater came about,[v] because whatever else it is, it is certainly not natural: I can think of no terrestrial animals or primitive tribes who give birth naturally in rivers or ponds. I have to assume that it all came about because warm water can aid relaxation and ease pain. It is not without risks however. Very definite dangers include unexplained deaths, drowning and near-drowning, asphyxiation, water intoxication (hyponatraemia) causing seizures, water aspiration leading to respiratory distress syndrome and respiratory failure, pulmonary oedema, broken umbilical cords, brain damage from lack of oxygen, pneumonia, and other infections including septicaemia.

I know that in a (typically mealy-mouthed) joint statement issued by the Royal Colleges of Obstetricians and Gynaecologists and Midwives, water birth was *not recommended in cases of complications.*[106] I always find it very irritating when the Americans can be shown to do something better than the British, but I found that the American Academy of Paediatrics (who have clearly been

---

[v] Igor Tjarkovsky a Soviet researcher and swimming instructor pioneered the idea of giving birth underwater in 1960.

taught to be very cautious, because of all the litigation) are much less worried about upsetting the Whole-Earth Mother lobby and stated quite didactically at the same time that *underwater birth should be considered an experimental procedure.*[107]

Mary found the pool business quite comfortable (unlike one of my other daughters, Alice, who said that instead of just being in pain, she was in pain and also too hot!) Anyway the birth of Mary's second child went well, although she admits to great apprehension about being so far away from proper medical back-up. She was warned that she would receive no pain relief in the Birthing Centre (at least they don't spell it *Center*), but told that only three ladies a year needed to be sent to Gloucester Hospital Maternity Unit (aka *Women's Centre*).

As she was lying in the pool, she realised that she personally knew all three of those unlucky women. Indeed she reckoned that in the last couple of years, at least seven of her friends had started their labour in the Cheltenham unit with every good intention of a pain-relief-free birth experience. Then, as she puts it *"the birthing plan gets shredded,"* when a decision is made mid-way through labour for them to be sent to the real hospital unit in Gloucester. They then have to get out of the pool, dry themselves off and zoom off to Gloucester Royal. This means they need to be driven ten miles in their bewildered husbands' cars (and during the second stage of labour) across the city centres of Cheltenham and Gloucester, looking for the hospital and then when they find it, not knowing where to go, since they had never been before.

Perhaps she thought they had meant three a week. Mary says that if she had a first pregnancy again, even though it is further away from home, she would certainly go straight to Gloucester (where incidentally, on 29 December 2010 Her Majesty's first great-grandchild[w] was born).

As it happened my daughter went to Gloucester Royal Hospital the very next day anyway. It was New Year's Day

---

[w] HRH Princess Anne's baby girl (weighing 8 lbs 8oz) and named Savannah Phillips.

and (as we shall see in a later chapter) bank holidays are never good days to go to hospital. She had gone back to the Birthing Centre to get baby Belle's neonatal paediatric check-up done. The experienced midwife looked at the one day old child and suggested that because her breathing was too fast, she should be seen by a doctor and so that meant a traipse across two city centres to Gloucester. After hours waiting at the real General Hospital, Mary and little Belle were seen by a specialist, reassured that there was absolutely no problem at all and sent home.

By sharp contrast their sister, Alice happens to live near me and her mother. Her ante-natal (and post natal) care for both her babies was by a consultant obstetrician, who was delighted to do this for his colleague's daughter. There were no problems in her confinements, which were both supervised by him and he personally delivered two more granddaughters (Lily and Mabel).

LORNA AND ROSE CHEEKED LAURA
I am all the daughters of my father's house.
William Shakespeare (1601) *Twelfth Night. II, 4,122.*

I am relating stories about births in my family because that seems a fair way of selecting a random small group. My reader can then compare the *OldSchool* experiences of my wife and eldest daughter, who both had the personal attendance of consultant obstetricians with the younger girls who didn't. They were under the care of midwives. We also have two sons, both of whom have done their bit for the gene pool. My older son Bertie was the first to provide us with a grandchild, which was over ten years ago. My younger son, William is married to Lorna and she too has had one baby. I told them both to demand to see a consultant obstetrician, but like their siblings, they did not want to make a fuss and since they did not live in the same town, I did not have the opportunity to have a few words with my hospital colleagues.

Lorna went a couple of weeks overdue. Now an *OldSchool* GP would have known that she had been recorded at a pre-conception family planning clinic (by a doctor, who took a proper clinical history) that her father had very high blood pressure and also that at that time she had a high blood pressure herself. The *OldSchool* obstetrician would very probably have got her into hospital at that point and started her off. But of course nowadays there is no doctor around. A couple of days later, she rang the midwife to say at last she had started to have contractions every 6 minutes. The midwife told her to hang on until they were every 5 minutes and then go to the Birthing Centre. Four hours later, the contractions stopped. Shortly after this, the baby stopped kicking.

Lorna had lost faith in the midwife and so made a telephone call to me. I told her to get along to the hospital as quickly as possible. At first they tried to fob her off (again) but when they checked her blood pressure (which was extremely high) and did a urine test, these tests showed that she had an extremely dangerous condition of pregnancy called *pre-eclamptic toxaemia*. She was immediately admitted. This PET (pre-eclampsia) is a hazardous condition to both mothers and babies and is still the second major cause of mothers' death in Great Britain.[108] Only urgent intervention can prevent it from turning into full blown *Eclampsia*. This is what happened with poor Lorna. Although she was stable, nothing positive was done until the following morning, when her face started to swell up and she started to have convulsions. These alarming signs are the typical indications of this terrible condition. At last an emergency Caesarian section was performed. Amazingly they wanted her to go home the following day, but she refused. You might say all's well that ends well, but is it? Poor little Ernie was a runt of a child and did not seem to thrive for a number of weeks. Happily he is now flourishing.

What about poor Laura?

She had been struggling in the second stage of her first ever labour for hours. She was in hospital, getting exhausted and thoroughly fed up – pushing and pushing, but to no avail. It was her first time, so she had no experience of what things should feel like. Eventually the busy over-worked midwife, who had examined Laura half an hour previously, decided that she had gone over the maximum time limit and told Laura and her mum (an experienced child-bearer) that she would arrange for a "C section." (This is the lay term for a Caesarian section.) The midwife gave Laura's mum a pair of those nice white stockings to put on her daughter for the operating theatre. Lo and behold! What did she find as she pulled them on her feet? She could see the baby's little head coming towards her. After initial disbelief, the midwife agreed and little Isabella was delivered vaginally.

So there you are, dear reader. I leave it to you to decide for yourself. Was the elimination of the GP and gynaecologist from the *OldSchool* system a good thing? Is the *NewSchool* touchy-feely system equally as safe for mother and baby? I was speaking to one of the new commissioners, (a GP) who reminded me that women have been having babies with the help of midwives (or wise women, or even doulas) for millennia. I told him he had clearly gone to the dark side and missed the point. I reminded him that maternal mortality in UK is soaring and we are now trailing behind countries like Albania, Poland and Slovakia. My point is that the only possible way to improve it is to go back to the *OldSchool* practice of having all deliveries in hospital and under the care of an obstetrician.

That would also (on the balance of probabilities) improve the soaring rate of cerebral palsy in newborn babies, because one of the main causes of this is a delayed second stage of labour.

The *NewSchool* midwives will not agree with this, since it takes away their new found kudos. My cynical wife says that the specialists themselves have not fought against it, because of course it makes their lives a lot easier now than their *OldSchool* predecessors, who used to work much longer hours and frequently get called in in the middle of the night.

THE SAD CASE OF LITTLE KATE
But none of us cared for Kate
William Shakespeare (1611) *The Tempest.* II, 2, 52.

The Stasi of course are pushing for more births in community hospitals where no obstetricians are available and the care is entirely in the hands of midwives. This would of course work out a lot cheaper and leave more money in the pot for the huge salaries of the managers. Hardly surprisingly the promotion of these midwife-led centres is strongly endorsed by the Royal College of Midwives. (Well they would wouldn't they?)

The parents of a baby who died in a midwife-led maternity unit in Shropshire in 2009 and had to wait until 2012 for a full coroner's inquest have strong views to the contrary. The mother and father of Kate Stanton Davis have called for improvements after an inquest jury found that their baby would probably have survived at a hospital with obstetricians.

Kate's parents believe that the Ludlow Community Hospital and units like it should provide ante-natal and post-natal care but not be used for deliveries.

It seems that the jury agreed with them.

Kate Stanton-Davies died just six hours after she was born. Experts at the inquest advised the jury that her mother, Rhiannon should have been categorised as high risk and she should never have been sent to Ludlow Community Hospital. Asked whether being delivered at Ludlow contributed to her death, the jury unanimously said yes. The mother said, *"Throughout the various stages of my pregnancy and Kate's birth we, as a family, have been let down by the various organisations within the NHS. Knowing what we know now I would never have consented to have given birth at Ludlow maternity unit.*[109]

Rhiannon had been seen several times by midwives in the two weeks before Kate was born, because she was worried that something was wrong with her unborn child. She was admitted to "hospital" twice.[110] When the baby was delivered by the midwives, she was cold and floppy. But at the inquest, the midwife in charge of her admitted that she left Kate in a hypothermic state in a cold cot for a prolonged period of time while she went about routine ward work.

The pathologist who had performed the post-mortem on the baby told the inquest that Kate was extremely anaemic: she had evidently suffered a rare complication which led to haemorrhage inside the womb. But he also said that this could have probably been corrected by a transfusion in the womb or immediately after she was delivered had she been in a hospital run by doctors.[111]

Some two hours later, the midwives eventually decided to send the floppy baby to a neonatal intensive care baby unit at Shrewsbury Hospital, but things just got worse. The air ambulance set off for Shrewsbury but was told as they approached that they could not land, because the hospital helipad was closed! The doctor on board then suggested they go to Birmingham Children's Hospital. He can perhaps be forgiven for making the presumption that they would have a neonatal unit there. You might think that the air ambulance helicopter pilots might have been able to set him right in his mistaken assumption, but when they approached the Birmingham Children's Hospital they were informed that this was not the case and sent on to Heartlands Hospital.

Birmingham Children's Hospital does not have a neonatal unit. It might seem almost incredible but it was closed by the Stasi years ago.

As they flew in to Heartlands, they were then told that the helipad there too was closed and they could not land! As though matters could not possibly have got worse, the mobile team had discovered that the baby airway tubes held on the air Ambulance were not fit for purpose. The poor baby was in a grave state by now and the helicopter pilots decided to land in a nearby field. Meanwhile the frantic parents had been driving about the West Midlands making calls to find out where their daughter had gone.

The paediatrician on call at Heartlands said she *was "angry; by the time Kate got to me she was virtually dead. There was nothing I could do to save her."* The information sent by the midwives was a bit scanty; *"When Kate arrived at the hospital, there was just a pink slip with the mother's name and Kate's birth weight."* No clinical notes had been made by the midwives.

Richard arrived in time to hold Kate for a few minutes as she died, but Rhiannon never got to hold her daughter whilst she was alive. She did not make it in time. She said to the inquest: *"I was met by a nurse. I said, 'she's dead, isn't she?*

because I just felt that she had gone, and the nurse just nodded. I collapsed."

Notwithstanding the ante-natal concerns that Rhiannon had experienced, I just cannot understand how a first time delivery would ever have been considered for a midwife unit rather than a hospital.

When this was reported on the Channel 4 Television News, the chap with the hideous neckties said sanctimoniously afterwards, *"A shattering account of medical failure."* This surely underlines the misconception that the general public has about midwives and the essential difference between them and obstetricians: he did not say *"a shattering account of midwifery failure,"* which is what Her Majesty's Coroner had said earlier.

REFERENCES

[81]. ARNOTT, Stephen (2004) *Eating Your Auntie is Wrong, The World's Strangest Customs.* Ebury, London, p.21.

[82]. DORKENOO, Efua (1994) *Cutting the Rose.* Minority Rights Publications, London.

[83]. PANDEY, U; LINDOW, SW (2006) *Should obstetrics and gynaecology be separate specialities?* J Obstet Gynaecol. 26(4):305.

[84]. PINKI P, SAYASNEH A, LINDOW SW: (2007) *The working relationship between midwives and junior doctors.* J Obstet Gynaecol. 27(4):365.

[85]. PERSONAL COMMUNICATION (2013) Louise Silverton, Director for Midwifery, RCM.

[86]. OFFICE FOR NATIONAL STATISTICS. (2009) *Infant and perinatal mortality* 2008: health areas, England and Wales.

[87]. ERASMUS MC (2010) *Care given during pregnancy and childbirth can and should be improved.* 5 July.

[88]..THE SKEPTICAL OB (2010) *The Netherlands, homebirth and the high mortality rate.* July 19, (Blog)

[89]. WALKER, JJ (2010) *Confidential enquiries into maternal mortality.* BJOG;117:379–381.

[90]. BASTIAN, Hilda; KIERSE, Marc; LANCASTER, Paul, (1998) *Perinatal death associated with planned home birth in Australia:* BritMedJ*; 317:384*

[91]. BEWLEY, Susan; HELLEUR Angela (2010) *Rising maternal deaths in London, UK.* The Lancet, Volume 379, Issue 9822, Page 1198.

[92]. THE GUARDIAN (2010) *Maternal mortality: how many women die in childbirth in your country?* 13 Apr.

[93]. LAURANCE, Jeremy (2012) *Doubling of maternal death rate blamed on shortage of midwives.* Independent. 30 Apr.

[94]. http://hurtbyhomebirth.blogspot.co.uk. Thursday, January 17, 2013

[95]. BEWLEY, Susan; HELLEUR Angela (2010) *op. cit.* (n.11)

[96]. MANDER, R (2001). *The doula. Supportive care and midwifery.* John Wiley. pp. 113–33.

[97]. HWANG, S (2004). *As 'Doulas' Enter Delivery Rooms, Conflicts Arise: Hired to Help in Childbirth, They Sometimes Clash With Doctors and Nurses.* The Wall Street Journal. 19 Jan.

[98]. CARROLL, Helen (2013) *Is this the craziest (and most reckless) birthing fad ever?)* Daily Mail. 26 Sep. p. 46.

[99]. YOUNG, SM, BENYSHEK, DC. (2010) *In Search of Human Placentophagy: A Cross-Cultural Survey of Human Placenta Consumption, Disposal Practices, and Cultural Beliefs.* Ecol Food Nutr. 49(6):467-84.

[100]. KRISTAL, Mark B. (2013) *Placentophagia: A Biobehavioral Enigma:* Neuroscience & Biobehavioral Reviews, Vol. 4, pp. 141--150.

[101]. BAWANY, Afsha. (2013) *Steamed, Dehydrated or Raw: Placentas May Help Moms* Post-Partum Health. February 27

[102]. PERSONAL COMMUNICATION (2013) Department of Health Helpline (Rachel Corby) 23 Oct.

[103]. WILSON, IH; ALLMAN, KG (2006) *Oxford Handbook of Anaesthesia.*
Oxford University Press. p. 21.

[104]. BORLAND, Sophie (2014) *Hospitals sent us home too early, say 40% of new mums, with some saying they were rushed out just two hours after giving birth.* Daily Mail 24 August

[105]. WILLIAMS, Hazel (2011) *£250,000 to give new mums 'perfect' space.* Gloucestershire Echo. 11 Jan.

[106]. ROYAL COLLEGE OF MIDWIVES/ROYAL COLLEGE OF OBSTETRICIANS AND GYNAECOLOGISTS. (2006) *Immersion in water during labour and birth.*

[107]. BATTON, D. G.; BLACKMON, L. R.; ADAMKIN, D. H.; BELL, E. F.; DENSON, S. E.; ENGLE, W. A.; MARTIN, G. I.; STARK, A. R. et al. (2005). *Underwater Births.* Pediatrics 115 (5): 1413–1414

[108]. WILLIAMS, D, CRAFT N; (2012) *Pre-eclampsia.* BritMedJ. Jul 19;345

[109]. SHROPSHIRE STAR (2012*) Fury at NHS over death of Ludlow couple's newborn baby.* 17 November

[110]. TEMPLETON, Sarah-Kate (2012) My baby's dead, isn't she, nurse?' The Sunday Times *18 November 2012.*

[111]. MACDONALD, Victoria (2012) *Call to make midwife-led maternity units safe.* Channel 4 News 19 Nov XII

CHAPTER 5

COME BACK DR SNODDY, ALL IS FORGIVEN

IN A NUTSHELL; OldSchool vs. NewSchool:
OldSchool: School doctors went into schools and vaccinated and immunised school children. The take-up rate was excellent. Doctors examined every single school child and picked up things which might well have been missed by the GP. Sight, hearing and growth were all checked at regular intervals.
NewSchool: School doctors have been discontinued. The percentage of children immunised in the community has dropped to such alarmingly low levels that mumps and measles outbreaks are increasing. Schoolchildren no longer get a routine medical examination and diseases and disabilities such as undescended testicles and foreskin problems in boys are commonly being missed. Children are frequently still bedwetting when they reach secondary school. No child ever gets his vision checked at school nowadays.

DR FINLAY'S CRUSTY DETRACTOR[a]

My mother's life was a canopy slung from the three tent poles of dirt, disease and the lavatory.
Alan Bennett (1982) *Intensive Care.*

Dr Finlay's Casebook was prime time television viewing during the sixties and I am reliably informed by an old lady who lives in our village that it was not only better but more popular than its lineal successors, *Casualty* and *Holby City.*[b] It

---

[a] This is how poor old Dr Snoddy is described in Wikipedia.
[b] These are both BBC prime time medical soaps, but set in hospitals rather than rural GP.

was based on a book written by Scottish physician, social critic and novelist, A. J. Cronin. The long running BBC series (which was in sparkling black and white) ran for nine years and was based on Cronin's own experiences about a general practice in the highlands of Scotland. One of the memorable characters was Dr Snoddy, the Medical Officer of Health (MOH) for Tannochbrae. Dr Snoddy was never really shown in a very good light, but was always immaculately turned out in morning dress, which was slightly offset by the fact that he was usually carrying a small glass vial containing faeces or sputum. Perhaps this was a reflection of the (unfair) way that quite a lot of medical colleagues used to view public health doctors.

They were usually called *drain sniffers*. This pejorative epithet probably takes its rise from the time when the old Medical Officers of Health appeared to concern themselves mainly with dirt, sanitation and the lavatory. In fact, Dr Snoddy and the appointment of MOH were relics of Sir Edwin Chadwick's Public Health Act of 1848. Chadwick was a barrister and believed (quite rightly) that effective sanitation, improved drainage and water closets for all, would radically improve the health of the nation. His report[112] was mainly concerned with sanitary reforms, but also separated public health doctors (the drain sniffers) from the rest of clinical[c] medicine (a schism which still persists).

Medical Officers of Health were doctors of the *OldSchool*, but at least they were medically qualified and intelligent. Quite a lot of them had been excellent clinicians in the past and understood clinical problems. The latest "good idea" of government has been to appoint a layman as the *NewSchool* chief executive of PHE. Yes that's the new name for it, I haven't made this up; the official name for the layman-led service is *Public Health England*. The chap who was appointed in July 2012 (Duncan Selbie) will be paid £180,000-£185,000 and he is definitely not medically qualified. His previous job was the chief executive at the hospital in

---

[c] From the Greek κλίνη (*cline*): bed.

Brighton, where "Dr" Spiers worked before him. It is important to clarify the "Dr" Spiers business. John Spiers was definitely not medically qualified either: he had however received a D.Mus. (hon.) from Sussex University. Although it is generally considered a bit naff to use the title "doctor" when honorary – particularly when working in a hospital where there are a lot of physicians about, your author will refrain from any interpretation of his motives in this respect.

Spiers attained national notoriety when he was designated by the British Medical Association as the *Man Doctors Love to Hate*[113] for publicly stating that *he would not choose to travel in a railway carriage* with consultants from the Brighton hospital. They must have been a sensitive lot because they considered that this statement by Spiers (and broadcast on the 6 o'clock television news) was disrespectful and inappropriate. At the next Medical Executive Meeting at the hospital a vote of no confidence was passed (which would have been unanimous, but for the medical director who declined to support it – see also *Quislings* in Chapter 7). He then left and became Chairman of the Patients' Association. After that he took the rôle as head of PHE and eventually his job was taken over by Mr Selbie.

One qualification which Mr Selbie appears to have is his grasp of the use of English. The Stasi's poor English is as stereotypical as a doctor's poor handwriting. Mr Selbie said (and I have been very careful to get this verbatim), *"The bit that I don't so easily recognise is that folk are being asked to do jobs they didn't – because almost 95% - maybe 97% are moving exactly as they are into the new system."*[114]

I wish him well.

THE PUBLIC DETERIORATION REPORT

Video meliora, proboque:
Deteriora sequor[d]
Ovid (43BC – 17AD) *Metamorphosis*, vii, 20.

---

[d] *I see better things and I approve of them, but sadly I follow the worse.*

The first ever health visitors were the *Ladies' Sanitary Reform Association of Manchester and Salford.* They were more concerned with the welfare and feeding of babies and were originally "good sort" volunteers, who visited nursing mothers in slums to advise them not to give cabbage water to the newborn. They were usually gentlefolk driven by a philanthropic Christian ethic. Some were the wives of aristocrats (and the *nouveau riches* wives of millionaire mill owners, who were trying to emulate them) and they all had to be wealthy enough to take on unpaid work during Victoria's glorious reign. These Salford *lady sanitary inspectors* became salaried in 1890 and fell under the auspices of the Manchester Medical Officer of Health (MOH). The city of Worcester also appointed *lady health missioners* and towards the end of the nineteenth century a number of other local authorities began to appoint similar ladies. In 1896, *"The Women Sanitary Inspectors Association"* was formed,[115] which then became the Health Visitors Association.[e]

Their specific task was to work with mothers and promote infant and child care and the prevention of the spread of infection. This mainly involved going out to the homes of young mothers and advising them on breast feeding, weaning and the importance of cleanliness. We were told at medical school that they warned mothers against giving cabbage water to their offspring, but they did give general advice on nutrition and other aspects of what has now become known as "parenting". This neologism did not exist when I was a student.

The first school doctor in the UK was appointed in 1890 in London,[f] with Bradford following three years later.[116] Initially his main task would be preventing malnutrition in schoolchildren but medical examinations in schools started in

---

[e] Actually it is now called the *Community Practitioners and Health Visitors Association*, but your author thinks the word *Practitioner* is rather misleading and smacks a bit of a medical qualification although it only includes health visitors, school nurses, nursery nurses and other community nurses.

[f] The first in the world was in Germany; two school doctors were appointed in Frankfurt-am Main in 1883.

1907. Medical Officers of Health had been in existence for quite a few years prior to this, since 1872.

There had been a national scandal following the outbreak of the Boer War in 1899 when it was even obvious to the recruiting sergeants that many of the British working class men were not fit *enough to bear arms in defence of their realm.* In 1902, General Maurice announced that *"out of every five men that are willing to serve* (in the Army) *only two are fit to become effective soldiers."*[117] It was even worse than this. There was already a popular belief that there had been a massive deterioration of the health of the nation, since the Industrial Revolution. This was not thought to be due to social deprivation, being forced to live in slums and the exploitation of the poor, but it was believed that there was some *hereditary* result of the migration of people from the countryside into the towns and cities. Whatever the cause, the manhood of Britain was now withering on the vine and two out of five young men were unfit for military service.

Could anything be done to combat this plummeting deterioration of the nation's health? After all, the defence of the realm was at stake.

In 1903, as a result of General Maurice's plea to Parliament, the *Public Deterioration Committee* was set up. Its findings were most reassuring. Although there were *"unfortunately very abundant signs of physical defect traceable to neglect, poverty and ignorance,"* there was no evidence of *"any hereditary effects!*[118]*"* In fact, the Public Deterioration Report marked an important turning point in the history of the provision of public health. The Government decided to make a much greater investment in the welfare of its children. It started to provide school meals and free school medical examinations and on 1st January 1908, the School Health Service was established. This *represented a major new development ... and can be regarded as one of the most important single steps on the road to the creation of the 'welfare state'.*[119]

MATERNITY, CHILD WELFARE AND SCHOOL CLINICS

There is no finer investment for any
community than putting milk into babies.
Winston Churchill. (1943) *Radio Broadcast.*

After the Second World War, babies and young children were regularly reviewed in maternity and child welfare clinics. These were run by clinical medical officers and health visitors. My wife was a CMO in Manchester and worked at one of these welfare clinics. The health visitors were the worker bees and in those days their basic training was longer than that of a doctor; they had to be a State Registered Nurse (which took three years), a State Registered Midwife (another two) and then do a final year's specialist training as a health visitor. This was six years when most doctors only did five. The health visitors were (and perhaps still are) the élite of the nurses.

They were of course the lineal descendants of the aristocratic sanitary reformers. They provided a vital rôle in the clinics, advising the mothers of young babies on nutrition and monitoring whether or not the infants were thriving by measuring weight and height and recording it on growth charts. These *OldSchool* growth charts, which were kept in the child's clinic medical records, until the late nineties, when one of the senior drain sniffers got a "good idea" and got rid of them. They were replaced by the *NewSchool* "Red Book."[g] This is like the French system of medical notes, where the patients keep their own. A little red booklet is given to the parents, who are expected to bring it with the child every time he sees the doctor. This of course does not happen and the red book inevitably gets lost so that if an adolescent develops a

---

[g] Not to be confused with other famous Red Books. The most famous was the pocket-size edition of *Quotations from Chairman Mao* Tse-Tung, from the People's Republic of China, but there were other less well-known political or ideological red booklets (all predictably socialist). There first was an Albanian one written in 1911 and there was even a Canadian *Red Book* (1993). The Danish *Little Red Schoolbook*, (which targeted schoolchildren inciting them to anarchy) published in 1969 was banned in France and Italy.

growth problem, the *NewSchool* community paediatrician has no idea about the previous patterns of growth, which are no longer kept in the safety of the child's notes.

The clinic health visitors also checked on the immunisation and vaccination status and did examinations of both eyesight and hearing. Any child that the health visitors were worried about would be referred to the clinic doctor, who was right there on the spot, rather than to the child's GP, who might indeed never get to see them. The welfare clinic doctors also gave the immunisations and did developmental checks on every single pre-school child.

When the child started school at five years old, the health visitor would hand over to the school nurse. It was her responsibility to then make sure that every child was offered a routine medical examination at the ages of five, eleven and fifteen years old. This was done by the school doctor. The height and weight charts, which had been handed over by the health visitor were filled in and any discrepancies in growth would be picked up. Importantly the vision and hearing were also checked at these ages. Booster jabs were given and remember this was a captive audience. There was no extra fag of the parents remembering and making a special visit to the doctors. All the children were at school in those days.

This was a particularly important consideration in immunisation programmes for as we shall see later, when this captive audience was lost and the parents had to take their children to the GP, the rate of uptake fell. All eleven to thirteen-year-old girls would be given their German measles jabs and all thirteen-year-olds of both sexes were tested to see if they needed BCG[h] vaccine. All the children were checked to see that all their other immunisations (polio, diphtheria, tetanus and measles) were up to date and if for any reason they were not, the school doctor would immunise them on the spot.

The BCG vaccination was for tuberculosis. Believe it or not, even though there were more than 6,000 people diagnosed with the disease in 2002 (an increase of 25% over the previous

---

[h] Bacille Calmette-Guérin is a vaccine used to inoculate against tuberculosis, named after the two French bacteriologists.

decade), routine vaccination was stopped a few years later in September 2005. Only a mere 350 people a year were dying and they were clearly not enough to warrant costly prevention. Since stopping the vaccination, the rate has continued to increase and is now among the highest in Europe (8,751 new cases in 2012).[120] The official reason why BCG was terminated was evidently because *experts say that is hugely cost-ineffective* and *for every 5,000 children vaccinated, one case of TB would be prevented.*[121] I am not an accountant but that doesn't seem such a bad option to me. I bet it sounds an even better option to the parents of every poor unlucky little devil who gets it.

The CMO (clinical medical officer) worked at both the maternity and baby clinics and as the school doctor. They would also do family planning clinics (which should really be called contraception clinics), "Well Women Clinics,"[i] occupational health medicals, adoption medicals, geriatric medicals and sex education in schools. In a move to make more money for their pets, the GPs, the BMA suggested to the Minister of Health that all these jobs should be done by general practitioners, who of course would be paid per item of service. The Government (knowing no better) believed them.

This was a (not even thinly disguisedly) purely mercenary manoeuvre and the public health of the nation suffered accordingly. Let me give you one eloquent example. The clinical medical officers were often specialist developmental paediatricians and had had years of experience assessing whether or not children below the age of five under their aegis were developing normally (or not). When the job was transferred to the GPs, countless thousands of pounds were spent on sending them all on two-day courses (to learn in a couple of days a very specialised subject). When they first returned from these courses, they may well have done a few developmental medicals, but would you be surprised to learn that when the novelty wore off, this job was quickly relegated to the poor health visitor (who had not even been on a two day

---

[i] Even though men have always had a shorter life expectancy than women, "Well-Men Clinics" did not start until at least twenty years later.

course). Nowadays any form of under-five developmental paediatric check by *NewSchool* GPs has virtually ceased. Once again I leave my readers to make their own decision as to whether things have improved.

OldSchool health visitors were reasonably happy because they used to be attached to a named GP. Then the Stasi got the good idea that health visitors should be designated as *professionals in their own right.* They were probably pleased when they heard of this new accolade until they found that they were to be taken out of GP medical centres and stuck in with the school nurses. Like every other player in the NHS, morale plummeted and at present there is a nationwide problem in recruiting them.

They tended to keep an eye on the pre-school children and the under-fives, advising young mothers on problems of parenthood (I adamantly refuse to use the *NewSchool* word, *parenting*) such as potty training. Because of the shortage of HVs, there are now myriads of five-year-olds starting primary school, who are unable to speak properly, dress themselves, feed themselves using basic cutlery, or use the lavatory (for either defaecation or urination). My daughter who is a teacher at a primary school, informs me that in every intake class of four-year-olds, there is at least one child who is wearing a nappy. A few years ago, children were not even allowed into the pre-school nursery unless they were fully potty trained. Then because of the politically correct dogma of *inclusion*, this policy was abolished so that special needs (NewSpeak for *handicapped*) children were not excluded. When I was a medical student, we were taught that normal children should all be potty trained by 2 years and 9 months (when they were about to go to nursery). Because of the PC *inclusion* business, things appear to be going backwards and this is one target which sadly no longer needs to be met.

THE IMPORTANCE OF COUNTING TESTICLES
If you've got them by the balls, their hearts and minds will follow.
John Wayne, US Cowboy Film Star. (1907 – 1979)

For nearly forty years, I served in the Territorial Army. Most of this time was during the "Cold War" and the "Big (Regular) Army" particularly valued the volunteer medical services, since they knew that *if the balloon went up* on the inner German border, the need for medical services would suddenly be enormous. They were always very kind to us and allowed us in on the more *fun* side of being in the Army; they would always let us drive Chieftain Tanks and Warrior APCs.[j] You were allowed to fire ground to air missiles and artillery pieces. You got to shoot live ammunition from pistols (the medical officer's personal weapon) as well as automatic self-loading rifles and sub-machine guns. We were always particularly welcome to join in big exercises in Germany and go on trips to work in places like BMH (i.e. British Military Hospital) Hong Kong, Gibraltar, Belize, West Berlin and Cyprus. They certainly liked to keep *sweet* those surgeons who had joined the TA and it was never difficult to get an invitation to a Buckingham Palace garden party.

One or two doctors had clearly joined wholly and exclusively for the peacetime benefits of the TA however, and when the Falklands War balloon did go up, immediately resigned their commissions. They had not read the small print on their contracts with the Ministry of Defence (the *very OldSchool* used to call it the War Office). If you resigned from the TA, you automatically went onto the Reserve List. Unlike the TA, these officers could be called up at the whim of the MoD. Remember, the Falklands *conflict* never officially became a war and the TA were not mobilised. Some of the reserve doctors however (particularly ones who had just left either the Regular or Territorial Army) were *put on stand-by*, including the lily-livered white-feather brigade who had resigned on the day Galtieri invaded Her Majesty's island. They were then much more liable to being called up!

Whilst at a Royal Marine cocktail party (*not*, I hasten to add, at Buckingham Palace), I found myself talking to an Air

---

[j] Armoured Personnel Carriers. A Warrior was a tracked armoured vehicle with a turret carrying a small cannon.

Chief Marshal.[k] He was not in any way medical and had just retired from the Royal Air Force. As a retirement job, he had just been appointed as the Chairman of the Healthcare Trust (which in those days was nominally in charge of the hospital) where I was working. I should perhaps point out that the Chairman is an honorary lay post and his rôle can be compared with that of the Queen. They are advisory and have little if any power. The Stasi in fact usually either ignore them or drive them intothe ground like cricket stumps. I am pleased to say this was a very rare instance when they actually took notice. In line with good cocktail party protocol, the Air Marshal soon got round to asking me what was my wife's occupation, and when I told him that she was a school doctor, he looked a bit worried and said that it was his understanding that the School Medical Service in the area was about to be disbanded. I told him that this indeed was the case.

What then happened was quite interesting. He had evidently been told the party line that school doctors did little else than counted little boys' testicles. For some reason, he seemed most interested in this particular subject. I told him that it was extremely important to ensure that boys' testes "descended" into the scrotal sac during childhood, because if they were impeded in their journey of descent and remained trapped in the groin, there was a definitely proven high chance that they would undergo cancerous change. Evidently the Air Chief Marshal had a friend whose son had gone to Eton College (where they had no nice NHS school doctor to come round and feel at their balls) and this poor lad had an undiagnosed undescended testis, which remained outside his scrotum and later went on to develop a cancer.

Our new chairman had never before fully realised the great importance of having your balls checked by the school doctor and of course, that's the big NHS problem with most things: the medically-unqualified managers have no idea at all about medicine. That is precisely why they make so many mistakes. I

---

[k] A full Admiral in the Royal Navy is equivalent to a definitive General in the land forces or an Air Chief Marshal in the RAF. There is only one rank higher than this (Marshal of the RAF).

must say that although the likelihood of finding an undescended testicle is not very high[1], it is very important to those who have got one (or indeed should one say those who have not got one).

By this chance cocktail party meeting, the School Medical Service in the area was saved from extinction for over twenty years and my dear wife continued to perform this valuable task for the local community. Since North Devon is a small community, it did occasionally lead to amusing situations in our family. My wife and I have been blessed with three daughters and two sons. This meant that from time to time, boyfriends would call at the house to take the girls out. Their faces would often show shock and horror when they met the wife. Since there are only two school doctors in the area, there was almost a 50% chance that she would already have had them by the balls and as one of them told me, this is not something you quickly forget! No-one in fact (I hope!) knows this better than me.

Eventually however, in the summer of 2008, the School Health Service was taken over by nurses. Female nurses have traditionally never really hit it off with lady doctors. (The often quoted reason that they are seen as rivals in the mating game for male doctors cannot of course possibly be true) The last remaining school doctors in the south west of England were then stopped from going into schools and the reason given by the health visitor Stasi was completely and typically illogical. Nobody anywhere else in the UK did it, whether it was better or not.

Now things would be bound to get worse.

They did and the people responsible had already moved on.

Not only are far more children left with undiagnosed undescended testes, but the school doctor no longer gets chance to look at the little boys' willies to check their foreskins. More circumcisions at a later age are therefore being

[1] 1.6 -2.2% of boys. Int J Androl. 2008 Feb; 31(1):1-11. *The frequency of undescended testis from birth to adulthood: a review.* Sijstermans K, Hack WW, Meijer RW, van der Voort-Doedens LM.

performed. A far more serious omission is the diagnosis of heart problems, which are notoriously difficult to diagnose and certainly should not be left to the poor school nurse. Bedwetting is a problem which is becoming increasingly common in children starting secondary school, because it has not been picked up by the *OldSchool* school doctors.

OLD-SCHOOL SCHOOL HEALTH VACCINATION

Cruell and unpartiall Sickesse,
Sword of that Arch Monarcke, Death,
That subdues all strength by Weaknesse,
Whom all Kings pay tribute breath
Thomas Spillman (1602) *Upon his Ladie's Sickenesse of the Smalle Pockes*[122]

The word, *vaccination* comes from the Latin word for cow, *vacca* and vaccination, as everybody knows was discovered by Dr Edward Jenner in 1796, who had noticed that milkmaids who caught a mild viral disease (called cowpox) from the teats of infected cows seemed to develop a definite immunity to the killer disease, smallpox. But was it Jenner who discovered vaccination? In fact during the Ming Dynasty in China,[m] scabs from smallpox sufferers were ground into a powder and then blown up the nose of someone who had never had the disease. The patient would then develop a mild case of smallpox, after which he would become immune to it. There was evidently a slight (0.5-2%) mortality rate, but that was considerably less than the 20-30% mortality rate of full-blown smallpox.[123]

Jenner's work, of course has saved countless millions of lives, but the introduction of vaccination had a very stormy course. It was initially derided and rejected. A famous cartoon by Gillray lampoons the idea and shows vaccinated patients developing cows' horns and hooves. Then in 1853 an Act of Parliament was passed making vaccination compulsory. From this time and until the end of the seventies, most

---

[m] (1368 to 1644.) Said to be *one of the greatest eras of orderly government and social stability in human history.*

schoolchildren were vaccinated. This was usually done at the maternity and child welfare clinic, rather than in the schools.

I was always personally very confused by an old family story told by my grandmother about my father's vaccination. The old lady completely baffled me by the oft repeated tale about her son being vaccinated in his arm and when he woke up the following morning the scab was in the middle of his back! It was not until I had my own vaccination that I realised what she was on about.

In 1977, the disease was declared by the World Health Organisation to have been eradicated. What a brilliant result this was, considering that the disease was estimated to have caused around 2,000,000 deaths only thirteen years earlier in 1967. Routine vaccination stopped shortly afterwards. There were no cases reported from anywhere in the world between 1977 to 1980 with two prominent and embarrassing exceptions. The two last cases of smallpox ever to be confirmed were reported in England in 1978. They were caught from a virus in a British laboratory. The smallpox virus is still kept in four secure laboratories throughout the world and this is done so that vaccines could once again be made, should it ever be necessary.

When children in schools were vaccinated or immunised, the "*hit-rate*" (i.e. percentage of schoolchildren in the community who actually got the vaccine in their arm) was little short of 100%.[124] There they all were sitting in their classes at school – a "*soft target*". The only reason for the small percentage of children slipping through the net was failure of the parents filling in the consent form. This might well have been mainly due to illiterate parents of dysfunctional families. They might well not have understood the concepts of *herd immunity* and *communal responsibility* even if they had been given/bothered to read the letter sent home to them from the school doctor. Some immigrant families too, whose parents might not have understood the consent forms fell into this category. In these cases the health visitors would visit the houses and try to explain the importance, since it could well be argued that these were the very children who were at the greatest risk.

In another attempt to improve the health of schoolchildren, during the Second War (1944) pre-school children were given their own "rations" of orange juice and cod liver oil and malt, and when they got to school all school children (even the 17 year olds got a free third of a pint bottle of milk every day. This continued until 1968 when Harold Wilson's Labour government stopped it in secondary schools.[n] For some reason, he did not suffer the outcry which Mrs Thatcher received in 1971, when she restricted it to the under seven year olds, (earning her the nickname by the Bolsheviks, *milk-snatcher, Thatcher*). It was later restricted to children of families on the dole and now it is still available but on medical grounds only.

Children who were not old enough to go to school would attend the state-run baby clinic (*syn.* school *and child welfare* clinic) to get their free powdered baby milk. Whilst they were there gossiping usefully with the other young mothers about how to bring up toddlers, they would be weighed and measured. A developmental and health check would then be done by one of the clinic's doctors. They would have their hearing and sight assessed and would be brought up to date with their immunisation programme.

In the mid-eighties, the Ministry of Health made a disastrous blunder (now there's a surprise!) which might well have been based on the good intention/eternal bonfire principle. To be fair,[o] they had clearly realised the public health benefits of vaccination, perhaps from the fantastic news that the WHO had eradicated the scourge of smallpox from the world by just such a programme.[p] Surely if smallpox could be eradicated from the Third World,[q] then it would not be beyond

---

[n] When at Sheffield City Grammar School, I was the senior school milk monitor, and drank up to 14 one-third pint bottles every day.

[o] You will no doubt have now realised that your author *is always punctilious* in his attempts to remain fair and equitable.

[p] Geneva, Switzerland, May 8, 1980 - The 33rd World Health Assembly declares solemnly that the world and all its peoples have won freedom from smallpox.

[q] We all know about the First and Third World, but where, you might well ask, is the *Second* World? The term *Third World* arose during the Cold War to define countries that remained non-aligned with either

the wit of the NHS to get rid of all those other nasty diseases, such as measles, tetanus, diphtheria, mumps, etc. for which vaccines exist. Where they went monumentally wrong was to consult the British Medical Association.[r] Since this is almost exclusively a GP organization and the GPs have an excellent track record of making the maximum amount of financial gain (for themselves) whenever consulted about almost anything, they came up with a solution, which made them lots and lots of money, but in fact, what they suggested did not achieve anywhere near the previous vaccination rate, when the work had been done by school doctors.

The BMA told the Government that it would be a much better idea if GPs did the immunisation programmes rather than the school medical officers. The Health Ministry did not realise that this was merely a ploy to make them loads of extra cash without even raising a finger (because unlike the school doctors, they would not be going to do it themselves, but delegate a nurse down the corridor to actually give the injections). Apart from anything else, this would take inordinately longer.

An *OldSchool* school doctor in Bideford once vaccinated a full class of 30 pupils (with the combined measles, mumps and rubella jab) in eight minutes.[125] In nearby Great Torrington a few years later, her *OldSchool* colleague (assisted by her nurse) vaccinated one thousand pupils against meningitis C in the compass of one day. Goodness only knows how much this would have cost the NHS if it had been done on by the Torrington *NewSchool* GPs on an item per service basis.

The corridors of power have been duped. Somewhat amazingly, they clearly never realised it would cost them a lot more money. School doctors were salaried. They used to get paid the same amount if they vaccinated twelve or two thousand pupils. They would not get any bonuses if they got a

---

capitalism and NATO (which along with its allies represented the First World), or communism and the Soviet Union (which along with its allies represented the Second World). Who would have thought that Poland was part of the Second World?

[r] Always a tower of strength and bastion of support in times of trouble!

good "hit rate" or not. They would visit a school and just vaccinate almost everybody there (and if they had any spare vaccine left over at the end of the afternoon, offer it to the staff). The GPs however were going to charge for piecework and then get bonuses if they reached certain percentage targets. It was a brilliant ploy, but sadly cut down the numbers of children who actually got their jabs and eventually (when the percentage of immunised children dropped below the critical level) led to predictable but sporadic outbreaks of disease.

It was even worse than this. There was even a case of a mother taking her children to the GP and asking for vaccination, but being refused.[126] Yes that's right; they were not given their free vaccination, because the poor children were not in the right age group to be counted in the target to earn the practice its financial bonus. They were sent away.

THE SPOTTED SICKNESS[s]

Love's like the measles – all the worse when it comes late in life.
Douglas Jerrold (1859) *Love.*

The inevitable epidemics came.

By 1996, the immunisation rate of measles in the population had fallen to such a critically low level, that there was a serious measles outbreak in the United Kingdom. Measles like mumps is usually a very unpleasant disease and also like mumps can be fatal. In 2011, the World Health Organization estimated that globally, there were probably 430 deaths from measles *every day*. In measles the causes of death are usually pneumonia, hepatitis and encephalitis and around one in five who catch the virus will need admission to hospital. In the United Kingdom by the middle of the last century, around 500,000 children a year caught the disease, and about 100 of these died as a result.

---

[s] Sir E.Wilson reckons that the word *measles* derives *from an ancient English word 'mesel' used in the time of Edward III synonymous with leprosy.* The German word, *maschel* means the spotted sickness (or indeed leprosy)

Maternity and child welfare clinics in the UK started to give measles vaccine to two year olds in 1968. In the mid-seventies, when my wife was working as a school doctor in Manchester, children on entry to school were a captive audience. They all received a *proper* medical examinatiom conducted by a medically qualified physician and she offered a measles jab to any children who might have slipped through the net three years previously. This meant that in those days, very few children would remain unvaccinated. It did not rely on the mother having to go to the trouble of taking her youngster to the GP surgery. This ensured a good immunity in the community. By 1981 however the BMA had bamboozled the Department of Health into stopping measles jabs at school (so that the GPs would get more money) and during the next ten years the uptake rate had plummeted. By 1988, there were still 80,000 cases of measles a year among children in England, including 16 deaths. This was the year that the combined MMR (measles, mumps and rubella) vaccine was introduced. The uptake rate was still nowhere near what it had been when the children were vaccinated at school. Although the number of clinical cases of measles continued to fall reassuringly (less than 4,000 in 1998), the number of children who had been left unprotected was probably higher than before 1980. The *herd immunity* was falling to below the critical limit and in 1994 an epidemic was predicted.[127,128,129] Then to make matters worse, in 1998, a study published in *The Lancet* linked the jab with autism and bowel disease.[130] Although this was later totally discredited (and its author struck off!), take-up rates plummeted further with people making such misinformed and alarmist (but predictable) statements as "*I'd rather have measles than be autistic!*"

The 1994 outbreak of 16,375 cases of measles (mainly in the north of England) precipitated a government programme of measles and rubella vaccination for all children between four and sixteen. GPs were sent into schools to do this, but the *NewSchool* ticking the boxes (mercenary) ethos had clearly already taken hold. Some sixth-formers in one of my daughter's schools, who were above 16-years-old (and quite able to give informed consent) were refused because they were not the correct age for the target. She would have to go to her own GP (and pay). The rot had set in.

After this mini-epidemic in the nineties, the Damoclean[t] thread broke in South Wales where there was a serious measles epidemic. It all started at the end of 2012 and there had been an alarming 2,016 confirmed cases in the country. Clearly the predictions had been right. It was estimated that in Wales there were 43,000 unvaccinated children within the crucial age group, who were all at serious risk of catching this highly infectious illness. It is estimated that a child with measles passes it on to another fifteen susceptible targets.[131] Welsh parents were urged to act immediately. The Chief Public Health Officer for Wales said: *The efforts to vaccinate susceptible young people children across Wales have been excellent, with non-routine vaccinations being given in their thousands by GPs, in schools and in emergency drop-in clinics.*[132]

If only they hadn't stopped the routine school doctor vaccinations, this might never have happened at all.

DON'T WORRY, LOVE; I'VE HAD MUMPS[u]
Ne aggódj Drágáni; nekem már volt mumszom.
Hungarian version.

An epidemic of mumps[v] had the UK in its grip in 2005, with almost 5000 new notifications of the disease in the first

---

[t] In Greek mythology, Damocles was invited to a banquet by the tyrant Dionysius. During the sumptuous dinner, he looked above his head to see a sword suspended by a single horse hair. The lovely meal then became a torment to him. Thus a Damoclean Sword is a metaphor for an expected and dreaded event which is almost inevitable.

[u] As a medical student, I was able to say this useful sentence in fourteen different languages.

[v] The etymology of the word mumps was not easy to trace. To *mump* evidently is to speak, eat or move the lips with the mouth nearly closed. In Scotland, the disease is also called *branks*. Personally I remain unconvinced. Perhaps because as you can see, interestingly the word in Hungarian above, *mums* (-*zom* is a first person pronoun suffix) is almost identical.

month alone.[133] Most patients were aged between 19 and 23 Mumps is a very unpleasant disease and as an ear, nose and throat surgeon for most of my working life, I was exposed to quite a lot of it. Indeed, two of my colleagues, when I was a registrar working at the Manchester Royal Infirmary had the misfortune to contract it. Both of them had serious complications.

Inflammation of the testicles (properly called *orchitis*[w]) occurs in 20% of young men who get mumps. That's one in five and I think quite high. It usually only involves one side, but in my workmate, it affected both his balls. The poor devil could hardly walk; it was so painful. He staggered around with a sort of bow-legged gait. The rest of the department found it hilariously funny: doctors are not well known for sympathy to their colleagues (and if the truth be known, he was not very popular anyway). Telling him he could not stop a pig in an alleyway and giving him adverts for wheelbarrows cut from the *Manchester Evening News* did little to cheer him up.

The other chap was far more unlucky. He didn't get orchitis, but finished up on intensive care. Peter was a very keen cricketer and was down in Somerset playing on his cricket club's tour, when he collapsed at the wicket waiting for the bowler to bowl! He had got mumps encephalitis, a particularly nasty inflammation of the brain by the mumps virus. It only occurs in 1 in 6000, but as he said magnanimously, "*Somebody's got to have it!*" It can be fatal but Peter recovered and went on to play many, many more wickets (and become a consultant surgeon in Lancashire).

There are other unpleasant complications of the virus. Permanent unilateral deafness occurs in 1 in 15,000 (one of my own daughters unfortunately got this) and another potentially fatal complication, in which the pancreas is attacked by the mumps virus (*pancreatitis*), occurs in up to 5% of cases. During my career as a doctor, I have seen two people die from mumps, one from pancreatitis and one from encephalitis.

---

[w] The word orchis (ὄρχις) is Greek for testis. Interestingly the early English word for orchid (flowers) is, believe it or not *ballockworts*. If you have ever seen the tubers, you will understand why.

Not surprisingly, I was a bit worried (being well in the firing range, as it were) that I might catch the dreadful disease myself. My mother was adamant that although my brother had been very ill and mumpy, I never caught it. I went for the vaccination, willing to pay if necessary. (Adults were not on the GPs' target list and indeed after the 2005 epidemic was over, the NHS announced that they could not possibly be to blame because most of the afflicted persons *had not been eligible for routine mumps vaccination*.) The consultant virologist suggested that I have a blood test to see if I had ever had the disease and, I am delighted to say that it came back strongly positive and not only that: my luck was certainly in because it had been quite recent. I must have had a *subclinical* attack. I had certainly not realised that as many as 30%[134] of people can be infected by the virus and develop antibodies (preventing them from getting it again) without actually being poorly and looking like a hamster.

LOCKING THE STABLE DOOR
For whan the grete stiede Is stole,
Thanne he taketh hiede,
And makst the stable dore fast.
William Caxton (1484) *Æsop. ii*, 245.[135]

In *OldSchool* university medical faculties, there would be a Department of Preventive[x] Medicine. My old alma mater, Sheffield certainly had one (in fact it was the Department of Public Health and Preventive Medicine).

It has now gone.

Public health physicians seem to have forgotten about the old adage about prevention being better than cure. On the contrary, they seem to wait for a disaster to strike and then bodge it up. Sadly an excellent example of this was the Swine 'Flu Epidemic in 2009. In fact this had affected so many parts of the world that in June of that year, The World Health

---

[x] Although both *preventive* and *preventative* both are valid English words, Fowler's *Use of English states* that "*the shorter is better.*"

Organization deemed it a *pandemic* rather than a common or garden *epidemic*. A pandemic[y] is defined as *an epidemic occurring worldwide or over a very wide area, crossing international boundaries, and usually affecting a large number of people.*[136]

Despite being called *swine flu*, the disease could not be caught by eating pork. In fact, the connection with pigs was tenuous and it was probably called this because it was a similar virus to the terrible Spanish swine 'flu' epidemic of 1918. In 2009 some keen British virologists eventually isolated the strain from a few pigs in Ulster. Some countries (interestingly mainly muslim states) went a bit overboard. On 29th April the Egyptian government ordered the slaughter of all pigs in Egypt[137] and Azerbaijan imposed a ban on the importation of meat from both North and South America.[138]

It always comes hard to have to grudgingly admit that the Americans got it right when we got it so badly wrong, but once again I leave you, dear reader to judge for yourself.

The pandemic started in Mexico and then two children died in California. Panic in North America started when the virus was identified as the deadly H_1N_1 influenza virus. This was the same virus as the so-called Spanish 'flu of 1918, which had killed far more people than the Great War, which had finished earlier that fateful year. That pandemic had infected 500 million people across the world, and killed 50 to 100 million of them (*i.e.* 3% to 5% of the world's population at the time) making it *one of the deadliest natural disasters in human history,*[139] worse than the Black Death.

It was certainly cause for grave concern and not only because most influenza outbreaks disproportionately kill the very old and the very young, but in contrast the 1918 pandemic had killed predominantly previously healthy young adults. Ironically a lot of the victims had just survived the horrors of the trenches and the First World War only to come back to their homes and be cut down in their prime by 'flu.

---

[y] From the Greek πᾶν (*pan*) which means *all* and δῆμος (*demos*) which means *people*.

Smalle Pockes was described above as a *Cruell and unpartiall Sickesse*. Swine 'flu is certainly cruel, but it is far from impartial; it has a very definite predilection for healthy young people. Thirty six per cent (36%) of deaths in the 2009-10 pandemic were less than 16 years old and only five per cent (5%) were aged above 65.

The Americans acted quickly and decisively. They targeted children and young people for fairly immediate vaccination, closing down 600 schools in 19 of their states. The response in the United Kingdom was typically ponderous and dilatory and of course the onus was on the patient rather than on the authorities.

What should have happened is that teams of doctors and nurses should have been sent into all schools and vaccinated all schoolchildren as soon as possible. This would not only have meant that the fit young people, the ones who are known to be likely to die, had been protected. It would also have meant that a huge proportion of the population had been quickly rendered immune. Then, when and if the virus arrived and tried to strike, that it would have had nowhere to go. A virus (unlike a bacterium) cannot survive outside the body. This is what happened in America but not in UK.

Instead of concentrating on the most vulnerable and threatened part of the population, the vaccine was first offered to the usual target groups: chronic chesty invalids, the elderly and diabetics. (Remember these were 5% of the deaths) There were no school doctors to go to the schools and give mass vaccinations to all the children anyway. It is amazing how effective and rapid this had been in the past. My wife has been boring the family for years with her story of how in the year, 2000 she and the *OldSchool* school nurse vaccinated five hundred children against meningitis in the morning and another five hundred in the same afternoon. When the school doctors were banned from going into schools, the school nurses (who still remained because were cheaper to pay!) were then stopped giving injections on school premises. They probably felt that they did not have the responsibility in case there were any untoward reactions and the whole issue was referred to the GPs. The family doctors of course relegated the injections to their surgery nurses, but at least in the Medical Centre (*NewSchool* name for GP Surgery) a medically qualified person was at arm's length. The surgery nurse however was not likely to give one thousand vaccinations a day; they allow for one injection every ten minutes.

Whilst the UK vaccination programme was tediously taking its time getting into action, some pregnant women and young people were being struck down and dying. How surprising!

As we have seen the Public Health UK made a spectacular bodge-up of prevention. They then went on to make a stunning job of bungling attempts at treatment. They probably realised that they hadn't acted fast enough to prevent the virus attacking and so decided to make amends by making Tamiflu tablets available to everybody who developed 'flu like symptoms during the epidemic. The Department of Health had made large stockpiles of Tamiflu in 2006 when they were worried about bird 'flu decimating the population of the UK and they probably wanted to get rid of them before they went out of date. As a drug, it is probably better than nothing, although there is some doubt over its ability to reduce complications and hospitalisations. It might speed up recovery (or then again, it might not).

The manner in which the Tamiflu tablets were dispensed was a definite Health Department masterpiece. You couldn't really make it up. Let me tell you what happened in Barnstaple. Because a fairly high demand was expected, a girl called Rachel was designated to man the local NHS helpline. I am not quite sure why Rachel got the job. She had had absolutely no formal training or experience. In fact her previous job had been as a wedding photographer. She was delighted with her evening job for which she was well reimbursed. She answered the 'phone and told patients to stay in their home in the warm and not to come out and spread the virus around the community. Instead they were told to send a friend to get their tablets for them. The GPs of course were very pleased; when anyone phoned them, they simply passed it on to Rachel, who then dispensed the tablets if it sounded to her (as a photographer) that they had got 'flu symptoms!

Tamiflu tablets are not without their side effects. The usual ones are nausea, but some rather strange effects have been reported. *Nightmares in children* was reported in UK during 2009, but when the drug was used in Japan for bird 'flu, the Nipponese government warned doctors that Tamiflu should not be prescribed to teenagers. They suggested that it can lead to bizarre and self-destructive behaviour. This was after they had investigated the deaths of 18 Japanese children in March 2007. One British teenager who was given Tamiflu has been left disabled. Ironically it is thought that she did not even have the virus. Samantha Millard, 19, was advised to take the tablets *by the controversial NHS helpline*. Within 72 hours of taking three pills, she was in hospital and doctors had put her on a life support machine. She developed the life-threatening Stevens Johnson syndrome, which caused all her skin to peel off, and she went on to develop toxic epidermal necrolysis syndrome, which damaged her sight.[140] She might not have had swine 'flu but she spent a month critically ill in hospital.

As it happened, swine 'flu hit North Devon and there were a few tragic deaths. One of my daughter's friends, a 32-year-old girl with a two week old baby died, but the massive carnage, which had been feared thankfully never happened. Lots of Tamiflu was dispensed by Rachel.

It was later disclosed that a quarter of the 40 million units of Tamiflu held had to be written off, because the Department of Health was unable to verify that they had been properly stored. The Government was bitterly criticised for its handling of the whole affair. The Public Accounts Committee chairman, Margaret Hodge, said that the mistake had cost taxpayers £74 million. She described it as *"shocking example of incompetence."*[141] This is another spectacular example of the Stasi's bungling incompetence.

VIRGIN TRAINS, BABCOCK ENGINEERING AND A FRENCH FOOD FIRM
Curiouser and curiouser
Lewis Carroll (1865) *Alice's Adventures in Wonderland.* ch.2.

I remember well the absolute incredulity when my wife told me of her surreal day at work. It was not just she who found difficulty in believing it, but I too. Instead of getting on with her school health medicals, she had been dragooned into attending a meeting, which she described as a bit like a cross between "Dragons' Den" and "Blind Date" on the television. The Dr Quisling with whom she worked, was a definite managers' man and had cancelled all the clinical work that day, so she had little choice. Evidently as she put it, the NHS had at last realised that it was totally incompetent and had decided to let somebody less incompetent do the actual job. The NHS plan in a nutshell was that rather than lose hundreds of thousands of pounds through their own ineptitude, they would give that amount of money to a private concern and tell them what they wanted doing. If the private company did a good job and there was some money left over, they could keep it as their own profit.

They had already done it for years in North Devon with the catering services in the hospital. In 1998, the chief executive had given the catering contract to a multinational French food service corporation.[z] The hospital catering officer, all the kitchen staff and dining room workforce no longer worked for the NHS and 300 workers at the North Devon Hospital had been drawing their wages from the French for fifteen years. After a lifetime's experience in the NHS, I have a very strong conviction that managers do not really have the first idea of how a hospital works. An example of this was when the hospital chief executive amalgamated the paediatric dietician in with the kitchen staff. I suppose he thought they all deal with food.

Well it appeared that since this privatisation had worked with the catering, they would extend their net. Who knows, if they manage to contract everything out, the managers will have to do even less work that they appear to do at present?

What my wife could not credit is just who the *NewSchool* contenders for the *OldSchool* school health department were.

---

[z] Sodexo whose headquarters are in the Paris suburb of Issy-les-Moulineaux, France.

Virgin Trains, Dr Barnardo's Home and Serco had all put in bids. Her brother had worked for HM's Prison Service and had not been in the least bit impressed by Serco, who evidently started life as in 1929 as a United Kingdom division of an American radio corporation, but now run four private prisons in Britain and also supply the electronic tagging devices for offenders and asylum seekers. The wife, an *OldSchool* paediatrician of many years' experience felt quite bizarre sitting listening to these big commercial firms trying to sell their services to the NHS for the provision of children's health services. It just seemed all so wrong to her. Of course she was not asked for her opinion. She had been sent to the meeting so that the commissioners could later say that *as many stakeholders as possible were involved in the evaluation process.*[142]

Virgin Trains won the contract (even though that same week Sir Richard Branson lost the tender for the rail network in the north east of England). As one door shuts, another one opens. That means that now Virgin have the responsibility for 2,400 children with disabilities, and employ 1,100 staff including school nurses and health visitors, children's mental health services, physiotherapists, speech and language therapists and occupational therapists.

After this, nobody was too surprised when shortly afterwards Babcock Engineering took over all the educational services for special needs children (*NewSchool* term for mentally and physically handicapped children). Quite appropriate you might well think for a company who specialises in refuelling our nuclear submarines. One of my wife's colleagues suggested a logo for the new department of a Polaris submarine with a little baby sitting on it. Also Babcocks had a very good name in North Devon and had saved the local shipyard[aa] from closure in 2007.

[aa] The Appledore Yard was founded in 1855 on the estuary of the River Torridge. It was the biggest covered shipyard in the World until the Japanese built a bigger one during the eighties, when Appledore then claimed to be the biggest shipyard in industrial Europe.

The Stasi said that the winning bidder would be *able to deliver the best possible outcomes for children and young people across Devon.* Who knows? Was this an inspired statement? After all, they can't possibly make a worse job than the incompetent Stasi themselves.

REFERENCES

[112]. CHADWICK, Sir Edwin (1842) *Report on the Sanitary Conditions of the Labouring Population of Great Britain.*

[113]. BMA NEWS REVIEW (1999) August page 19.

[114]. BMA NEWS REVIEW (2012) January page 8.

[115]. SMITH, J (1995) *Illustrations from the Wellcome Institute Library .The archive of the health visitors association in the contemporary medical archives centre.* Medical History 39, 1995, pp 358-367.

[116]. HORN, Pamela (1989) *The Victorian and Edwardian Schoolchild.* Sutton, Gloucester. p 84

[117]. MAURICE, JF (1902) *Where to get Men.* Contemporary Review. (81) p79.

[118]. HMSO (1904) *Report of the Interdepartmental Committee on Physical Deterioration.* Cd 2175,xxxii

[119]. HARRIS, Bernard (1995) *The Health of the Schoolchild.* Open University Press. Back cover.

[120]. PUBLIC HEALTH ENGLAND (2013) *Tuberculosis rates remain among highest in Western Europe.* 21 August 2013.

[121]. BBC NEWS Wednesday, 6 July, 2005,

[122]. YOUNG, John Riddington (2009) *Poetry, Physick, Pestilence and Pox.* VDM Saarbrücken. p. 117.

[123]. NEEDHAM, J (1999). *Science and Civilization in China: Volume 6, Biology and Biological Technology. Medicine Part 6.* Cambridge: Cambridge University Press. p. 134.

[124]. YOUNG, Elizabeth (2013) *Personal Communication.*

[125]. NYMAN, Valerie (2005) Personal *Communication.*

[126]. YOUNG, Elizabeth (2013) *Personal Communication.*

[127]. RAMSAY, M.; GAY, NJ, MILLER, E.; et al. (1994) *The epidemiology of measles in England and Wales: rationale for the 1994 national vaccination campaign.* Commun Dis Rep CDR Rev; 4:R141–6.

[128]. BABAD HR, NOKES DJ, GAY NJ *et al.* (1995) *Predicting the impact of measles vaccination in England and Wales:* Epidemiol Infect 114: 319–44.

[129]. GAY NJ, HESKETH LM, MORGAN-CAPNER P and MILLER E (1995) *Interpretation of serological surveillance data for measles.* Epidemiol.Infect 115: 139–56

[130]. GODLEE F, SMITH, J, MARCOVITCH H (2011). *"Wakefield's article linking MMR vaccine and autism was fraudulent".* BritMedJ 342: c7452

[131]. MACRAE, Fiona. (2013) ed. *Measles cases at 18-year high because parents are failing to get children vaccinated.* Daily Mail. 8 February.

[132]. PRESS ASSOCIATION (2013) *MMR vaccination drive targets 43,000 children as measles epidemic spreads.* The Guardian, 2 May.

[133]. HEALTH PROTECTION AGENCY. (2005) *National increase in mumps cases continues.* Press release; 4 February.

[134]. LEINIKKI, P. (2004) *Mumps* In: ZUCKERMAN AJ, BANATVALA JE, PATTISON JR, GRIFFITHS PD, SCHOUB BD, eds. *Principles and practice of clinical virology.* 4th ed. Wiley, Chichester: 459-66.

[135]. APPERSON, G.L. (1993) *The Wordsworth Dictionary of Proverbs.* Wordsworth. Ware.

[136]. PORTA, Miquel (ed) (2008) *Dictionary of Epidemiology.* Oxford University Press. Oxon. p. 179

[137]. ABC NEWS (AUSTRALIAN BROADCASTING CORPORATION) (2009) *Egypt orders pig cull .* 30 April.

[138]. TREND NEWS AGENCY. (2009) *Prevention against "swine flu" stabile in Azerbaijan: minister.* 28 April

[139]. TAUBENBERGER, Jeffery K.; MORENS, David M. (2006). *1918 Influenza: the Mother of All Pandemics.* Centers for Disease Control and Prevention. Washington.

[140]. DAILY MAIL REPORTER (2012) *Side effects and effectiveness of 'wonder-drug' Tamiflu under the microscope as Department of Health faces awkward questions over mass prescriptions.* Daily Mail. 17 January.

[141]. LISTER, Sam (2013) *Shocking example of incompetence over stockpiled flu drug Tamiflu.* The Independent. 21 May.

[142]. RAMESH Randeep; LAWRENCE, Felicity: (2012) *Virgin Care to take over children's health services in Devon.* The Guardian, 12 July.

CHAPTER 6

GUIDE, PHILOSOPHER AND FRIEND

I do not like thee, Doctor Fell,
The reason why - I cannot tell;
But this I know, and know full well,
I do not like thee, Doctor Fell[a]
Brown, Thomas. *Translation of Martial's Epigrams, I,xxxii*

IN A NUTSHELL; OldSchool vs. NewSchool:
OldSchool: People had their own GP. More than
that, they actually *chose* which doctor they wanted to
look after them. They would go and see him
whenever they liked if they were ill, or if they were
very ill, he would actually come to their house and
see them. You would be able to see *your* local GP,
whom you had probably known for years (and might
well even have come to your home and delivered you
into the world) at any time of day or night.
NewSchool: People no longer have a GP as such
but are registered with a Medical Centre. They now
have difficulty getting an appointment to see one of
the doctors, but might if they are lucky be able to see
a nurse that same day. After the surgery shuts in the
evening, they have to start telephoning a call service
which is usually manned by a layperson and is usually

---

[a] This rhyme was written by Thomas Brown (1663-1616). It is said that
when he was a student at Oxford, he was caught doing mischief by the
dean of his college (one Dr John Fell), who expelled Brown; but offered
to take him back if he could extemporaneously translate the thirty-second
epigram of Martial from Latin. That epigram is viz. *Non amo te, Sabidi,*
nec possum dicere quare; Hoc tantum possum dicere, non amo te. It is Dr
John Fell, who Hannibal Lecter chooses for his pseudonym, remember!

so unsatisfactory that they have started to use the local hospital casualty department instead.

DOCTOR GILBERT WOOD

General practice is at least as difficult, if it is to be carried on well and successfully, as any special practice can be, and probably more so; for the G.P. has to live continually, as it were, with the results of his handiwork.
Sir Henry Howarth Bashford

Many years ago before I was a surgeon, I was a general practitioner in a small mining village in South Yorkshire. I was full partner[b] to a bluff Yorkshireman, who was trying to entice me away from hospital medicine to go into full-time general practice with him. His usual partner (again no sexual connotation) was an Indian lady, who had gone back to the vast subcontinent on maternity leave (and it was widely suspected in Mapplewell that she would never come back!). They were in fact right; she never did. These were the days before the British coal industry had entered into a self-destructive conflict with the (Tory) government and the little village had a thriving colliery and most of our patients were coal miners. Between the two of us, we had to look after 14,000 men, women and children. When I tell this to a *NewSchool* doctor, I can tell that they do not really believe me. Nowadays an average practice is between one and two thousand patients per GP.

But that's only during the day and during the week. Whereas, the *OldSchool* doctor would have taken it for granted that he would be expected to provide a duty of care for his patients 24 hours a day, and although it might well have been a bit tedious from time to time, it was a matter of *noblesse oblige.*[c] It was a strange unenviable sort of privilege that just

---

[b] In those halcyon days before political correctness had started to insidiously corrupt even intelligent people's minds, the word *partner* had no sexual connotation (except perhaps when dancing).
[c] Taken literally this is French for *nobility imposes certain obligations*, but it has taken on a more figurative meaning. The *Dictionnaire de*

went with the job. The reward (which of course was never sought) was respect from your patients, which you had earned. You knew what being a doctor entailed before you started to go to medical school and as sure as hell, you would not start to quibble about being on call when you qualified. *OldSchool* doctors certainly never considered the job to be "nine till five". If you didn't fancy looking after poorly people at unsociable hours, then perhaps you would be better suited to being a double glazing salesman. Nurses worked shifts; doctors got on with the work until it was all finished.

The *OldSchool* populations now pale into inconsequentiality when we look at how cost-cutting Stasi have left out of hours *NewSchool* GPs to care for astronomical numbers of patients and areas which stretch over hundreds of square miles.[143] It is estimated that at night nowadays, the ratio drops unbelievably in some cases to one GP for 535,000 patients (Cornwall). In Mid Essex, numbers were slightly better at 325,000 per GP between the hours of 7 in the evening and 8 the next morning.

PEOPLE ARE MORE IMPORTANT THAN PLACES.

The first [quality] to be named must always be the power of attention, of giving one's whole mind to the patient without the interposition of anything of oneself. It sounds simple but only the very greatest doctors ever fully attain it.[144]

Wilfred Trotter. *The Collected Papers of Wilfred Trotter, FRS* (1941), 98.

I shall never forget arriving at the GP Surgery for my first morning's work. Gilbert (the senior partner) and I were sitting in the back of the car after having eaten a healthy breakfast[d] at Gilbert's farm. The surgery was a converted butcher's shop situated next to one of the village pubs. If the sun was at the right angle in the sky, you could still see where the French

---

l'Académie française defines it thus: *One must act in a fashion that conforms to one's position, and with the reputation that one has earned.*

[d] The metaphorical meaning of "a healthy breakfast" as usually in "*the prisoner ate etc.etc.*" is of course a very unhealthy (full English) fried breakfast

embossed windows proudly proclaimed, "*Co-op Butcher*" under the more recently painted and superimposed solitary word "Surgery". At that time however, there was no sun in the dull smoky sky and even if there had been, I could not see any of this frontage because of the massive queues snaking out of the surgery door and onto the pavement quite a long way past the Talbot public house and down the main road. Gilbert, noting the look of mild alarm on my face, laughed quietly and said, "*I teld thee, lad: tha's cum 'ere t'work!*"[e]

In fact, the reason for the long queue was because it was the first day of the month. Quite a lot of the people had turned up for their follow-up long-term sick notes and regular repeat prescriptions. There were a lot of miners on long term sick with miner's lung (pneumoconiosis), who were required to attend at regular 14 week intervals for a certificate, signed by a doctor, which they referred to as a "*Lloyd-George*".[f]

Inside the place were just four tiny rooms. The largest was the waiting area and that wasn't very big. When it had been a butcher's shop, that was probably the space[g] occupied by the customers. There were no more than twelve chairs. There was a tiny WC in which your knees pressed on the door when you sat down and the two consulting rooms were very small. Gilbert had a wonderful Brazilian mahogany roll-top desk in his. It was a family heirloom and was quite attractive in itself. He would sit at it and write out prescriptions (in Latin) in illegible writing using a fountain pen. (There were of course no computers in those days.) The problem with the desk was that the room was so small that there was hardly any space left for anything else.

---

[e] Translation from the Yorkshire dialect: *I told you, young man: you have come here to work!*

[f] David Lloyd-George (1863–1945) was Prime Minister of the United Kingdom before the introduction of the NHS.

[g] I have tried to avoid this use of this highly fashionable word, but in this instance have used it to avoid repetition. In a recent visit to the Glasgow School of Art, the girl guiding us round the building used the word *space* over forty times in the first twenty minutes (instead of room, studio, corridor, building, staircase, library, etc. etc. etc.). Then I stopped counting!

Nobody was ever turned away from that surgery. If they were willing to wait, they would be seen. Another amazing thing about *NewSchool* GPs is that not only do they now have a strict appointment system, but nowadays, if you have two problems about which you wish to consult your *NewSchool* doctor, you have to book two separate appointments. For example, if you have gone along with a bad cough, but wanted a bit of advice about your piles, whilst you were there, you might well be told that you need to book another appointment on another day.

There was no appointment system of any sort in Gilbert's *OldSchool* surgery in the mornings. However having said this, Gilbert told me that if I considered that anybody "really needs seeing" to bring them back in the afternoon. In fact the arrangement worked brilliantly. I certainly worked very hard, but I learned a great deal, particularly about dealing with and talking to patients. In those *OldSchool* days, doctors never had any training in talking to people. The medical school curriculum was far too full of things that really mattered (like human anatomy). I am sure that Gilbert, who was one of the best GPs I have ever come across, never had any training in communication skills (or any other touchy-feely claptrap). I really do have to say that students who need that sort of training are probably better suited to a career in biochemistry. In the *OldSchool* days of course, they would never have got through the all-important *interview* to even get into medical school.

Despite this massive discrepancy in numbers, I honestly believe that my old partner, Gilbert provided each and every one of the patients under his care with a better standard of care than the *NewSchool* replacements. His patients had the deepest genuine affection and admiration for him. He was not just their physician, but acted as their guide, philosopher and friend. I remember one night after the evening surgery, we went to the little pub next to the old butcher's shop and it had been all trimmed up for his birthday. Gilbert himself was surprised, because I think he had forgotten. The villagers and miners' wives had made cakes and sandwiches for him and of course, Clara (the landlady) had made him a birthday cake. When nowadays would this ever happen? When would anyone know when it was their GP's birthday? When indeed would a GP live in the midst of his flock and go for a drink in the local pub? I have heard *NewSchool* family practitioner colleagues say (somewhat nastily) that they want to get as far away from their patients as possible when they are off duty

Gilbert's patients thought the world of him. I worked with him during the "Winter of Discontent," when the coal miners made the almost suicidal mistake of trying (unsuccessfully) to bring down Edward Heath and his Tory government by repeatedly going on strike. Nobody could get hold of any coal, but I have personally never seen so much in my life. The patients kept bringing him a sack round to the house and just leaving it anonymously outside the back door. They didn't want their doctor to be cold. Gilbert had got an old railway truck in a field round the back and as soon as we got home from evening surgery, the first job was to wheel the coal round to the truck in a wheelbarrow and dump it inside the truck out of sight.

One of my consultant colleagues reckons that GPs are now essentially (very effective) businessmen: they certainly earn more and can expect to get more in their pensions than the harder working hospital consultant surgeons.[h] He went on to say that it is the nurses at the medical centres who do all the day to day work anyway, whilst the physicians just sit looking at screens and working out how to get even bigger salaries. Of course your author would wish to distance himself completely from this somewhat jaundiced view of his valued colleagues in so-called primary care. Another scurrilous suggestion is that the GPs are completely supernumerary and nowadays merely act as a valve to slow down the flow of patients going to hospital.

YOU MISS MORE BY NOT LOOKING
The examining physician often hesitates to make the necessary examination because it involves soiling the finger.

---

[h] As a surgeon myself, I have purposely used this term rather than any other.

A general surgeon from Harrogate once told me that one of the truest rules in clinical medicine is the old saying; *you miss a lot more by not looking, than not knowing.* My old GP mentor, Gilbert put it another way: he used to call it, "the Laying on of Hands". It is as important now as it ever was and it is as essential in a hospital ward round as it is in a GP home visit.

NewSchool young doctors look a bit perplexed when I tell them, *"You have to touch your patient – to make some sort of physical contact with them."* It doesn't matter if you just pull their lower eyelids down and check the pinkness (or yellowness) of their conjunctivae – at least you have *examined* them. There used to be no worse indictment of a physician than *"the doctor never even examined me!"*

I remember once when I had been sent on a home visit and I could hear the old collier wheezing as I walked up his stairs, before I even got to the bedroom. I told Gilbert that I did not really need to put the stethoscope on the chest to know what was wrong. He was in acute heart failure. Gilbert chuckled and said I was starting to learn about general practice. He was even more delighted to know that I had gone through the ritual of putting the bell of the stethoscope on the bare chest wall and pulling a grave face while I listened. The truth of the matter is that the *OldSchool* stethoscopes were often so battered that you could hardly hear anything anyway. And sometimes they weren't even switched on.

One old patient visiting my hospital clinic was bewailing the fact that he no longer saw *his own* doctor when he went to the GP. He went on to say that even if he did, she never examined him; " *'er never took 'er eyes off that danged computer thing!"* I did wonder if a *NewSchool* GP would miss a case of jaundice[i] nowadays.

---

[i] Jaundice is a yellowness of the skin (from the French *jaunisse* – yellowness) indicating liver disease and often diagnosed by pulling the lower eyelid downwards.

It isn't even as though reliance on the *danged* things does not give rise to quite serious errors anyway. A rather alarming recent finding showed that the computer's use for repeat prescriptions gets significantly compromised by *a barrage of unspecific and extraneous computer alerts.* Evidently the largest ever analysis of primary care prescribing data showed that 4% of GP prescriptions contained prescribing errors and a further 1% monitoring errors. One mistake in every twenty prescriptions is certainly not insignificant. Even more worrying is that it would seem that *common errors included prescribing the wrong dose*! They also contained blunders like not checking to see if there were any drug interactions with other medications the patient was already taking, and not routinely organising blood tests and blood pressure check when the prescribed drug had well known side effects.[145]

I have long thought that the GMC has lost its way. A source of intense irritation to most doctors is getting a patronising little GMC booklet[146] offering guidance to doctors, who have more than likely been doctors, since the authors of this odious little book were still at primary school. It is unusual to get doctors to agree about anything, but this nasty little booklet which is set out like a *Janet and John* book[j] seems to have united them. The very mention of it elicits unanimous scorn.

It has really succeeded in irritating doctors. It is so outrageously condescending that a few years ago I took the trouble to write to the GMC (I didn't actually send the booklet back to them, although I was sorely tempted). I pointed out that most experienced doctors would, more than likely be offended to be talked down to in such a manner. I got an equally terse and disdainful reply. It was pointed out to me that most doctors who faced disciplinary charges were in fact very experienced. The reason for these booklets then became blindingly obvious: what a pity that Freddie Shipman (a very experienced doctor, after all) never read his copy of "*Good*

---

[j] Evidently since 1964, these Ladybird books which teach children to read are called *Peter and Jane* books.

Medical Practice". Evidently he would have behaved himself a lot better if he had!

On the title page, just underneath the heading, the condescension begins in earnest. Remember that this book is meant *solely and exclusively* for doctors, who if selection criteria have kept up their standards should be in the top 3% intellectually. It actually states on its opening page, *This guidance has been edited for plain English.*[5] That is just in case one of the doctors reading the book (and bearing in mind that it is the more experienced ones who are more likely to face disciplinary charges) cannot understand words of more than one syllable.

I was absolutely horrified to hear from my wife (who actually looked at her copy!) that the current copy states that among the *Duties of a Doctor* is taking a history. Well how patronising is that? It gets better however; it goes on to say (no doubt for the PC *NewSchool* doctors) *including the symptoms and psychological, spiritual, social and cultural factors, their views and values*; and then almost as an afterthought *and* **where necessary**, *examine the patient.* (My emphasis).

In 1601 the newly formed Royal College of Physicians found it necessary to pass a statute proscribing members from giving advice without personally examining the patient.[147] This edict was intended to stop the doctors of the day prescribing treatment after seeing a sample of urine rather than seeing the patient himself. Sadly this did not stop the practice, even among college members.[148] One wonders whether or not looking at your patient's urine is so much worse than delegating a nurse (or even *a trained call-handler or health information adviser)* to talk to them over the telephone, where no doubt their spiritual and perhaps even political values can be taken into consideration.

The cornerstones of modern medicine are based on the sound (and fairly obvious) principles of examining the patient. The pioneering giants who brought medicine out of the Dark Ages and into the light of the Age of Reason – Thomas Sydenham, Sir William Osler and many more, stressed the importance of learning medicine at the bedside. My learned professors, for whom I still cherish the greatest respect, always taught us that, *"The patient is the best textbook of medicine."* Doctors learn their art best by *doing* and the practice of medicine should always therefore begin with the patient and end with the patient. Books and lectures are only supportive tools to this end. One of the cardinal differences between a doctor and a nurse is that nurses are not trained how to make a diagnostic examination of their patients.

Physical examination is the basis of good clinical excellence and even the shyest old maiden lady would rather suffer a moment's indignity and embarrassment to gain the secure knowledge that she has been properly clinically examined. Many years as a doctor have left me in no doubt that it is the reassurance of *having been examined* is what most patients really want from their medical attendant. As we have already said, *you miss a lot more by not looking than by not knowing.* Any deviation away from this fundamental principle cannot possibly be seen as progress and the suggestion that patients do not now get seen and examined by a properly trained doctor has to be seen as a gross deterioration of service. In the *OldSchool* general practice, this would never have happened.

I remember when I was a medical student in the Sheffield Royal Infirmary and had just examined a young man with a lump in his neck, but I had not gone on to examine his groins. There are 800 lymph nodes in the human body of which 400 are situated in the neck. The others are mainly under the arms and in the groins and a full examination of the lymphatic system should certainly include the armpits, groins and abdomen. The senior registrar on the firm was really unpleasant to me because I had omitted to do this. The public scorn and humiliation which he poured onto me would nowadays I am sure be designated as "bullying." I did not consider it to be bullying; it was part of my education. Indeed, I am grateful to him for instilling this useful principle, which I have never forgotten. I went on to become an ear, nose and throat specialist and not once did any of my patients with a lump in the neck get out of my consulting room without having their groins felt. Indeed, on one occasion, fairly surprisingly I found a hernia in a young nurse, who had come to see me about her tonsils!

NOT EVEN LOOKING
There is only one cardinal rule: One must always listen to the patient.
Oliver Sacks[k]

The *NewSchool* GP must have taken Professor Sacks too literally in his interpretation of the advice above about listening to the patient, because as often as not nowadays, he just talks to them on the telephone! When it was first brought out it was called NHS Direct, but it has changed its name and number more than once since then.

The worst ever nuclear disaster in the United Kingdom was at a nuclear reactor in a place called Windscale in Cumbria in 1957. It was later estimated that the fire at this nuclear reactor (which scored level 5 on the seven point International Nuclear Event Scale) released so much radioactive iodine (Iodine 131) into British air space that no less than 240 cases of thyroid cancer were directly attributable to the catastrophe.149

The first thing that the government of the day did was to change the name of the place from Windscale to Sellafield. That is why you have probably never heard of it. No figures are available to show whether NHS Direct has killed more or less than 240, but the Government have changed the name of NHS Direct to NHS 111.

NHS Direct was a Stasi brainchild launched in 1998. It was principally to save money (but sadly not lives) and represented a monumental deterioration in the standard of care one would expect from the *OldSchool* system. Instead of having a quick word with your GP or if necessary getting a house call, this Samaritan type telephone answering service

---

[k] Oliver Wolf Sacks, CBE, is a British neurologist and writer, who sadly now lives in the USA. He was formerly the Professor of Neurology at New York University School of Medicine. He wrote *The Man Who Mistook His Wife for a Hat.*

was *staffed by nurses and trained call-handlers or health information advisers.*

It didn't seem to impress anybody!

But at least it was free. The 'Fair Telecoms' campaign found that nine hundred and thirty eight GP surgeries (*OldSchool* term for medical centres, but I suppose one should be glad at least they don't spell it centers) were still using costly 0844 numbers in 2013, even though the Department of Health had outlawed the practice three years earlier. When it was also found that the offending GPs were taking a cut of the profits and actually making income from their patients' phone calls, this gave rise to even more animosity. The fact that NHS Direct was free however might have been the only good thing about it.

An undercover study in March 2003 opined that the service by then was more likely to put patients' lives in danger.[150] The research was done by the Consumer Association magazine, *Which?* who made 33 phone calls to 11 of the 22 *NHS Direct* regional call centres asking for help in three different hypothetical situations.[1] It would appear that you don't always get through to one of these highly skilled telephone answerers straightway. Presumably there is a "queuing[m] system."

Needless to say, the Stasi had set a "target" (well, they would have, wouldn't they? That is what they do best!) for NHS Direct and that is that 90 per cent of callers get to speak to a nurse (or a trained call-handler – whatever that is) within five minutes. The target was certainly not reached: 21% of cases took longer than half an hour and in 10% there was no return call at all! When the calls were eventually returned, the quality of the advice given did not impress the panel of expert judges. The hypothetical questions which the researchers tested the system with described three supposed patients. One was an angina sufferer requesting a repeat prescription for the

---

[1] Whether or not Ethical Committee approval was applied for in this piece of research is not stated.

[m] For any North Americans struggling to understand this book, a *queue* is a *line*.

painkiller for his attacks of chest pain, which he said had become more frequent. The second was a female who described symptoms that might well have been an ectopic pregnancy. The last one was a back pain sufferer.

Which? said: *"Many nurses missed 'red flags' pointing to unstable angina, thus leaving the 'patient' at risk of collapse or death. Only one of nine nurses spoken to stressed to our researcher the risk of ectopic pregnancy."* In more than 50% of the cases in the trial, the nurses failed to ask relevant questions about the caller's medical history and in only four of the 33 calls were all the key questions asked. The problem is of course that there really is no substitute for proper medical care and there is no doubt that this ill-conceived idea represents a massive deterioration in the care which patients used to receive from the *OldSchool* on-call GP.

The patients' GPs were not even informed about the calls on the following day: they could not have been because their details were hardly ever requested from the researchers and in the eight cases where they were taken, no information was subsequently passed on.

Six years after its inception a group of family doctors in Kent were so unimpressed with NHS Direct that they described the helpline as offering a *chronically poor service to patients*; they called it *unsafe, slow and inaccurate in logging patients' details.* They found an even worse response time than the *Which?* investigators, saying that in Kent patients had to wait up to two hours for a nurse to ring them back and were then sometimes told they should call an ambulance urgently. They cited two very harrowing tales.[151] One told *how a four-week-old baby girl died of meningitis after a helpline operator said 'she only had colic'.* The other was a sad death of a 60 year old diabetic lady, who died after a nurse on the helpline failed to spot she needed immediate hospital treatment and instead told her daughter to give her lemonade.[152]

What occurs to your author is that surely this group of Kentish[n] GPs should perhaps have opted out of the system and

_____

[n] Since Dartford and Gravesend lie to the west of the River Medway, the term *Kentish* (cf. *Men of Kent)* is used advisedly.

informed patients in their practice that they would continue to provide an *OldSchool* type service, where poorly patients could talk to a doctor and even get – nay, perish the very thought – an emergency medical visit if thought fit.

In Hertfordshire, however a mother was admonished by her GP for using the wonderful service even though the hardworking general practice had closed down for the weekend (something an *OldSchool* practice would never have done). Her little boy was so poorly he couldn't even get out of bed; he had a fever and had become sensitive to light. The concerned mother rang NHS Direct, who said it might well be meningitis and advised that she should take her son to the hospital as fast as she could. Happily, the lad was diagnosed with a viral infection and sent home on appropriate medicine. A few days later, a letter addressed to the seven year old little lad arrived from the GP practice and the mother's relief turned to outrage, when she read that her son had been rebuked for going to A&E instead of the surgery. The practice said it had received a letter from the hospital about his visit, and continued: *'A&E is for life-threatening situations such as a heart attack or stroke and for the care of people who show the symptoms of serious illness or who are badly injured.*[153]

The transition from NHS Direct to its new daft name was far from smooth; it inspired the editor of BMA News to come up with the page 1 headline, *"NHS111 Meltdown Mires Launch"*. Members were told how the phone triage scheme had failed monumentally across the nation. The North West Ambulance Service had been completely inundated by 999 calls *because people were fed up of waiting or couldn't get through*. In Shropshire, South London, and Northern Ireland, GPs were pleading with the NHS to defer implementation of the system.[154]

A particularly poignant little cameo took place in the north of England, when an *OldSchool* GP, who had served his community for some 30 years was let down dismally by the new so-called service. His daughter visited him and found him to be very ill (he was actually dying) and so she had no recourse but to telephone NHS111. After quarter of an hour, she became so frustrated with the *trained call-handler* she was speaking to, that she hung up and sent for an ambulance by dialing 999. Here was a dedicated *OldSchool* doctor, who himself had attended his patients in all weathers and at all hours. His poor daughter pointed out that he *was from a generation of GPs who were used to working every hour. He worked every other night on call and every other weekend on duty. And he always made sure he put his patients first. It is obviously a source of some regret that he did not have similar access to a GP in his own hour of need.'* [155]

KWOFFING
to drink something quickly or in large amounts
Definition of verb: *to quaff*
Cambridge Dictionary & Thesaurus

It is always fascinating to hear what my colleagues find the most appalling deterioration in the quality of the care they are now allowed to give in the NHS. I had never heard of QOF until I met a GP from Basildon (in the transfer area of Bangkok Airport). We had a couple of hours to kill and inevitably started talking about the inexcusable way in which the care of patients is being destroyed by NHS administration. I asked him to single out the nastiest feature and he had little hesitation in citing QOF (which he pronounced *kwoff*). I hesitate to admit that I had no idea what he was talking about, especially when he told me that QOFs had evidently been in place since 2004! When I got home from holiday, I asked my own GP and he immediately agreed that QOF was the worst thing since sliced bread.[o]

In the early 2000s, there was a serious shortage of GPs and QOF was evidently part of a cunning government scheme to attract more doctors into general practice by offering huge financial benefits. It certainly worked. Prior to then, hospital consultants had usually received higher yearly earnings than family doctors, but the new GMS (General Medical Service) contract in 2004 (which included QOF) marked the turning

---

[o] Sliced bread was first introduced in 1928 in (hardly surprisingly) America.

point. It's probably true to say that the lifetime earnings of GPs has probably always been higher than specialists, owing to the much longer period of hospital training in relatively low paid posts. The GPs have always carped on about private practice, but in the present financial climate, that has not been a great consideration. Anyway I can certainly remember that round about 2004, some of my more puerile GP colleagues tried to wind up me and my hospital mates by telling us just how much more this new deal from the Government would be giving them (than us!)

QOF is short for *Quality and Outcomes Framework.* Evidently there is already a new noun in use, *QOFability*[p] (pronounced *kwoffability*) but the same article in the British Medical Journal[156] also talked about QALYs (quality adjusted life-years)! Sadly most *OldSchool* doctors quickly lose interest when trying to read such goobledegook.[q] At the time of its introduction, senior Stasi said that it was intended to improve the quality of general practice and described it as *a system for the performance management.* Ostensibly a system of rewards for introducing "best practice" in their surgeries, it was a successful ploy to get more physicians to become family doctors. It worked. By 2008, there were 4000 more GPs in Britain, all lured by the promise of *filthy lucre.* Benjamin Bradshaw, the (socialist) Health Minister said, *The GP contract ... has stemmed the haemorrhaging of GPs from the NHS and improved the quality of care for the public. Longer consultations, quicker appointments and being able to book ahead are improvements valued by patients.*[157]

In fact it cost the Government a lot more money than they had reckoned on. True to their Stalinist philosophy, the system was based on achieving targets. The GPs however were hitting far more targets than had been expected. It was thought they would achieve only 75% of the available points but in their first year, they actually got a 90% score rate. This cost £1.76

---

[p] *Reasons why certain issues can or cannot be made into QOF indicators* (sic).
[q] Interestingly this now innocuous term was once used to denote a prostitute who performed fellatio!

billion more than the Government had predicted.[158] Participation by practices was entirely voluntary, but not to join was (according to the local BMA rep) a *no-brainer.*[r] I had always believed that GPs are extremely financially motivated. When they saw that QOF could make a vast difference to their income, almost every practice in the UK participated.

Although my own father was a bank manager (and always despaired about my *lack of financial awareness*), I have never been good with money and even have difficulty in filling in my travel forms. I was one of the first students ever to get into Sheffield Medical School without an O-level in basic mathematics.[s] I found the business of QOFs totally confusing and thought that the GPs would need the assistance of accountants to work it all out. It was all based on a points system and the value of points was evidently further modified by the prevalence of that condition in particular practice - this was measured as the square root of the ratio of the national prevalence. (Honestly, I have not made this up!)

My own GP said he had just about come to understand it and cited an example of the proportion of patients in the practice with coronary heart disease, who had had a blood test to measure their cholesterol during the financial year. The practice would be paid more money for a bigger percentage of appropriate blood tests. A Belfast GP recently said,

QOF is all about counting and not what counts. The targets move priorities away from patients.

At the same conference, her colleague summed up the whole potty idea beautifully with his story about his practice being worried that they might not meet their targets because they had not yet managed to find an elderly patient from their practice with a broken bone due to osteoporosis who would fit into one of the required categories. He said, *The time I realised*

---

[r] It was in fact the first time I had ever heard this expression and immediately assumed it to be an American intrusion into our language and berated the representative accordingly. He later however assured me that it is not quite so dire. The expression is evidently Canadian and was first used to mean an *easily made decision* in the Canadian newspaper *The Lethbridge Herald*, January 1968, in a report on an ice hockey game.
[s] US *Math*

the QOF had lost the run of itself was when we were really struggling to get our orthopaedic points as we didn't have an over-75 patient who had a fragility fracture in the last year. Then I got a text message from one of our GPs, who was in the A&E to tell me our problem was solved because an older woman from our practice had a broken wrist.[159]

Most practices got, and still get, a significant proportion of their income through the QOF system.

As to whether the wonderful new system has improved the health of the nation, even the BMA admit that they don't really know.[15.] It has been so expensive and has caused so much disaffection and strife in our GPs (who cannot afford not to adopt it!).

Let us all hope that it does.

HOME VISITS

I was sick and ye visited me.
St. Matthew, 25, 36.

And in the time of their visitation, they shall shine and run to and fro like sparks amongst the stubble.
Wisdom of Solomon, 3, 7.

I was at the retirement party of a dear old pal who is a well-known and well-loved GP of the *OldSchool* and I took the advantage to ask lots of his colleagues what they considered the worst change in the NHS. I was surprised when one of them said that she was such an old dinosaur, she had to say it was the removal of out of hours service. I was even more surprised to hear two of her colleagues agree, but add the codicil that it might well have been the worst change for the patients, but perhaps the best thing for the doctors. They were all of one mind that this marked the end of an era in the doctor-patient relationship; that GPs were no longer as *close* to those they looked after.

The patients usually appreciated the fact that you had visited them, but I have to admit that the system was occasionally abused. I once did a GP locum in a place called East Dereham in deepest Norfolk and was summonsed for a home visit by an ancient beldam who lived at the back of beyond. It was, I think, the most difficult house I ever did have to find. I had to leave my ancient Rover motor car at the end of an impassable rutted lane and paddle through deep mud carrying my doctor's bag, to get to the isolated cottage. And when I eventually let myself in, the only thing I could get out of the old crone who had sent for me was that she wanted her toenails cutting!

Home visits during the day were not too bad. It was the ones at night which were the big bugbear. Not just because you had been wrenched out of a warm bed, fireside chair or out of the pub, where of course you would be engaging in social intercourse with the locals, whilst drinking a few half pints, rather than two or three quarts.[t] The big problem was that nine times out of ten you didn't know where the patient lived. Having an address did not always get you to the right house. Often as not there were no numbers on the houses and when there were, they didn't always follow the rule of odd numbers down one side, starting at number 1 nearest town, with the consecutive even numbers straight opposite. Of course, the ailing patient would try to be as helpful as possible and hang a white towel out of the bedroom window. I can remember quite a few occasions of driving slowly down a road, which I believed to be the subject road with one hand on the steering wheel and the other with a torch either shining it at bedroom windows looking for a towel or at front doors trying to spot a number. It was easier when you could get a relative to hang the towel over the front gate or better still to meet you at either the end of the road or outside the pub (even if it was shut) or the nearest church or chapel (or perhaps nowadays in some areas of Yorkshire, it might be the mosque).

It was not just finding these places; it was the unsocial hours that people chose to be ill. A GP colleague was

---

[t] A couple of pints are a quart and in the north of England, a gill was half a pint, although in some regions there are 4 gills in a pint. There were always 8 pints (i.e. 4 quarts) in a gallon. It is suggested that any Americans still struggling with this book had better ignore this footnote and press on.

reminiscing about when he was a 24-year-old GP in South West London. He tells a lovely story about standing in a back garden in Mortlake at 5am one morning, holding a healthy newborn baby and having stitched up the mother whilst holding the torch to illuminate the procedure between his teeth.[160]

CORONARY AMBULANCE
I held my tongue and spake nothing...but it was
pain and grief to me. My heart was hot within me
and while I was thus musing, the fire kindled...
Lord let me know mine end and the number of my days.
Psalm 39, v.3

Nowadays the public complain about the deterioration in the service provided by their *NewSchool* GPs, but when I was a houseman even the hospital doctors sometimes made house calls. In the early seventies, I worked on the only coronary ambulance unit, which England ever had. Heart attack still remains the greatest killer in the UK and accounted in 2012 for 300 deaths a day. During the first hour after the attack, the chance of death is highest.

Professor Frank Pantridge from Belfast, in an attempt to cut deaths from heart attacks during this crucial 60 minute period, transformed emergency heart medicine by inventing the portable defibrillator and setting up a mobile coronary ambulance unit in Northern Ireland. This fully equipped dedicated wagon raced to the patient's house with a flashing red light and an illuminated sign saying "Cardiac Emergency." It carried not only a defibrillator but a doctor, a senior nurse, an ECG machine and controlled drugs for analgesia. An intravenous infusion would always be set up in the patient's home. It certainly saved lives by the treatment of ventricular fibrillation during that first crucial hour.

The Belfast Coronary Ambulance Unit was featured on national television and in the Sunday papers. The NHS never took it on: it probably didn't save quite enough lives to be *cost-effective*, but the Miners' Welfare Institute in Barnsley had heard all about it and seen it on the telly. Because heart disease was prevalent in colliers and the local cardiologist (a disciple of Pantridge) told them that it would save up to thirty lives a year, the committee decided that they should have one of their own and then went on and bought a dedicated coronary ambulance. They approached the editor of the *Barnsley Chronicle* and between them[161] they raised the money to pay for it by public subscription – flag days, sponsored runs, darts matches and the like. I can remember people throwing coins into a large sheet held by buxom Barnsley wenches outside the town hall. Enough brass was raised and the second (and final) emergency coronary ambulance service in the world was set up in that small mining town in South Yorkshire.[162]

I had done an attachment as a medical student at the Barnsley General Hospital,[u] where it was based and thought it was such a great experience that I would try and get my first house job there. Luckily for me, I was successful. The ambulance would be activated by either a call from a GP or even a 999 call. If you dialled the emergency services in Barnsley during 1970 and asked for an ambulance, you would be asked if the patient had chest pain. If so, the coronary ambulance would be mobilised. The emergency hospital team of a doctor and a senior nurse carrying the bag of controlled drugs (they didn't trust the doctor to find them) would go to the hospital gate and wait. The ambulance station was only a few minutes up the road from the general hospital.

I remember one patient (a fishmonger from Barnsley Market), who had a cardiac arrest on the way from his home to the coronary unit in the back of the ambulance. We pulled in and stopped the van at the side of the main road and successfully defibrillated him and started his heart working again. When we arrived at the hospital, he certainly looked worse for wear and his relatives, who had been following the wagon in their family car quite reasonably asked me why we had stopped for quarter of an hour on the way to the hospital. Before I could get a word in, the nurse (who was a beautiful redhead) said in her throaty Yorkshire accent, *"Dooant thee werry, luv; he just 'ad a bit of a funny turn in t'back o'*

---

[u] In those days it was called Saint Helen's Hospital.

t'waggin, but he's reight enough naa![v] When I mentioned it to her later, she chuckled and said, "*Aa didnee think they'd knooa what ventricular fibrillation warr.*"[w] The man had a further attack on the ward and was once more defibrillated. He then made a full and uneventful recovery. I have no doubt that had it not been for the ambulance, he would have died. After that, he went back to work in the fish market for quite a few years and I never paid for wet fish in Barnsley again.

We did get a number of false alarms, but as the boss said, if they had all been kosher myocardial infarctions, not enough people would be coming through and we would be missing some. There were two particularly memorable cases of heartburn. The first was a definite abuse of the service by a GP. He told me over the 'phone that he was performing heart massage and mouth to mouth resuscitation on a lady in her front room. As we rushed up her garden path some minutes later, we found a somewhat surprised housewife pruning her roses. The boss was rightly furious and I heard him berating our colleague and asking him if they had not heard in Ireland the fable of the boy who cried wolf.

The second was more excusable, because the patient himself told the 999 operator he had chest pain.

I well remember the evening of a murderously busy day on call, when I had not managed to eat any dinner because the canteen had closed whilst I was dealing with the on-call emergencies (not an unusual occurrence). The pub up the road from the hospital was called *Tom Treddlehoyle's*[x] and the landlady there had just said she would make me a hot meal. Before she had cooked it for me however, the landlord shouted over to tell me that that the coronary ambulance had just left the ambulance station and would be picking me up to go to the home of some poor devil with crushing chest pain. Seconds later, the frosted pub window was lit up by blue flashing lights

---

[v] For any American readers, this can be translated as, "*Don't you worry, my dear: he just had a funny turn in the ambulance, but he's alright now.*"

[w] *I didn't think they would know what ventricular fibrillation was.*

[x] The pub is still there. Its strange name (which, not unsurprisingly is unique) is the pen name for a local journalist, Charles Rogers (fl. 1820).

193

outside, as the vehicle stopped. In my haste, I spilled beer down my chin, before I climbed on board and we zoomed off into the night. This was pure *OldSchool* and would never happen now.

We picked up the nurse and the drugs from the hospital and sped to a terraced house about twelve miles away to find our patient sitting at his kitchen table. In a way I was relieved to hear the familiar history of acid regurgitation. At least this chap was not likely to arrest and his outlook was very good. We did an ECG and confirmed a healthy heart trace, but protocol demanded we set up an intravenous drip and take him in for further tests. I was so famished by this time that my belly was rumbling (rather embarrassingly) and the man's wife asked me if I wanted something to eat.

There was evidently a well-reckoned fish and chip shop very close nearby and on the way back to the hospital, so we stopped the wagon outside and I went in for some fish and chips. The fryers were a bit alarmed, but quickly reassured when I told them all I wanted was a fish supper. Then my own heart nearly stopped when the nurse suddenly dashed into the chip shop. I was so very glad to hear that the only reason she had come was to tell me my patient had asked if he could have a bag of chips! I was so relieved that I actually bought him one, even though "nice greasy chips" are about the worst thing for heartburn.

The coronary ambulance service continued for quite a few years and unquestionably the *OldSchool* coronary team saved the lives of scores of people (the fishmonger being one who would otherwise have died). The *NewSchool* doctors however are no longer willing to invest medical manpower in it. They have delegated this lifesaving work to the paramedics, who clearly do a wonderful job. It was eventually discontinued in Barnsley during the eighties. I once again leave you dear reader, to make your own decision as to whether or not in the frightening moments at what certainly would seem like (and indeed might definitely turn out to be) the last minutes of your life, you would choose a cardiologist or a paramedic to come to your home.

Although he is known worldwide as the "Father of Emergency Medicine," Frank Pantridge is almost unknown in his own country (Northern Ireland). His groundbreaking contributions to emergency care, the portable defibrillator and a mobile coronary domiciliary ambulance service undoubtedly saved many lives, but Pantridge himself was saddened that it took until 1990 (over twenty years) before all front-line ambulances in the Great Britain were fitted with defibrillators and of course nowadays there are no coronary ambulances (with doctors and nurses).

OUT OF HOURS
Airline pilots and pizza delivery boys work all hours.
How arrogant of GPs to think it's beneath them.[163]
Dr Martin Scurr. Medical Ethicist and London GP. (2013)

Although I look back with a certain pride and sense of a job well done to the days and nights when I used to be called out in the middle of the night (in both GP and hospital medicine), I would be the first to admit that it was very hard work. I know that they used to send little boys up chimneys, but I still feel that when a young person applies for a place at medical school, he should be willing and aware that part of the job he will be expected to do will include enough dedication to his profession to work long hours and not Monday to Friday, nine to five. He will also be expected if he chooses to specialise in family medicine to do house calls and some of them in the middle of the night.

The public perception of the medical profession has deteriorated in recent years almost wholly and exclusively because of their inability to get a doctor out of hours. They believe that physicians have given up on their moral obligation to provide out of hours services. I have heard colleagues say that they never again intend to work out of hours. As a young doctor, I never thought I would hear this attitude expressed by so-called colleagues and I must say that I have little respect for them.

The truth however is that the majority of patients can no longer get in touch with their GP once the surgery has closed for business at the end of the afternoon. Instead, the poorly patient in desperate straits is relegated to a call centre. If you ever get called back, it is most unlikely that you will talk to a doctor and even if you do, it will not be someone you know, nor even somebody with access to your case notes and previous history. It will be some poor over-worked, (overpaid) under-experienced young chap with a monumental workload and absolutely no idea at all of your personal circumstances. It is more likely that your only hope will be one of the governmental helplines, which are so notoriously bad that many patients do not even bother with them. Rather than waste valuable time and eventually hang up having lost the will to live anyway, tens of thousands of frantic and distressed patients go straight to the local hospital accident and emergency department. The marmalade salesman himself[y] was severely criticised for taking his own child to a casualty department in November 2014, after having advised everybody else that poorly folk should not do this. Evidently he said that he *"didn't want to wait for the GP surgery to reopen"* and that people did not always know whether an illness is urgent or not[164]. This was less than two weeks after he had made a ststement urging the public *to make more use of pharmacies when unwell, to reduce "unprecedented" strain on GPs and casualty units.*[165]

Since 2004, the number of patients arriving at A&E in UK has risen by four million. It was estimated that in 2012, 37,000 patients, that's up to 100 patients a day were being forced to wait more than an hour outside bursting casualty units, in ambulance 'jams' with delays of up to four hours at some hospitals.[166]

A spokesman for the British College of Emergency Medicine said in March 2013 that this has driven them to a crisis point and likened A&E units to war zones. He went on to say that worse still these were war zones where *your heart sinks, because essentially you are fighting a losing battle. He said too many patients were arriving in hospital as emergency cases when they should have received help much earlier, because of a lack of community services, and the decision by*

---

[y] Rt. Hon. Jeremy Hunt MP. Secretary of State for Health was a former (unsuccessful) exporter of marmalade (not to Peru, but to Japan).

the last government to allow GPs to opt out of providing out-of-hours services.[167]

The Patients' Association would agree: they say that the present crisis in the casualty departments is due to *a complete lack of faith in local GP out-of-hours service.*[168]

That is not likely to improve. In May 2013, the GP magazine, *Pulse* said that a survey, commissioned by the Bedfordshire and Hertfordshire Local Medical Committee had found that six out of ten GPs would consider resigning if the UK government forced GPs to take back out-of-hours commitments. Somewhat alarmed by this result, shortly afterwards a blog poll was run for all the family practitioners throughout the country. This showed that the majority of GPs *said* that they would indeed resign rather than go back to doing *OldSchool* GP work (i.e. actually working irregular hours and *(perish the thought!)* doing house calls in the evening. Only 18% seemed to have any Hippocratic commitment and said that they would not abdicate their responsibilities. There were of course a fairly predictable third (34%) who said they could be tempted back to proper doctoring, but only if the Government made it financially worth their while.[169]

The introduction of the new contract by the 2004 Socialist government has meant that GPs now get much more money (averaging around £110k a year in 2013) and now never have to do any more out of hours visits for the privilege. There is no doubt whatever in my mind that most GPs do work reasonably hard. I am also absolutely sure that they do not work anywhere near as hard as they used to ten years ago. Having been a GP myself, I am also quite certain that the *OldSchool* GPs in the last years of the 20th century used to work a damned sight harder. GPs are not stupid (and unfortunately they have been shown to be financially both shrewd and greedy). Are they likely to want to work any harder than they have to, just to regain the public confidence?

Ones I have spoken to recently all agree that they have lost that wonderful and close doctor-patient relationship, which used to exist ten years ago. *NewSchool* GPs, who have never visited the household (certainly never in the evening), are clearly unlikely to fully understand the family dynamics. They might be blissfully unaware that their anorexic young patient has an alcoholic father and a brother who has just overdosed on cocaine; that her house is an insanitary hovel and that her mother, understandably ,is in a deep black depression.

What is profoundly depressing to me is that the GP situation is never likely to get any better in the foreseeable future either.

MY MEDYK

Lepsze zdrowie niż pieniądze.
Polish proverb: *Good health is above wealth.*

The obvious dissatisfaction of the public with the *NewSchool* NHS GPs has led to the setting up of private (that is non-NHS) clinics where one can be seen by a doctor without having to wait for weeks. *Research showed that in 2013, two thirds of Health Service patients have to wait more than 48 hours for a doctor's appointment and few slots are available outside the regular working week.*[170]

The main reason people cite for using these clinics is that they can be seen at their convenience rather than the convenience of the NHS GP practice and patient continuity is ensured because you can see the physician of your choice, every time you go. One such successful medical centre in London was opened in West London by a group of Polish immigrant doctors and dentists. It is called *My Medyk*[z] and by mid-2013, it had 30,000 patients on its books (6,000 of whom were British disaffected with the *NewSchool* NHS). It is doing so well that it has already opened a second clinic and has plans for a third. It opens until 11pm every night (except Sunday, when it closes at 6pm) and the appointments (which cost £70 for a half hour consultation) are three times longer than a routine GP session on the NHS. For comparison, at the time of going to print, a specialist private appointment would be around £250 and a BUPA GP service would cost £67.49 for a 15-minute appointment.

---

[z] Interestingly, the Polish word for doctor is *lekarz*; *medyk* means *medical.*

The spotlessly clean modern clinic is proud of its motto: 'Put Patients First' and is quick to point out that this certainly does not happen with its rival, the NHS. If any scans, however chemotherapy, surgery or other procedures are thought by the Polish doctors to be indicated, My Medyk will usually refer patients to their closest hospital, where the investigations will be funded by the NHS. A spokesman for the ginger group[aa] Patient Concern said that he was *not surprised this clinic is attracting so many patients. I know people who are having to wait three weeks* for *a GP appointment. At my own NHS GP you normally have to wait at least a fortnight. Patients will rarely see the same doctor twice and this is particularly hard on the elderly or those with long-term conditions.*

REFERENCES

[143]. BORLAND, Sophie (2012) *Just One GP for 500,000 Patients.* Daily Mail. 29 September. Page 1.

[144]. TROTTER, Wilfred. (1941) *The Collected Papers of Wilfred Trotter, FRS*, 98.OUP, Oxon.

[145]. PRAITIES, Nigel (2012) *Computer alerts contribute to GP prescription errors.* PULSE. 13 Feb.

[146]. GENERAL MEDICAL COUNCIL (2013) *Good Medical Practice 2013.*

[147]. SIMPSON, R.R. (1959) *Shakespeare and Medicine.* Livingstone, Edina & London. p. 22.

[148]. YOUNG, J.R. (2009) *Poetry, Physick, Pestilence and Pox.* Verlag Doktor Müller, Saarbrucken. 158.

[149]. BEARDSLEY, T. (1983) *'Windscale; increased cancer incidence alleged'.* Nature vol 306 Issue 5938 Nov 3 1983 p. 5.

[150]. POULTER, Sean (2003) *NHS Direct 'errors put patients at risk'; Callers face long delays and missed danger signals.* Daily Mail 3 July

[151]. www.dailymail.co.uk/health/article.../NHS-Direct-unsafe-say-GPs.html

[152]. CARVEL, John (2002) *Baby death coroner criticises NHS Direct.*The Guardian, 15 February.

[aa] Like "to ginger up", the term comes from the use of ginger root to make a horse seem more lively.

[153]. LEVY, Andrew (2012) *Family who rushed boy, 7, to A&E with meningitis symptoms are stunned to receive letter accusing them of wasting NHS time.*Daily Mail. 6 December

[154]. BMA NEWS (2013) *NHS 111 Meltdown Mires Launch.* Apr. 6. p.1.

[155]. BORLAND, Sophie (2013) *My dad was a GP. But in his hour of need the 111 helpline let him down.* Daily Mail. June 8. Page 21

[156]. GILLAM, S: STEEL, N (2013) *QOF Points: valuable to whom?*Brit.Med.J. 346, 21.

[157]. HAWKES, Nigel (2008) The Times. 28 Feb. 34.

[158]. TIMMINS, Nicholas. (2005) *Do GPs deserve their recent pay rise?* Brit.Med.J.; 331:800.

[159]. SMYTH, Lisa. (2013) *BMA News* Saturday 20 April. p.5

[160]. SCURR, Martin (2013) Airline *pilots and pizza delivery boys work all hours.How arrogant of GPs to think it's beneath them.* Daily Mail. 17 May. page 15.

[161]. BOOKER, Donald (2013) Personal communication.

[162]. G. SANDLER AND A. PISTEVOS (1972) *Mobile coronary care. The coronary ambulance.* British Heart Journal, 34, I283-I29I.

[163] SCURR, Martin (2013) *op.cit.* (n.160)

[164] GUARDIAN (2014) *Jeremy Hunt jousts with Labour shadow over children's A&E visit.* 26 November.

[165] DONNELLY (2014) *Public warned to keep away from hospitals as pressures mount.* Telegraph 14 November.

[166]. SHIPMAN, Tim (2013) *Hunt pledges to hire 2,000 extra GPs and casualty doctors to ease the A&E crisis.* Daily Mail. 27 May.

[167]. DONNELLY, Laura. (2013) *A&E units have become like warzones, top doctor warns.* Daily Telegraph. 9 May

[168] SCURR, Martin (2013) *op.cit.* (n. 160)

[169]. Doc2doc (2013) 30 May.

[170]. INFANTE, Francesca; BORLAND, Sophie (2013) *Patients shun NHS for clinic run by Polish GPs.* Daily Mail. Jun 8. page 1.

CHAPTER 7

LIONS LED BY DONKEYS [a]

*Suppose you were an idiot. And suppose you were
a hospital manager. But then I repeat myself.* [b]
Mark Twain.

> **IN A NUTSHELL; OldSchool vs. NewSchool:**
> ***OldSchool* Hospitals:** Hospitals used to be
> happy places to work; morale was good. The
> doctors and nurses were part of a well defined
> hierarchy for which there was universal respect.
> Doctors wore spotless starched white coats and
> nurses wore immaculate uniforms. Matrons and
> ward sisters ensured a system of discipline,

[a] The title of this chapter is taken from a conversation reported in the
Great War *Memoirs* of General Erich von Falkenhayn, (1861-1922) Chief
of the Imperial German Staff. Erich Friedrich Wilhelm Ludendoff, (1865
-1937) Prussian General who was mainly responsible for Germany's
military policy and strategy in the latter years of World War I commented
during a hard fought battle that,
The English soldiers fight like lions!
His Chief of Staff, General Max Hoffmann (1869 - 1927), widely
regarded as one of the finest German staff officers and greatest tacticians
of the Imperial period, sagely replied,
True. But don't we know that they are lions led by donkeys?
Alan Clark wrote a book in 1961 called *The Donkeys*, about the British
Army officers in the Great War. Your author tried to use this title for a
book on managerial incompetence published in 2008. The publishers
however did not like this and actually wished to call the book, *Meltdown*.
After much arguing, *The Hospital Revolution* was settled on. The original
title then was *Lions Led by Donkeys* but on reflection this was changed,
and the word *"led"* was by *driven* replaced because, of course at present
there is absolutely no leadership!
[b] What Mark Twain actually said referred to *a member of Congress.*

cleanliness and order. Ward Rounds were part of traditional rituals evolved through decades which guaranteed patients' safety. There were a few administrators, who administrated the wishes of the doctors and nurses. Everyone knew their place and was happy with it.

NewSchool **Hospitals:** The administrators (Stasi) who like to be called managers have destroyed decorum and respect completely in their attempts to control the clinical staff. Morale is at an all time low. These Control Freaks have tried to make doctors and nurses wear pyjamas to work and sadly some have conformed. Hospitals are no longer happy places to work.

WATER, WATER EVERYWHERE, NOR ANY DROP TO DRINK

Water, water everywhere,
And all the boards did shrink,
Water, water everywhere,
Nor any drop to drink.
Samuel Taylor Coleridge, *The Rime of the Ancient Mariner.* (1798)

In July 2012, the country was horrified to learn that a 22 year old lad had died of dehydration on the ward of a London teaching hospital. He had become so thirsty that he had dialed 999[c] from his hospital bed to ask the police for a drink of water. No water came from either the police or the nursing staff and poor Kane Gorny died a slow unpleasant death the following day. The Westminster coroner said at his inquest that he had died from dehydration contributed to by neglect.

---

[c] In UK (and also Kingdom of Swaziland, Ireland, Poland, Saudi Arabia, the United Arab Emirates, Macau, Bahrain, Qatar, Bangladesh, Botswana, Ghana, Kenya, Hong Kong, Malaysia, Mauritius, Singapore, Zimbabwe, and Trinidad and Tobago) this is the emergency free telephone number. It is the world's oldest emergency call service and was introduced on 30 June 1937. For some reason, the Canadians decided on 911 as their emergency number in Manitoba during 1959. Evidently USA also use this.

Kane was suffering from a rare condition called diabetes insipidus, in which the kidneys no longer conserve the body's fluid but allow it to be lost as urine. As this happens, the patient gets progressively drier and thirstier. They also typically become aggressive as they get more dehydrated. This had happened in Kane's case and he had evidently thrown a urinal at his doctor. Nobody realised that this aggression was a tell-tale symptom and because of it, he had been placed in a side room and sedated.

I have very little doubt that in an *OldSchool* hospital, this *cascade of individual failures*[171] which led to the young man's death would probably not have happened. Her Majesty's Coroner Dr Shirley Radcliffe said that after two years of "*being with the case*" it had been a very difficult issue because it was so emotive. She summed up by saying, "*Kane was undoubtedly let down by incompetence of staff, poor communication, lack of leadership, both medical and nursing.*[172]"

If an *OldSchool* morning ward round had taken place on the Holdsworth Ward in St George's Hospital where poor Kane Gorny died just before lunch, the medical and nursing staff would have been fully apprised of the specific clinical situation and this tragic death of a 22 year old might well have been prevented. The importance of the daily ward round in the *NewSchool* hospital has become sadly neglected. It used to be the cornerstone of the day's work and included all the key staff of the ward. The Stasi blame *huge pressures in terms of staffing, a rising tide of inpatients and emergency admissions, and particularly the financial constraints on the NHS at the moment.* These might be reasons, but they are not valid excuses for the neglect of the basic principles of hospital medicine and nursing. Apparently, nobody on the ward at St George's seemed to know what was happening and the endocrinology specialist doctors who were nominally responsible for the treatment of Kane's diabetes insipidus did not even know that Kane was in the hospital![173]

The direct blame must of course be laid at the door of the Stasi, but the medical staff are certainly not inculpable. They are guilty of incompetence by association. Why on earth do they take notice of unqualified persons, when they are told to cut down the amount of time they spend on rounds? Indeed I often wonder why any of my gutless colleagues ever listen to the Stasi at all? It has even been suggested that by 2015, Stasi financially driven directives could lead to doctors being told to reduce the length of time they spend on ward rounds by more than half (from three hours to an hour and a quarter).[174]

THE SURGICAL FIRM SYSTEM

It is the function of science to discover the existence of a general reign of order in nature and to find the causes governing this order. And this refers in equal measure to the relations of man - social and political - and to the entire universe as a whole.[175]
Dmitri Ivanovich Mendeleev. (1869)

A colleague of mine, a very experienced general surgeon, who worked for many years in the same hospital as me, considers that the worst deterioration in the way he is allowed to get on with his work in recent years is the erosion of the surgical firms in the NHS and the loss of propriety of patients. This has been a direct intrusion of the Stasi to humiliate surgeons and assert their power. In an *OldSchool* hospital, an individual consultant would be responsible for his "firm" (*i.e.* his surgical team). He was the boss of that firm and the junior doctors worked for him (even when I was a houseman, I did not work *with* a particular boss, but *for* him). The firm would usually have (in rising order of seniority): a houseman, a senior house officer, a registrar and then a senior registrar. They would be directly responsible *to* the consultant and he would certainly be responsible *for* them. He would be paternalistic towards them and if they served him well, he would do his utmost for them. He would try to teach them all the surgical skills and tricks he knew and when he had achieved this he would then try to advance them in their own careers. They would be his protégés.[d]

---

[d] Strictly speaking this is the French word for *protected.*

As for the propriety of the patients, they would have been referred to a specific consultant by their GP or they would have been admitted as an emergency on a night when that particular consultant was on call, but one thing was quite definite: those patients *belonged*, as it were, to that consultant and his firm would be absolutely dedicated (in more ways than one) to the welfare of that patient. Each member of the firm would be very well aware of the details of every patient under the boss's care. When they did a ward round, they would not pause at every bed in the ward, but only those under their care – those beds, which had their boss's name actually written above them.

If this system of propriety of patients were still in place, I believe it is most unlikely that poor Kane Gorny would have died in a hospital bed for want of a drink.

This loss of propriety has in the opinion of many experienced *OldSchool* surgeons led to a deterioration of patient care. Together with the European Working Time Directive (described in the second chapter) intended for long distance lorry drivers but applied to junior doctors, it has meant that patients are banded around and might not ever see the same doctor more than once. This must represent a serious deterioration in individual patient care.

WARD ROUNDS

The trivial round, the common task
Will furnish all we ought to ask
John Keble, *The Christian Year.* (1827)

When I was appointed as a consultant surgeon in 1980, whilst I was working my three months notice at my teaching hospital, I received a letter from the ward sister at the hospital where I had been appointed, congratulating me on my preferment and asking me what time I intended to arrive at the hospital each morning. I wrote back to the good sister telling her that I always arrived at 8 o'clock (something which, in spite of everything, I did until the day I retired). On my first morning, I saw a very proper looking lady, wearing a smart dark blue uniform: she did not in truth wear an apron, but she did have a crisp white sister's cap and of course a Petersham belt with an ornate silver buckle, which I later learned had been a present from her very proud father, when she had qualified as a nurse (at St James's Hospital in Leeds just after the war). She had spotted me. My predecessor had evidently told her that I sported a large blonde moustache. This morning meeting was to define the pattern, which the good sister continued every morning at 0800 hrs excluding Saturdays for the next ten years, when sadly she retired. She met me at the main door of the hospital and while we walked together through the hospital, she would apprise me of any problems which might have occurred on *her* ward.

On rare occasions, particularly when we (I say *we* although in truth I should say *she*) had a visitor to the ward, we would all go back to her office after the round, and she would unlock the drugs cupboard and produce a bottle of *Harvey's Bristol Cream Sherry*[e] and some rather nice cut-glass sherry glasses and one would be given a small glass of this. I could never work out what I had done on these rare occasions to deserve a drink after my coffee and I never asked. On an aside here (unusual for me) when I was attached to the 1st Battalion Grenadier Guards as their Regimental Medical Officer, I was invited after morning muster parade on the first day of my attachment to take a (large) glass of port with the Regimental Sergeant Major.

That was when I was a consultant. Quite a few years before that, when I was a lowly houseman, I was allowed onto the ward by the sister first thing in the morning long before the boss arrived. It was then my job to make sure that everything was ready for his round. If the patients had had blood tests, I would not only have to make sure that they were available but *commit to memory* any abnormal results so that I could inform

---

[e] Bristol Cream is a brand of sherry that has been imported into and bottled in Bristol since 1796 by John Harvey & Sons. It was always in lovely sapphire coloured bottles made from Bristol blue glass. The wine is blended from three sherry types: Fino, Amontillado, and Oloroso. Finally some sweet Pedro Ximénez is added which gives the richness and creaminess that is the hallmark of the brand. It was typically a favourite of old ladies (including my mother).

my chief during the round. I had to make sure that all the appropriate X-rays were available on the ward and I had to have scanned them personally and apprised myself of the expert radiologist report on them. Woe betide me, if all these facts and figures were not at my fingertips when the consultant arrived on the ward.

The *OldSchool* staff nurses had a similar responsibility for the all the nursing charts of fluid balance, blood pressure, body temperature and pulse rate. In addition to doctors' rounds, the nurse also had to contend with the added spectre of matron's rounds, when the hospital matron would check up that everything was up to scratch on the wards in *her* hospital. Matron's rounds were usually unplanned, or rather unexpected in that she would not give the nursing staff any clue as to when she was likely to visit. That was just to keep them on their toes. On these fearful occasions, she would also check the cleanliness of the ward. I have seen the ward sister put on a pair of white gloves which she kept especially for this purpose. She would run her fingers along the tops of doors and cupboards to make sure there was no accumulation of dust. If she was not satisfied, she would then roll her own sleeves up and help the nurses to thoroughly clean the place from top to bottom.

Since the *OldSchool* system held the dated idea that the *patient* is the most important consideration in the hospital and that the daily ward round was essential to patient care, both doctors and nurses would all do their utmost to be present at this central event. It was the equivalent to a school assemby or a morning muster parade in the Army. Recent orders from the Stasi in Birmingham however, have actively *prevented* junior staff *from entering the ward to commence ward duties.*[76]Administrators there have instituted protected patient meal times. Nurses have therefore been instructed to prevent any ward round taking place until the patients have finished their meals. Surgical teams' ward rounds have usually started at 8 o'clock (they used to start at 8 o'clock when I was a houseman in 1970!). This was because the operating theatre list traditionally starts at half past eight. The administrator who brought in this thoughtful directive almost certainly did not know that folk going to theatre aren't allowed to eat anything anyway. Stasi will never have been on a ward round in their miserable embittered lives and in any case they doubtless do not arrive until around 10 o'clock.

I was particularly angered to be told recently by a patient in my clinic that she had read in the newspaper that *doctors and nurses now had been ordered to visit the patients on the ward every day*. I could hardly believe it when she dug into her bag and showed me that this was actually the case: it really said that we had been *ORDERED*[f] to do ward rounds and also commanded to *speak to patients for 5 minutes every day.*[177] This dear old lady had read this in the paper and of course understandably had believed that the Stasi had the right to order us about. Worse than that, she supposed that the majority of patients in hospital beds do not get visited by doctors and nurses and need to be told by some higher authority to do so. What sort of Control Freak had put this story in the paper? It was based on guidelines (not orders) issued by the two Royal Colleges of Physicians and of Nurses, who had quite rightly reiterated the axiom that daily ward rounds are essential for patient safety and care. Unfortunately I had to admit that although this sort of guidance would never have been necessary in the past, it is sadly no longer the case.

When a patient left the ward, the bed would be stripped down and the rubber covered mattress would be scrubbed with antiseptic. This was before anybody had ever heard of methicillin-resistant staphylococcus aureus (which appeared in the mid-nineties). Needless to say, there was never any problem with the dreaded MRSA in the sixties and seventies.

Let us contrast this with the woeful story told at the Kane Gorny Inquest in Westminster Coroner's Court in July 2012. The court was told that *many of the medical staff had not read his notes and did not even know he suffered a rare condition that required daily drugs to control it.* Almost unbelievably, it was also heard that *no one checked his pulse, blood pressure,*

---

[f] I was shocked even further to see that when I looked it up on line, it had been put in block capitals!

or breathing between 10am on May 27, 2009, and the following morning, shortly before he died.[178]

It is also difficult to credit that the fluid balance in a patient with known diabetes insipidus had not been fully monitored and that no intravenous infusion had been put up. Indeed poor Kane was not the only one to summon the police. A Metropolitan Police spokesman said: *Detectives from the Homicide and Serious Crime Command are investigating the death of Kane Gorny at St George's Hospital after this was referred to us by Westminster Coroner's Court.*[179]

On a *NewSchool* hospital ward, the sister (although she neither likes nor wants it) now has a badge with the epithet *Ward Manager* inscribed on it. The Stasi tried to get rid of archaic elitist titles like *Sister* and *Matron.* Sometimes the badge doesn't even include her surname (nor in some cases her proper Christian name and says something like *Jo* or *Sam*)! Contrast this with the *OldSchool* nurses whose badge (if they ever had one; rather they were told to introduce themselves in a courteous lady-like manner) just gave their initials[g] and they were taught fairly early in the school of nursing that if a patient asked for their first name, they should answer simply, "Nurse".

Nowadays there is usually little evidence of the sister when one goes on the ward anyway: she is probably in her office ticking boxes. The staff nurses are not usually by the beds of their patients, plumping up pillows, making new beds and giving bed baths. They are usually filling in forms. If a doctor visits a ward to see a patient, and asks the nurse in charge (or if he is particularly callow, the ward clerk), they will point over towards some distant bay saying "*She is in Bay 4*" (or wherever).

This would never have happened in the past. The senior nurse would have said, "*Please come with me, Doctor*" and accompanied the doctor to the patient's bed where she would

---

[g] I had a dear old army friend whose surname was *Hole.* It was always a source of puerile amusement to his fellow officers that he had called his daughter, *Angela Simone.* One would have thought with a surname like Hole that one would have been more circumspect in the choice of names for one's children. His daughter became a nurse and had a name badge, *Student Nurse A.S.Hole.*

then have introduced them to the physician and explained why he had come to see them. She would then have waited whilst the doctor took a history and stayed to help/chaperone the doctor during the physical examination. By doing this, she would not only have reassured the frightened patient, but also learned herself about the patient's condition and exactly what action the doctor advised. Perhaps written orders are better executed, but spoken orders are certainly better understood. The experienced practitioner will of course do both. This also allows the nurse to ask questions and clarify things.

THE OLD ORDER CHANGETH

The old order changeth, giving place to new,
Lest one good custom, should corrupt the world.
Alfred, Lord Tennyson. *Idylls of the King.* (1869)[h]

I remember very clearly some forty years ago when I started to work as a porter at the Sheffield Royal Infirmary. I had just left the old City Grammar School[i] and had managed somehow to get the requisite grades at A-Level to get into university to study medicine. Whilst waiting for the course to begin, I was delighted to have landed a vacation job as a hospital porter. It has always stood me in good stead; because of this, I know how the hospital works.

---

[h] In *The Passing of King Arthur* by Tennyson, when Arthur is about to die, Bedivere, one of his faithful followers, bewails the passing away of the old order - of the age of knighthood and chivalry-and complains that he has to live on in a different kind of society. Arthur consoles him with these well-known lines.
[i] Grammar schools were so called because they taught Latin grammar. Knowledge of Latin was (and to a much lesser extent still is) the hallmark of a good education. In order to gain entry to a grammar school in the second half of the 20th century, one would have to pass an IQ test as well as an exam in English and Arithmetic. This exam was called the 11-plus and was taken at eleven years of age. Those who failed would go to a less academic school called a Secondary Modern School. This was the most egalitarian system of education in the UK since the war. My class at grammar school had children of steel workers, and postmen, sitting next to the offspring of GPs and bank managers.

In those days (1965), hospitals were totally different from today. The main difference was the whole ethos of working. Despite the implicit burden of human misery in a hospital – let's face it people go into hospital to die and to have major surgery – despite all this, they were still happy places to work.

Everyone who worked there felt *valued.*

In those days the Stasi did not exist.

There was nobody who seemed to be always trying to make you feel undervalued and indeed threatened. You did not feel that Big Brother (in the Orwellian rather than the Channel 4 sense) was watching you.

Morale was great.

Forty odd years ago, there was an *esprit de corps* between the medical staff and the porters and indeed all the other workers in the place. We felt that we were all pulling together for the good of the NHS in general and the hospital in particular. Moreover we felt that our work was appreciated. The *OldSchool* consultants virtually ran the hospital themselves. The term *manager* or *management* were never used. There were a few *administrators*, who literally were just that. They were there to *administrate* the wishes and the needs of the senior doctors. Then as now, they were never medically qualified, but then they knew their place in the imperative hospital hierarchy. They would never dream of making impertinent suggestions to the consultants as to how best to run their practices.

Of course the hospitals ran very well. The complex ethical concepts which drove it had been in place for many years, even before the inception of the NHS in 1948. Sadly all this has now been forcibly changed. A revolution[j] has taken place which has been politically motivated and which like other political revolutions has set out to destroy the old order completely and replace it with a new (political) one. It has been achieved solely and exclusively by hordes of totally unqualified administrators. During their destruction of the old order, they have made monumental mistakes in most areas.

[j] For a full exploration of this see YOUNG, JR (2008) *The Hospital Revolution.* John Blake. London.

Most of the Stasi do not have any sort of classical education and so it would be unreasonable to suggest that they have ever heard of Edmund Burke. He was the politician who condemned the French Jacobins and wrote *Reflections on the Revolution in France* in 1790 suggested in a letter to their National Assembly: *Make the Revolution a parent of settlement, and not the nursery of future revolutions.* This is precisely what the Stasi have *not* done.

The best examples of their bungling incompetence are in their somewhat spiteful attempts to regulate and control doctors and nurses. This had hitherto always been a self-governing process, which had evolved over many years and was administered exclusively by other doctors or nurses in the same hospital or the General Medical Council (or in the case of nurses the General Nursing Council). It had absolutely nothing at all to do with financial considerations, but was based on old fashioned Hippocratic principles and was wholly concerned with ethics and patient care. This self-regulation has now been completely replaced by these power-mad bureaucrats, whose main drive in life seems to be fuelled by a malicious jealousy that they are not themselves medically qualified and so they try to humiliate those who are.

NURSE OF THE YEAR

The six Cs underpinning excellent nursing: **care, compassion, competence, communication, courage** *and* **commitment.**
Nursing Times.

I can still well remember waiting for the lovely blonde Pamela, outside the Royal Hospital, Sheffield in 1966. She came running towards me, with her beautiful smile turning my knees to jelly, but then all of a sudden, she looked horrified; stopped in her tracks and turned back. What had I done? She shouted over her shoulder, "I'll be back." I need not have worried. She had forgotten her gloves. She was on a split shift and we were meeting for a quick afternoon tryst. She was in her walking-out uniform (complete with two-tone red and navy) cape and if she had been spotted *incorrectly dressed*, (i.e. without her white cotton "Minnie Mouse" gloves) she might well have been reported to the school of nursing and would have no doubt been in trouble with Matron. The cape had a red lining with strange red criss-cross straps which served both to keep the cape on and accentuate the nurse's ample breasts.

Pamela later went on to be Nurse of the Year! I was flabbergasted, not of course to hear in the late sixties that Pam had become Nurse of the Year, but to find that the title still exists even in the PC twenty-first century. Mind you, I think that (in line with nursing in general) the criteria have become a lot more academic. When sweet Pamela won the title, as I remember, all she had to do was send in a photograph (not in a bathing costume, but in full nurse's uniform)! The award has always been run by the professional nurses' journal, *The Nursing Times* and I am now reliably informed that the award in 2013 will not require a studio picture at all and that the prize will go to the nurse who has written the best essay, which should show she (or indeed, he): *embodies the 6Cs identified as the values underpinning excellent nursing: **care, compassion, competence, communication, courage** and* ***commitment.***[180]

So that is now official. It has nothing to do with the prettiness of the applicant's smile, the loveliness of her hair (or indeed her bra[k] size). Although I have no doubt whatsoever that Pamela did indeed embody the six Cs laid out above, she certainly was a beautiful girl. Indeed she went on to be matron of a maternity hospital in the Emirates (and later to make top of the Celtic folk song charts in America.)

Nurse's uniforms in those days were far from straightforward. Of course they were allegedly derived from a nun's habit, although I have to admit, I have never seen a nun looking anything like that – but there again my experience of nurses is greater than that of holy sisters. They differed greatly from hospital to hospital. In London, each of the teaching hospitals had utterly different uniforms and it was easy for the junior doctor to tell on a quick glance which hospital

---

[k] US brassiere (pronounced *brazeer)*

individual nurses came from. The frilly caps were quite singular (and evidently a nightmare to keep up to muster).

The dresses too were different colours in different places. Even in the same hospital, nurses would wear different coloured frocks. In the old United Sheffield Hospitals,[1] student nurses would have a dress of blue denim with a starched white (detachable) collar. They wore starched white cotton caps too but in time, these became replaced by white cardboard (disposable) ones. They would always have a fresh starched white apron with a bib front which would be held up usually by a name badge (which did not include their Christian name) on their right side and a fob watch on the left. A fob or *pendant* watch was once considered synonymous with nursing. It left the nurse's hands free and prevented the necessity from removing a wrist watch every time one scrubbed up. Nurses were about the only people ever to wear fob watches and they were often a "rite of passage" gift from Dad, when the nurse left home for the first time to go and start work (and live in the nurses' home).

A first year student nurse would wear a humble blue denim belt (to match the dress). This had a button at the front and was worn over the apron. If the student survived the first year of training, they would get a much smarter Petersham[m] belt of navy blue, which fastened at the back (with hooks and eyes). At the beginning of the third (final) year of their apprenticeship, they would change the blue Petersham ribbon belt for a scarlet one. If and when they passed their final examinations (and there was in those *OldSchool* days a definite failure rate for examinations!), they would no longer be a student. They would become a staff nurse and get a nice new dress, which was pale purple in colour and of course, a dark purple Petersham ribbon belt.

---

[1] Which included the Royal Hospital, the Royal Infirmary, the Jessop Hospital for Women and the famous Sheffield Children's Hospital.

[m] Petersham is a thick rigid corded ribbon material, which is not named after the area of southwest London, but after Lord Petersham (1790–1851), a British army officer.

Their new belt however would not be fastened at the back, but at the front and it would be worn with a coveted staff nurse belt buckle. This buckle was a badge of rank. They were the only form of self-expression in the entire uniform. The one my outpatient staff nurse used to wear had two elephants locking tusks. They were often quite elaborate affairs and almost always made of sterling silver. Just as a nurse's father would buy his daughter a fob watch when she left home to start her training, now that she had qualified into that noble profession, proud Dad would often buy his darling daughter an expensive filigree silver belt buckle. Now that the odious Stasi do not allow nurses to wear them, they have become sought after collectors' items. Quite a few had the crest of the old teaching hospital incorporated into the design and some of the Boer War examples are miniature works of art.

In March 2013, there were one or two reports[181] that when Her Majesty left the King Edward VII Hospital for Officers, she was attended by a nurse wearing a "Masonic" belt buckle. The large ornate silver belt-fastener in question featured the Masonic square and compasses next to a pentacular star. It indicated to me that the nurse had probably qualified at the Royal Masonic Hospital[n] (which sadly closed in 1992). I found it very reassuring to discover that nurses are still wearing *OldSchool* (professional) nurses uniforms in one of the best hospitals in London. I also found it very amusing to read the conspiracy theorists wild conjecture about the Royal family and Freemasonry. They even suggested that the photograph shows Her Majesty giving the nurse in question a secret Masonic handshake as she left hospital.

In addition to the belt buckle from Dad, the young lady received another highly prized piece of jewellery as a direct gift from the hospital where she had trained. This was the much coveted hospital badge, of which nurses were rightly and inordinately proud. These are definite collectables and some sell for hundreds of pounds. They are very diverse in size and

[n] Where your author many years ago secured illicit entry to the nurses' home on Ravenscourt Road. He was let in from a very rusty fire escape at the dead of night.

shape. I remember the one nurses wore at the Manchester Royal Infirmary (where I did my postgraduate training); it was bigger than most. It was a beautiful bronze brooch with a bas relief depiction of the Good Samaritan complete with background mule and the motto *vade et tu fac similiter* (Go thou and do likewise).

Hospital badges (like military gallantry medals) always had the nurse's name and date of qualifying engraved on the reverse. Some of them do look like military medals and have ribbons. They are usually beautifully enamelled on sterling silver. Favourite designs are based on heraldry and biblical stories and there is often a background cross or star. At the same time the nurse got her hospital badge, she would also get another (smaller) badge to validate her registration on the General Nursing Council, (but she would have to pay for this). It was the GNC of England and Wales and so it was shaped like a Tudor rose (for England) but had (if you had a magnifying glass) a small leek on it somewhere (for Wales, of course). These were nowhere near as superbly decorated as the hospital badges, but should reassure the patients that their nurse was registered.

I have asked quite a lot of senior nurses about their uniform and was surprised to learn that what they miss most of all is their caps. Jennifer, a nurse from Belfast spoke nostalgically about a long-awaited cap with a "fall" down the back of the neck. Mary from the Radcliffe Infirmary in Oxford talked wistfully of the "*beautiful hat*" you were allowed to wear on qualifying and tried to explain to me how she had to press seven folds in the back of her cap with a roller. She said that those seven folds represented the seven virtues of a woman.[o]

WHITE COATS
Clothed in white samite[p], mystic, wonderful
Alfred Lord Tennyson, *Idylls of the King.* (1869) 284.

---

[o] Evidently Faith, Hope, Charity (these first three being the holy virtues), Prudence, Justice, Fortitude and Temperance.

[p] A rich silk fabric.

White coats are no longer available for doctors in most hospitals. When I retired from the NHS in summer 2013, they told me that I was the only one (out of sixty consultants) still insisting on wearing one and thus gave me mine to take home. Now that I am retired, they come in useful for umpiring village cricket matches.

When I was a medical student at the United Sheffield Hospitals, clinical students would go to the laundry at the Jessop Hospital for Women,[q] where they would get their white coats from a nice lady called Elsie. (Sadly hospitals no longer have their own laundries.) Elsie issued clean white coats – every morning if you wanted one. The coats were not just spotless but were freshly starched. They were so stiff that you could stand them up on the floor and they wouldn't fall over. The two sides of the sleeve were always stuck together with starch so that when you first put them on, you had to push your hand down to get the sides of the sleeve apart. I remember that this was a vaguely sensual experience. When I told this to my father, he asked me if it was better than wiping one's arse on a goose's neck. Father was a very well-read fellow and when I asked him what he meant, he just laughed and told me I ought to find out. It was many years later, when I found that Rabelais had suggested this wonderful early sensual alternative to toilet paper in his hilariously obscene 16th century book, *Gargantua and Pantagruel.*[182]

I remember working in one hospital, as a senior house officer in Norwich, where I had to have a separate white coat on each of the wards where I worked. When I went on the ward, I would doff my jacket in the ward lobby and put the white coat on. It was a bit of a nuisance, because I had to transfer the contents of the pockets. That was in the 1970s.

GPs usually didn't wear white coats, and I recall that when my senior partner referred a patient to the local hospital to see a specialist, he always used to say, *I'm afraid I will have to send you to see a white coat.* He was always appropriately

---

[q] The Jessop Hospital for Women was opened in 1878 with funds from Thomas Jessop, a wealthy steelworks-owner.

dressed himself, wearing either a tweed sports jacket or a well lived-in grey suit – and of course, always a collar and tie and clean polished dark brown brogues. In fact, he would have lost credibility if he had not . Doctors were gentlemen (or ladies) and were expected to dress as such and lady doctors never wore trousers. The patients expected it and if truth be known older patients *still* expect it. Any deviation from the expected and accepted standards would be interpreted by the patients as a casual approach not just to their attire but to their work.[183]

In most countries of the world (and up to a few years ago in the United Kingdom), a white coat is a symbol of a doctor.[r] In every medical school in America, the "White Coat Ceremony" is considered an important symbolic act in the medical student's career. It is attended by proud parents and is a sort of ceremonial "cloaking" of the doctor-to-be. It takes place when the student has finished studying the basic medical sciences (pre-clinical years) and is about to embarks on their apprenticeship in the teaching hospital. The professor of surgery at New York University School of Medicine recently said that the ceremony *welcomes those embarking on their medical careers to the community of physicians by giving them this powerful symbol of compassion and honour. It also gives them a standard against which they must measure their every act of care to the patients who trust them.*[184]

Not all Americans would agree. A contrary (liberal) view militating against the WCC (this is evidently what the Americans and Canadians call the White Coat Ceremony) opined that it creates *a sense of entitlement to trust and respect that is unhealthy and in turn may foster an elitism that separates patients from caregivers.*[185] I completely disagree with this modern attitude and strongly believe that trust and respect are the cornerstones of a successful doctor-patient relationship.

The history of the clinical white coat is interesting, since it started with the discovery of bacteria, germs and sepsis at the

---

[r] In Argentina and Spain, they are a symbol of learning and they are worn by schoolchildren. In Tunisia and Mozambique, teachers wear white coats to protect their street clothes from chalk.

end of the nineteenth century. Until that time physicians and surgeons would wear formal black morning dress. It was around this time that the value of cleanliness and the introduction of antiseptics became so important and that *the 'whiteness' or 'pureness' of medicine became reflected in the garb of physicians.*[15]

White has symbolically been associated with purity since classical times. It is significant that the word *candour* (truth) is derived from the Latin *candidus* which means white. The term *candidate* is also similarly derived: Romans seeking public office wore the white togas to indicate their truthfulness. It is gratifying to reflect that many years ago politicians were honest. The converse, of course, is evil or death depicted in black. Undertakers still wear black. Before my more PC readers go into self-righteous and indignant frenzy, I discovered on a recent visit to Ethiopia that Sunday best in that country is a white robe and church goers wear white to signify purity. Furthermore, the Patriarch of Addis Ababa wears a snow-white crown.

THE PYJAMA GAME
Everybody in Tunbridge Wells wears pyjamas![s]
Officer in Laundry Platoon, *Exercise Lionheart* (1984)

It was around 2008 that Stasi began trying to throw their weight around and impose dress restrictions on their betters (doctors and nurses). Ironically the research had just been released which stated that there was no definite evidence for any type of clothing or dress code making any difference at all to infection rates.[186] This did not stop their absolute affront to demand that doctors, nurses and midwives should wear *no jackets or ties, sleeves short or rolled up, no watches or wrist jewellery, no hand jewellery except plain wedding bands, no neck or ankle chains.*

A friend and colleague who works in the Emirates said at a recent hospital audit in Dubai, the hospital authority demanded that their clinical staff wear white coats. Why then you might

---

[s] US *pajamas*. The word itself is of Urdu origin and means *leg clothing*.

219

very justifiably ask have some UK hospitals (and all Scottish hospitals) banned them?

It certainly has no proven relationship to infection. Quite the reverse. The only people who wear white coats in the hospital nowadays are the bacteriologists. Mind you, they do actually have a working knowledge of germs, viruses, bacteria and microbes.

All the *OldSchool* doctors learned practical bacteriology, not just reading about the differences between streptococci and staphylococci,[t] but actually plating out cultures of bacteria on Petri dishes. We learned properly about aseptic techniques as well as staining bacteria and mounting them on microscope slides. We worked in the laboratories with real clinical specimens of blood, urine, pus, faeces and other body fluids. We learned how to actually grow colonies of disease causing bacteria and how to test them for sensitivity to various different antibiotics. The great medical teacher, Sir William Osler, hailed as the "Father of Modern Clinical Medicine" stressed the importance of all medical students working in the bacteriology laboratory. I certainly did and I have always considered it an extremely valuable experience.

Sadly the uninformed oafs who decided that doctors should stop wearing ties and roll their sleeves up to their elbows did not have that same privilege. There is absolutely no important *type 1 evidence* (I bet they don't even know what type 1 evidence is) that not wearing a tie and being bare below the elbow has any effect whatever on the incidence of MRSA (which in fact is what it was all supposed to be about). When I asked a bacteriologist about any scientific support for the new dress code, he said, "*There is definitely no evidence about this at all. I think the "Postman"[u] woke up one morning and*

---

[t] For the intensely interested, streps form long (bent) chains (*streptos, στρεπτός* means *bent*, not *chains,* as most people think) and staphs form clusters like bunches of grapes (*staphulē* σταφυλή means *a bunch or cluster of grapes*).

[u] I assumed he meant the Minister of Health at the time, the Rt Hon Alan Johnson MP, who had absolutely no knowledge of practical bacteriology, but who started life as a postman. Let us all hope that at least he used to be good as a postman.

wondered how he could best humiliate doctors, and came up with the idea of making them all wear blue pyjamas to work."

Chairman Mao, during his Cultural Revoltion made everybody except the police wear blue pyjamas (and face masks). Adolf Hitler had a similar idea in the 1930s about striped pyjamas, but not for doctors. I suppose they are all socialists.

From the day I was instructed by the Stasi to roll up my sleeves and throw away my tie, I started to wear full morning dress to work. It is a bit naff to call it a morning suit, although (hardly surprisingly) many do. A *morning suit*[v] is more properly worn to a wedding or the Ascot races. The difference is that all parts (morning coat, waistcoat and trousers) are the same colour/material, often grey and usually called 'morning grey' to distinguish it from the formal *morning dress*, where the trousers are striped (known as a "Cashmere" or even a "washbag" stripe). I never tired of being told by my patients that it is always so nice to see somebody who still looks like a doctor. The British Medical Association says that *patients want to know who is treating them and that they judge the professionalism and trustworthiness of doctors based on the clothes that they wear.* I think that is what Alan Bennett had in mind when he wrote, *The doctor wore a zip-up cardigan and this did not inspire confidence.* Can one indeed trust the clinical judgment of a doctor in a short sleeved shirt?

At some hospitals, my colleagues have been threatened with disciplinary action if they do not conform to the dress code and sad to relate they have crumpled to the will of the Stasi Control Freaks. Whether they are just too gutless to wear what they think appropriate or whether they are cowed by the "pervasive culture of fear"[w] which exists in most hospitals is difficult to assess. At a hospital in South Wales in 2007, however, the BMA stepped in when the local Stasi tried to

---

[v] This semi-formal variant may also be called a *Stroller* (which in Australia now is used for pram).

[w] This term *pervasive culture of fear* was used in the Francis Report (see Chapter 9) to describe the Stasi's Reign of Terror at present in NHS hospitals.

enforce a "pyjama game". Our trade union pointed out that uniform is not included in our Conditions of Service. Things have deteriorated since then although there is as yet no robust evidence to show that codes of dress make any difference at all, doctors are backing down under Stasi pressure. The official line from the Consultants' Committee and the BMA remains that *evidence is considered in a balanced way and not over-emphasised in the development of uniform policy and that the general principles of infection control are stressed.* The heroic Scots have bottled out altogether.

In some other places, my colleagues wore short-sleeved white coats and bow ties, but I continued to wear clothes appropriate to my profession (morning dress) right up to my last day at work in summer 2013. I must admit that I did not wear a wrist watch, but this not really for any bogus bacteriological reason. It was really because there was a little empty vertical button hole between the middle buttons of my waistcoat, which gave me an excellent excuse to wear the gold watch chain I had inherited from my granddad.

If there is any evidence at all in connecting mode of dress with hospital infection rates it would in fact suggest that wearing traditional "doctors' outfits" is associated with *a lower rate* of MRSA. In private hospitals, where the administrators do not seem to have such chips on their shoulders, the prevalence of superbugs is very low; in fact it is almost unknown. In private hospitals of course, consultants tend to wear conventional collar, jacket and tie or even a suit. (This is type 2 evidence.)

THE UNIFORM IS A TARGET
When my dad first started out in the police force,
wearing the uniform was a sense of pride,
Unfortunately today, the uniform is a target.
Jerry Doyle.[x]

---

[x] Jerry Doyle is an American right-libertarian political commentator, and television actor.

Long before the Postman tried to humiliate his betters (*vide supra*), the nurses had proved a soft target for the Stasi. They had been quickly de-professionalised at the beginning of the Hospital Revolution with the odious Salmon Report. Traditional titles like "Matron" were abandoned; they were considered not only élitist but genderist (that's evidently a new word for sexist, with which people now "feel uncomfortable"). There were in the seventies and eighties quite a few male nurses taking managerial rôles at the time. In the Royal Army Medical Corps, who quite honestly never have been genderist, the term lives on and the head nurse of a hospital whether male or female is still called, "Matron."[y] Private hospitals in the UK never got rid of them; they of course have a lot more sense and are not driven by spite but by a real will to provide a good service to their patients. In South Africa and its former mandated territory South-West Africa (today's Namibia), Matron is the rank of the most senior nurse of a hospital. Good on 'em!

There was a simultaneous attempt to get rid of the term, "ward sister" and substitute "ward manager" but in my experience, this has been fairly unsuccessful and the boss of the ward is still usually referred to by this cosy old archaic term, which of course derives from the times when nuns used to run the infirmaries. Americans evidently "feel uncomfortable" with this because in the colonies, the epithet, "Sister" is used disrespectfully *to any female whose proper name one does not know.*[187]

In 2001, it was announced by the BBC on the 6 o'clock news that in response to various complaints in the press of dirty, ineffective hospitals with poorly disciplined staff that matrons would be coming back on the wards.[188] Clips were shown of the 1967 British comedy film, *Carry On Doctor* with the stereotypical formidable matron played by Hattie Jacques.

---

[y] This applies to all Her Majesty's Services, the chief nurse is a matron, whether in the Queen Alexandra's Royal Army Nursing Corps, or the nursing branches of the Royal Navy, the Queen Alexandra's Royal Naval Nursing Service (QARNNS), and the Princess Mary's Royal Air Force Nursing Service (PMRAFNS).

223

The return of the matron was a potty attempt of the Stasi to dupe the public that they actually could bring discipline and order back to the wards. They decided to call this new category of nurses Modern Matrons. In an unprecedented and totally uncharacteristic burst of apparent care for what people actually wanted, the Stasi canvassed 152,000 members of the public and 58,000 staff on how to improve the NHS. The single most requested proposal was the re-institution of the matron. What they had intended *was a strong clinical leader with clear authority at ward level. Someone in charge of getting the basics right.*[189] That of course was never going to happen. The new administrators could not possibly let go of their power. Thirty years ago, matron's rôle was undisputed: she ran her hospital and wards *with a rod of iron*. She knew all her patients, her nurses, her cleaners and the porters - and had authority over every one of them.

I got to know the *OldSchool* matron of my first hospital quite well. She was not a tyrant but a very hard-working and caring nurse with years of experience. She was ex-Army and always proudly wore her Queen Alexandra's Royal Army Nurse's uniform (and medals) to work. She definitely ran a tight ship, but she was well respected by all her staff. She was a great *OldSchool* professional. She had a house in the hospital grounds, which was quite close to my accommodation and her boyfriend, who would often come and visit her was an ex-Rear Admiral. He too was a great character with "a very Royal Navy" clipped white beard. He suffered from gout and the consultant physician at the hospital (my boss) would not give him the medicine he wanted, when he had a flare-up. The very *OldSchool* treatment for acute gout was a drug derived from the autumn crocus called colchicine.[z] The Admiral swore by this stuff but because of all its severe side effects, the physician whom I worked for was very reticent to give him any.

---

[z] *Colchicum autumnale*, commonly known as autumn crocus, meadow saffron or naked lady, is a flower that resembles the true crocuses, but blooms in autumn.

The main problem with gout is the excruciating pain you get, typically in the big toe and the small joints of the foot. I have gout myself and know just how painful it can be. The way the colchicine worked is that the patient kept on taking it (every couple of hours) until it made him so nauseated that he could not swallow any more tablets, because of vomiting! But by that stage it had cured the terrible unbearable pain. I would be asked by the matron to smuggle a bottle of the wonderful colchicine tablets round to her house, together with a lotion (containing as I remember opium and lead) to apply as a poultice to his toe – and a bed cradle. This last was the most difficult thing to "smuggle" out of the hospital, since it was quite a large contraption that went into bed with the patient, under the sheets and prevented the sheets from touching the foot. The inflamed joint really was so intensely tender. It did put me in a difficult position; did I upset the matron – or did I take the chance of the boss finding out?

No competition. I got the key to pharmacy and took all the stuff round to her.

It always seemed to work within a half a day and the following morning I found a bottle of gin outside my door (with my milk) for my troubles.

The *OldSchool* matron very much saw herself as the patient's advocate; her opinion was sought and valued by the consultant on his ward round. If something went wrong or was not done, she took responsibility for everything in the hospital and the buck definitely stopped with her. This would be anathema to the Stasi (although I am sure they would value having a scapegoat, if anything went wrong). The *NewSchool* Modern Matron is not even a shadow of her former self. One lass from an inner-city London hospital said she couldn't go round telling people what to do; *it doesn't work like that any more*. Daphne saw herself less as a champion for her patients and more as a pacifier. *Patients, she said with an air of surprise, still demanded to see matron when something had gone wrong. She found a "softly, softly" approach the most effective. "I am here to defuse anger because there is so much anger among our patients.*"[19]

The wonderful nurses uniform's described earlier in the chapter were another obvious target. Let's be honest, some of them had remained unchanged since the redoubtable Miss Nightingale had come back from the Scutari Hospital in the Crimean War.[aa] The ostensible reason for abolishing them and making the nurses wear debasing Jeyecloth smocks or blue pyjamas would of course be cited as *modernity* and *inevitable progress*, but of course it would it be an excellent way for the Stasi to exert their newly found power over the very vulnerable nurses who did not have the power to strike back. The Stasi have always been and always will be control freaks. What better way to humiliate and de-professionalise the poor nurses and keep them firmly in their place. Totally unproven bacteriological arguments would be put forward by Stasi who did not even possess first aid certificates, let alone any knowledge of bacteria.

When I asked Victoria, the most professional nurse I have ever had the privilege of working with, what she considered the worst change in nursing in recent years, she had little hesitation in citing the loss of her cherished uniform, her symbol of being a nurse; her cap, her buckle and her badge. "*I suppose it would be difficult to argue for the return of things like starched aprons,*" she said, "*but you just cannot feel very professional in this!*" She pointed down at her sexless baggy impersonal blue pyjamas.

What do the patients think? I was interested that there has been a very definite outcry in the USA about nurses *wearing scrubs on public transportation* constituting a bacteriological hazard. I have heard more than one friend in UK make this same point. I think the best answer to this question however, is what happened a few years ago in Plymouth. When the Royal Naval Hospital (RNH) Stonehouse was closed (along with all but one of the military hospitals in the United Kingdom), the unit became amalgamated with the NHS Derriford Hospital in that city. The Royal Naval nurses moved there to work. Of

---

[aa] The old Barrack Hospital at Scutari is still in existence. Scutari was the Greek name for the district of Istanbul now known as Üsküdar (pronounced ew*skew*dar).

course, they were not subject to the petty NHS control freaks and they continued to wear their smart professional uniforms (maintained by themselves with much elaborate folding and starching) and were inordinately proud to do so. These uniforms include caps, and, during the winter, *tippets*![bb] This is in contrast to the drab Jeyecloth-like outfits which the NHS Derriford nurses are supplied with. Much to the chagrin of the nursing Stasi, patients at the hospital often complained when being looked after by the civilian nurses, stating that they would rather be treated by one of the "proper" nurses - i.e. one wearing a traditional nurse uniform.

Some "progressive" nurses might even welcome the end of uniforms.[cc] There is a strange feminist idea that the traditional uniform merely reinforces the rôle of the nurse as being somehow subservient to that of a doctor. Certainly, many nurses in administrative rôles are quick to divest themselves of anything which might recall their origins, and specialist nurse practitioners who work in outpatients can be seen wearing their ordinary civilian clothes with a white coat - *just like a doctor.*[190]

THE LYING DOWN GAME
There lies the doctor.
John Aubrey, *Brief Lives.* (1696)

OldSchool hospitals not only used to be happier places ; they were definitely sexier places to work. There was certainly always an extremely powerful frisson of sexuality on the wards of the hospital thirty years ago. Some of my colleagues think it was directly related to the nurses' uniforms with those delicious seamed black stockings. Whatever it was, there was an amazing amount of sexual activity which took place actually in the hospital – not only on the wards but also in the out-patients department and even the operating theatre. The

---

[bb] The other group of people who wear red tippets are, of course, Her Majesty's judges.

[cc] Your author has from time to time been lucky enough to meet with nurses who fall into this category (i.e. Nurses who like to have their uniforms removed).

ward linen cupboard and the bathrooms were the usual site of engagement. Linen cupboards, which were large walk-in affairs actually had door bolts on the inside. I was once naïve enough to ask an *OldSchool* sister why this was. In a look which was half nostalgic and half pitying (for me!), she told me that it was to prevent anyone working inside from getting a nasty bump on their elbows if the door opened on them all of a sudden.

I could not believe just how prissy and puritanical things have become under the Stasi. In the past few years, I was flabbergasted to read that the medical director at a *NewSchool* NHS hospital had actually suspended some of his colleagues and also some nurses for playing a fairly harmless internet game – the "lying down game[dd]" whilst on duty.

Shock! Horror!

How could responsible people even dream of doing that?

This highly reprehensible behaviour involved lying flat on one's belly in increasingly unlikely places. That's all. They *lie rigidly face-down on rooftops, postboxes, luggage racks and even in the engine of a jumbo jet.*[191] BBC reported that

...staff were pictured lying down on the hospital's resuscitation trolleys, ward floors and the air ambulance helipad.

These young hot-blooded casualty staff had had their picture taken lying prone (fully clothed) on the helicopter pad. Dr Quisling[ee] thought there was definitely a risk of infection! Perhaps the accident and emergency department had better stop admitting road traffic accidents: people get so very dirty lying about on the road!

One of the consultants at that hospital told me that the Stasi (unbelievably abetted by the medical director) had every intention of sacking them, although the general feeling among

---

[dd] *The Lying Down Game* is called *Planking* in Australia. It entails lying face down in an unusual or incongruous location. Both hands must touch the sides of the body. A photograph posted on the Internet is an integral part of the game. Rigidity of the body must be maintained to constitute good planking, which should mimic lying on a wooden plank.

[ee] This is the nickname for a medical director. (see Chapter 8)

all the medical staff was of course that this would be far too excessive a censure (if indeed any sanction whatever was appropriate). The suspended staff were all in fact reinstated. A scurrilous story (which your author rejects entirely as hearsay) went around that hospital concerning the imminent disclosure of some very old grainy photographs of a much younger Dr Jobsworth Quisling playing ersatz hockey inside a hospital with a walking stick and a bag of saline!

In the past the casualty officers and nurses would certainly not have been lying still and having their photos taken.

The Stasi were evidently up to it as well. A retired hospital catering officer rang me up in June 2013 to tell me that the indignant chairman of Treliske Hospital had resigned after an allegation that he *put his hand on the shoulder of a female colleague* was upheld as an infringement of part *of the hospital's dignity at work policy*.[192] My old chum the catering officer was tickled pink. He reminded me of the alleged shenanigans[ff] at the hospital where we once both worked, where a very senior female administratrix had done far more than put her hand on the shoulder of a youthful hospital porter, who was certainly young enough to be her son.

THE GREAT BED OF WARE
As many lies as will lie on thy sheet of paper, although the sheet were big enough for the bed of Ware in England, set 'em down.
William Shakespeare. *Twelfth Night.* (1601) III,2,51.

I remember a lovely blonde haired nurse, who had an old-fashioned outstandingly beautiful hour glass figure. She was one of the most caring children's nurses I have ever known. She was loved and respected by her patients and their parents, as well as the sister and other nurses on the ward. She had a genuine avocation for her job.

She lived life to the full and once told me about her terribly exciting hobby of copulating in the most bizarre

---

[ff] Evidently this word is derived from the Irish gaelic, *sionnach,* which means *to play the fox.*

places. They had ceased to be on the hospital premises, but that I think was because these had been rapidly ticked off the top of her list. (What infinitely better tick-lists in days gone by!) Who knows, perhaps it had all started off with a "knee-trembler" in the linen cupboard during Matron's ward round. Operating theatre tables and the mortuary slabs were definitely significantly more risqué (the former also being a lot more comfortable). The board room table was logistically even easier, because the safe timing of such an escapade in the middle of her night shift. Her extra mural carnal adventures were far more daring. They included the Guildhall steps, the Cathedral cloisters, Norwich Castle Art Gallery and the Cromer lifeboat. On another occasion, a long and hazardous climb up a metal ladder towards the cabin of a "hammerhead crane" followed breaking into a building construction site! Sadly, any hope of sexual congress had to be aborted when the door to the crane's compartment was found to be securely padlocked. In retrospect, one might have foreseen this, had one's critical sense not been blunted by half a gallon of beer!

This sweet nurse had once been (falsely) informed that an old inn in East Anglia still possessed the biggest bed in England in one of their guest rooms. This was of course an immediate and wonderful challenge. She had reconnoitred the exercise and she and I were taken up to "see it" by a chambermaid, whom I had to bribe (£2) for us to be left alone in the room for ten minutes. The maid thought that it was all a great prank and told me in a lovely Suffolk accent how difficult it was to put clean sheets on this huge bed, *"That ain't just big; that's king soize!"*

I later learned that the Great Bed of Ware[gg] had in fact been moved from the White Hart Inn to the Victoria and Albert Museum as long ago as 1931, but I thought it expedient not to tell the lovely nurse; I did not really fancy my chances either

---

[gg] The Great Bed of Ware is an extremely large oak four poster bed, carved with marquetry, that was originally housed in the White Hart Inn in Ware, England. Built by Hertfordshire carpenter Jonas Fosbrooke circa 1590, the bed measures ten by eleven feet and can "sleep" over fifteen people at once. Many of those who have used the bed have carved their names into its posts. Your author did not.

bribing the museum attendants at the V & A, or worse still breaking into the place after dark! Jane and I have long since lost touch, but I have often kept an eye open for her possible inclusion in the Guinness Book of Records.

Although I freely admit that the exploits of Jane were definitely out of the ordinary, sex whilst at work in the hospital were certainly not unusual. About fifteen years ago, one of my consultant colleagues was discovered by one of the porters *in flagrante delicto*^{hh} with the on-call laboratory technician. This discovery was in the middle of the night and in the hospital library. Nothing much happened apart from a lot of ribald leg-pulling about the unsuitability of the location ("*Did you take her there for a damn good book*" etc.). Neither was suspended and life went on as normal. There again, perhaps there was no danger about the risk of infection. What I remember very clearly is the bawdy gossip which inevitably took place in the surgeon's room, shortly after the event. Three out of the five surgeons present (who were also the older members of this small group) freely admitted to using the operating theatre table for purposes besides those for which it was primarily intended.

Talking to an anaesthetist colleague from one of our former colonies, I was amused to hear that one of the world's greatest pioneers in heart transplant surgery was regularly surprised in the linen cupboard.

"A bit of nookyⁱⁱ" was far from unknown in the out-patients too. It was most unusual for there ever to be a gap between patients. In fact perusal of the records shows that in the *OldSchool* hospitals, many more out-patients were seen than they ever are today. Consequently, when one or more of the expected patients failed to show up, doctors and nurses

---

^{hh} *in blazing offence* This Latin term is used colloquially as a euphemism for someone being caught in the act of sexual intercourse.

ⁱⁱ For the benefit of any Kiwi readers, *nooky* or *nookie* in UK (and I believe US) is slang for *sexual intercourse* or *vagina* (from the Dutch word, *neuken,* to fuck) and does not mean *short-arse* or *small boy* as I am reliably informed it does in New Zealand (from the Maori word, *noke,* small).

took full advantage of the time. After all, there were no computers to play with in those days.

It would seem that the patients were aware of this too. My old boss at the Doncaster Royal Infirmary was a urologist and often told the story about passing a cystoscope in an out-patient clinic. The lights were always darkened to help this procedure, which consisted of passing a rigid metal telescope with its own small but strong light source into the urinary bladder under a local anaesthetic. As the surgeon needed unhampered access to the old man's penis, he asked him to open his legs "*a wee bit*". There was no response and so, assuming the patient to be hard of hearing in his old age, the surgeon repeated in a louder voice,

"*I said will you open your legs a wee bit please, sir?*"

"*I'm terribly sorry*" the old chap's voice came out of the darkness, "*I thought you were talking to the nurse.*"

THE CHANGING RÔLE OF THE NURSE

And always keep a hold of Nurse
For fear of finding something worse!
Hillaire Belloc. *Cautionary Tales, "Jim"* (1907)

The fully qualified and highly trained theatre nurse, who was assisting me perform some very complex surgery, said to me (during an ear operation) that she had made the difficult decision that she was going to leave her job at the hospital to go and work in the community (Newspeak for at a GPs' surgery). I was so disappointed and taken aback that I nearly dropped my high speed drill! She would be such a loss to our theatre department. I asked her if she would be getting a lot more money in her new job, but she said it was not really because of the money and that she would get roughly the same in her new post. It was because that she had been made to feel so under-valued by the Stasi. The job was just not the same as it used to be when she was training. She felt totally de-professionalised. I must hasten to add that this was not a seasoned old nursing veteran; she was just short of thirty years old. What a loss she would really be. Sadly, this is not an isolated story. It is not unusual at all.

I then asked her what she thought had been the worst recent change in nursing and I was flabbergasted to hear her answer. I could hardly believe what she said. She said that the worst thing was nothing to do with her operating theatre work, but it really exemplified how absurd things had become.

Now that nurses are graduates, they are no longer allowed to give patients a bath!

They are evidently "too posh to wash! I couldn't believe it.

I asked the theatre sister and she confirmed it and then flew into a tirade herself about how patients were now being sent to her theatre from the wards dirty.

I feel very confident that the redoubtable Miss Nightingale herself would be horrified to learn that nurses no longer washed their patients. As a student I had the great privilege to work with Professor Pierre Durel, the foremost venereologist in Paris. The old professor told wonderful stories of how he used to work as Babinski's[jj] houseman at the Salpetrière in Paris, where the *chef d'infirmières* [kk] would carry a towel and a silver bowl of warm water to wash the patients before Babinski examined the soles [ll] of their feet. One cannot help but wonder if the present day "chip-on-their-shoulder" nursing Stasi would expect the great old man to carry his own towel and bowl. One got the impression that he would not have minded in the least, [mm] but the matron would have had an apoplexy at the very thought.[nn] It might be considered that she was acting as a handmaiden to the great man, but she never lost any dignity in

[jj] Joseph Francois Felix Babinski (1857-1932). One of the "Fathers" of neurology.

[kk] Matron.

[ll] Babinski's test is a famous and useful test in neurology in which the sole of the foot is stroked with a metal instrument. If the toes go up instead of down, this is very significant (Babinski J F F. *Comptes rendues hebdomadaires des séances de la Société de Biologie*, Paris 1896;3:207).

[mm] Professor Durel told another story that Babinski went home precipitantly in the middle of one ward round, when the matron told him that his wife's soufflé was nearing perfection. Babinski was over 6 ft tall and loved his food.

[nn] Which, of course, Babinski would have been eminently able to diagnose!

washing feet. Indeed, she was following a very illustrious example.[oo]

That same evening I met a colleague's wife at a leaving party for a local GP. She was a nurse and when I told her how amazed I had been to learn about this "too posh to wash" ruling, she said that she worked at a peripheral cottage hospital, where a lot of the patients are very old and infirm and many have had strokes. She told me that she just completely ignores the directive and lets common sense and humanity prevail. She said she had broken the rules earlier that day by giving two bed baths and washing an old lady's hair.

The rationale for this absurd ruling is that nurses are graduates and clearly above giving bed-baths and wiping arses. They plainly have more important things to do than caring for incapacitated, ill, old people in bed. OldSchool nursing was a vocation in which they did just that. One of the best general nurses I have ever come across was a wonderful compassionate Irish lass. She had won the coveted Gold Medal for her year at the Barnsley Becket Hospital. I remember being at first surprised when she told me that she wanted to specialise in psycho-geriatric nursing because that was what she considered proper nursing; that was why she had become a nurse. I know what she meant. It also underlines the massive difference between doctors and nurses. If a prospective doctor does not manage to be accepted into medical school, he would never dream of becoming a nurse instead. He would more likely to do something like dentistry, engineering, or pharmacology. Medical students and student nurses are different animals.

The really sad truth is that so many nurses have recently become so demoralised and felt so unvalued that they have left the NHS. The Stasi have driven them all away with their bullying and incompetence and now are at a loss about how to staff the hospital service. In May of 2014 the Stasi admitted that they were 12,566 nurses short.[193] Their first plan to fill this staggering shortage was

---

[oo] *Jesus... laid aside his garments; and took a towel and girded himself. After that he poureth water into a basin, and began to wash the disciples' feet, and to wipe them with the towel wherewith he was girded* (Gospel according to St John Ch 13 3-5) - *gird* means to wrap around like a girdle.

to appeal to ex-nurses to come back. The potential recruits might not have worked in the NHS for more than 20 years having qualified in the 1980s – and they would not have a degree [194] but at least they would know how to give a bed bath. The ploy did not work. By the end of the year, the number of unfilled jobs had risen and it was estimated that the NHS were now so drastically short of nurses *that as many as 20,000 full-time posts – one in 20 – are vacant.* They might be short of nurses but they do not seem to be short of cash. Some hospital Trusts turned to recession-hit Spain and Portugal for recruits and have paid private recruitment firms *up to £50,000 to hire nurses en masse – on a commission basis of £2,000 per nurse.*[195] The fact that these girls cannot communicate in good English is no bar to recruitment. EU legislation prevents the Nursing and Midwifery Council regulator from checking the English-speaking ability of European nurses, as it is deemed to restrict 'freedom of movement.' Indeed forty Portuguese nurses from Porto were told that *it didn't matter since people would 'speak slowly' on hospital wards.*[196] This evidently was not the case in Colchester the previous year. At the Colchester Hospital in 2013, a whistleblower revealed how most of their 50 recently-hired Spanish nurses were so inept at reading drug charts that had been banned from working without a supervisor.

I have lost count of how many colleagues (and by that I mean other doctors) I have asked as to what they think is the main reason for the decline in morale in the NHS. It is noteworthy that not one has ever said that he does not think that there has been such a marked change in feelings. Most would agree with your author that it is the fault of the Stasi, but there are a good handful (mainly, surprisingly lady consultants) who attribute the demise of hospital happiness to what is usually referred to as "the extended rôle of the nurse." The lay person will doubtless find it difficult to believe, but in order to save money and because it degrades the status of the doctor, the Stasi (backed by the Royal College of Nursing) have successfully introduced nurse practitioners, who in certain small and designated circumstances take on the rôle of a qualified doctor, including (though you may think it beggars belief) the prescription of dangerous drugs!

Nurses are now (like indeed almost everybody else) taking university degrees and clearly needs must be specialists in their own right. Some nurses are so professional that they are called nurse specialists; yet other (presumably even more professional) are nursing consultants. The reader should not be too surprised therefore to discover that there are even professors of nursing.pp

Since they are not paid on a similar scale to doctors, this is, of course (not even a thinly veiled) attempt to save money. The nurses understandably have embraced it with open arms. At last they can play at being doctors, without needing to acquire any of the great knowledge base, which doctors are required to have. Is this newly-found nurse independence a development marking the modern nurse graduate of the new millenium, or is it a return to the days when the doctor in the village cost too much and it was much cheaper if one felt ill to *carry his water to the wise woman*?qq

In 1967, an American alienist coined the term *'doctor/nurse game'*rr to refer to the *implicit or explicit relationships of power between doctors and nurses, and the social game played by both parties to maintain that balance.*[197] That relationship has traditionally been a simple hierarchy: doctors are superior to nurses. This is perhaps based on the totally rebuttable presumption that doctors are more clever than nurses – just because they have a much greater knowledge base; just because it was (and of course, it still is) much more difficult to get into medical school (at university) than a school of nursing (at a hospital) and perhaps because the medical

---

pp There are even chairs of chiropody and physiotherapy (Rao D S. *Nurse Rôle Row Goes On*. Hospital Doctor 15 January 1998, p25).

qq In *Twelfth Night* when his two friends feared Malvolio had gone mad, they sent a specimen of urine off to the uroscopist or water-caster who would diagnose, treat, and prognosticate on the appearance of the water alone!

rr This should not be confused with *playing doctor,* which is a phrase used colloquially for children examining each other's genitals. *"Is Your Preschooler Playing Doctor?* (BOYD, Keith M.; OSBORN, Kevin (1997-06). *The Complete Idiot's Guide to Parenting a Preschooler and Toddler, Too*. USA: Penguin Group. ISBN 978-0028617336)

course is five or six years compared to a three year nurse training. During this nurse training, the nurse is never taught how to make a proper diagnostic examination of her patient, nor for that matter how to take an accurate diagnostic history. Doctors have always been responsible for the planning of the medical care of patients. Similarly nurses have been in charge of the nursing process. This was described by a disaffected nurse as *'folding pillow cases and mopping brows'*[198] When they tried to reinvent nursing as an associate "science" to medicine ten years ago, one glaringly obvious question was debated in the British Medical Journal. Why didn't these new quasimedical nurses simply re-train as doctors? *Is it because they believed in the traditionally honourable and distinguishing nature of nursing? Or because they didn't have enough A-levels? Was the pursuit of equality motivated by a belief in the value of nursing or an inferiority complex?*[199]I (as an ear, nose and throat specialist with an experience of over 30 years) was horrified to see in my clinic, a patient who had been inappropriately and improperly prescribed antibiotics for a dangerous ear infection. When I asked if the GP had looked in her ear, she said that she had never been seen by a physician, let alone have a doctor look in her ear. She had been given the antibiotics by a nurse practitioner (and one who got all shirty, when I rang her up to question her). Inadequate or improper treatment of ear infections can lead to meningitis or brain abscesses or irreversible paralysis of the face. They are serious conditions and it is not only unfair, but I think negligent to ask a nurse to take on this responsibility. This is just what the Stasi (and not you will note the Government) have done.

I leave it once again for my reader to decide if they agree with me that this practice is an abrogation of duty, which definitely represents a serious and unsafe deterioration in patient care.

REFERENCES

[171]. BBC NEWS (2012) *Kane Gorny inquest: Hospital neglect contributed to death.* 13 July 2012
[172]. DAVIES, Caroline (2012) *London hospital blamed for man's dehydration death.*

The Guardian, Thursday 12 July2012

[173]. DAILY TELEGRAPH (unnamed reporter) (2012) *Kane Gorny inquest: doctors did not know patient, 22, who died of thirst was there.* The Daily Telegraph. 9 July 2012.

[174]. CAMPBELL, Denis (2012) *NHS hospitals neglecting ward rounds, say doctors and nurses.* The Guardian, Thursday 4 October 2012.

[175]. MENDELEEV, Dmitri (2005) *Mendeleev on the Periodic Law: Selected Writings, 1869 – 1905* (ed. William B. Jensen) Dover: Mineola, NY.

[176]. JUNAID, Mustafa (2012) *Farewell to Common Sense.* BMA News. 31 March. Page 9.

[177]. BORLAND, Sophie (2012) *Speak to patients for 5 minutes every day.* Daily Mail October 4.

[178]. DAILY TELEGRAPH (unnamed reporters) (2012) *Kane Gorny inquest: medics did not check pulse for 24 hours.* The Daily Telegraph. 11 Jul 2012.

[179]. JAMIESON, Alastair (2010) *Police probe death of hospital patient who begged for water.* The Daily Telegraph. 06 Mar 2010.

[180]. HART, Victoria (2013) (www.ntawards.co.uk)

[181]. TOP INFORMATION POST (2013) *Why is Queen Elizabeth's Nurse Wearing a Masonic Belt?* June 14th, 2013; DAVID ICKE'S OFFICIAL FORUM (2013) *Queen's Nurse Masonic Belt Buckle* May 3rd 201;VIGILANT CITZEN (2013)
March 8th 2013.

[182]. FRANÇOIS RABELAIS (1534). *Gargantua and Pantagruel*

[183]. ANVIK T. (1990) *Doctors in a white coat—what do patients think and what do doctors do?* Scand J Prim Health Care ;8:91-94.

[184]. HOCHBERG, M. S. (2007) *The Doctor's White Coat – an Historical Perspective.* AMA Jounal of Ethics.Volume 9, Number 4: 257-329.

[185]. RUSSELL PC (2002). *The White Coat Ceremony: turning trust into entitlement.* Teach Learn Med 14 (1): 56–9.

[186]. LOVEDAY, HP; WILSON, JA; HOFFMAN, PN; PRATT, RJ (2007), *Public perception and the social and microbiological significance of uniforms in the prevention and control of healthcare-associated infections: an evidence review.* British Journal of Infections Control, Vol. 8 No.4, (pp.10-21).

[187]. GREEN Jonathon (1998) *The Cassell Dictionary of Slang.*Cassell. London.

[188]. BBC News (2001) *Matrons back on the wards.* 4th April 6 o'clock News.

[189]. SERGEANT, Harriet (2003) *The Modern Matron* Daily Telegraph 02 Dec.

[190]. STRONG A. *Badges Can't Take Place Of A Uniform (letter).* Nursing Standard 1998;13(3):11.

[191]. http://www.dailymail.co.uk/news/article-1198572/Find-odd-place-lie-face--Is-pointless-internet-craze-yet.html#ixzz1iVTJbVlY

[192]. HARGREAVES, Andy (2013) *Chairman of Hospitals Trust Resigns.* Scillytoday. 20 June.

[193] NHS EMPLOYERS (2014) *NHS Qualified Nurse Supply and Demand Survey – Findings. Report produced for the Health Education England Nursing Supply Steering Group.* May 2014.

[194] BORLAND, Sophie (2014) *NHS begs old nurses to come back to solve staffing crisis: Officials draw up plans to entice back staff who left up to 20 years ago.* Daily Mail. 16 May.

[195] BORLAND, Sophie (2014) *Come and be an NHS nurse (and you don't even need good English.* Daily Mail Saturday, November 29, page 8.

[196] Ibid.

[197]. STEIN, Leonard (1967): *The Doctor-Nurse Game.* Arch.Gen.Psych.16(6):699-703.

[198]. RADCLIFFE, M. (2000): '*Doctors and Nurses: New Game, Same Result*' Brit.Med.J. 320,7241,1085.

[199]. BMJ (2000): Leading Article; *The Doctor's White Coat--an Historical Perspective* 320:1085.1

CHAPTER 8

YOU COULDN'T MAKE IT UP

IN A NUTSHELL; *OldSchool* **vs.** *NewSchool*:
OldSchool: In the past, consultants got on with their work without any interference, which they neither wanted nor needed. So did the nurses, led by their excellent and well-disciplined hierarchy. Things in the hospital ran smoothly and well. The only people who made suggestions for change were colleagues. There was no such thing as *political correctness.*
NewSchool: Control Freak managers (Stasi) have been installed by government. They have no "officer calibre" and are respected by nobody. Because they therefore have no leadership qualities and the organisational skills of an ostrich, they continue to make absurd suggestions, which are to the detriment of patients and the working staff. Some (insecure) doctors have gone to the dark side *for lucre vile* and become the "yes-men" puppets of the administrators. The term *skill mix* has been introduced to get cheap labour from non-doctors.

HAEMORRHAGE FROM THE NHS
A cancer kills by haemorrhage: the life blood flows away.
The NHS "Health Professionals" are its life blood, so they say
And more doctors and more nurses leave with every passing day;
There are now more cancerous managers than beds,
And all on the highest pay.

At the end of 2011, a leading consultant orthopaedic surgeon resigned from a top job at the Royal London Hospital in Whitechapel.[200] He was not the first consultant there to jack it all in: that same year, four others had already walked out, fed up and disillusioned by the dreadful worsening in the standards of care they were able to provide for their patients. Mr David Goodier, FRCS said that he could *no longer stand idly by* whilst patients came to harm through the incompetence of the managers.

He said that the supply situation was *dangerous* and that the working staff was *regularly out of kit, out of nurses ... and always out of beds.* He had resigned because he felt that if he stayed, he himself would become *complicit in a poor standard of care* and that he and his colleagues were *guilty of negligence by association.* When asked about this specific hospital situation, the current president of the Royal College of Surgeons, Professor Norman Williams (who also incidentally worked for the same Trust) said that there had been an *appalling deterioration* in the standards of care at the London Hospital.

One of the features of a cancer and one of the ways in which it kills is by causing haemorrhage. The life blood of the NHS is doctors and nurses and they can be seen to be leaving the service at a hitherto unprecedented rate. This exodus of surgeons from one of London's top teaching hospitals shows just how apt this metaphor of a cancer really is.

Another internationally acclaimed surgeon, whose innovative new surgical ideas altered surgical practice in this country and became famous all over the world resigned from the NHS for a much more personal reason. He is working in Dubai but then emigrating to Tasmania. He has been a friend of mine for more years than I care to remember. He happens like me to be a lover of cask conditioned beer.[a] I asked him what the main reason had been for him to leave UK and work in countries where the beer was either non-existent or dire. He said he had become so nauseated with the "*overwhelming and sickening hypocrisy*"[201] of a management system who

---

[a] Often known (erroneously in my opinion) as *Real Ale.*

professed unxiety about the care of patients when their only real concern was their own massive salaries.

LEADERSHIP
Order, Counter-Order, Disorder!
Neville Winter ("Bill") Gill. *Old Army maxim*

I am more afraid of an army of a hundred sheep led by a lion than an army of a hundred lions led by a sheep.
Talleyrand. *Remark to Napoleon (Attributed)*

This quote by Talleyrand places a true value on leadership. Charles Maurice de Talleyrand-Périgord was Foreign Minister to Napoleon Bonaparte (who is often mistakenly credited with referring to British army officers as *lions led by donkeys*). Although Boney never actually said this, he understood the link between leadership and morale and the annals show[202] that he did say, "*In war, three quarters turns on morale.*[b]" Napoleon was a great leader of men and of course, he had got it absolutely right here. It is not only armies that depend on morale. The effective running of any large organisation also relies on this fragile and intangible quality. The NHS is the sixth biggest organisation in the world[c] and employs 1.4 million people.

Morale in the NHS is at rock bottom.

Field Marshal Montgomery was a brilliant and successful British General in the Second World War and he too understood men, whom he described as *the raw material of his trade*. He was undoubtedly a great leader and imbued not only

[b] Of course, he said it in French and not in English. What he actually said was, "Ã *la guerre, les trois quarts sont des affaires morales, la balance des forces réelles n'est que pour un autre quart.*" Interestingly wrongly translated in at least two dictionaries of quotations. I hope mine (*ut supra)* is accurate!

[c] The figures in the *Economist* (2010) put the US Defence Department as the biggest (3.2million). Next in line came the Chinese People's Army (2.3m). Also ahead of the NHS were Walmart (2.1m), McDonalds (1.7m), Chinese Petroleum (1.7m), and Chinese Electricity Company (1.6m).

the men under his command, but the whole of the British people with morale and optimism. Morale depends absolutely and utterly on leadership. That is probably why the NHS is in such a bad way. There is absolutely no credible leadership and therefore the morale of the troops is non-existent.[d] The man in the street might know the name of the Minister of Health, but even workers in the NHS do not know the names of their so-called leaders?

When I have seen top Stasi make a rare appearance on television, they appear as the grey nonentities who they are. Nobody recognises them. I asked eight housemen randomly at a party what was the name of the chief executive of their hospital and not one of them knew! There is no morale without leadership.

The Stasi evidently have insight into the problem. A 2010 NHS Confederation poll claimed that 24% of hospital managers were *"losing sleep over maintaining staff morale"*!

The NHS is much, much bigger than Her Majesty's Armed Forces, but there are many parallels and analogies. Men and women are doubtless also the raw material of the NHS and as such also require good leadership to function effectively.

I was on the Army List for nearly forty years. During the whole of my long service, I never felt at any time the same oppressive management in the Army, which I now feel still pervades the NHS. Senior officers of course are vastly different in HM's Land Force. They are actually selected for their leadership skills at rigorous commissioning boards. When I reached the dizzy heights of Colonel[e], I occasionally sat on some of these boards, where one had to make the difficult decision as to whether or not someone was "officer calibre." Would he (or indeed she) command respect? Would she or he be able to give and take orders? In short would they make

---

[d] For a full investigation into failing morale in the NHS and its consequences, an entire chapter has been dedicated to this in YOUNG, JR, (2008) *The Hospital Revolution, Doctors Reveal the Crisis Engulfing Britain's Health Service*. Metro. London.

[e] Officer rank structure in HM's Army is; Second Lieutenant; First Lieutenant; Captain; Major; Lieutenant Colonel; Colonel; Brigadier; Major General; Lieutenant General and General.

good leaders? Sometimes the demanding selection board process would last for the whole weekend and there are always more applicants than places. Even then, the talented minority who survive might still not make the grade. I have always been impressed however with the Army's ability to assess people and to recognise potential and this is borne out by the low dropout rate of 14 per cent of each intake after selection.[203] I first worked in the NHS in 1964 and during the whole of that long service, I can honestly say that I have never once known one (*nay not even one*) Stasi who has had "officer calibre" and would pass officer selection.

I suppose leadership goes hand in hand with respect. Nobody ever respects the Stasi. People despise them. Sadly the managers compensate for this by simple old fashioned oppression and bullying. Most hospital workers (and unfortunately that includes some of my colleagues) *fear* the Stasi. As a very senior consultant at the hospital where I worked until I retired earlier this year, it fell my lot to do some of my colleagues' annual appraisals. I was horrified to learn how many surgeons for whom I had great respect were held in thrall to the Stasi. As a lifelong forthright critic of NHS so-called managers, I have been implored by my friends and colleagues not to be so outspoken and warned that I was in danger of losing my job.

Not all doctors make good leaders, but at least they have the respect of their peers, which of course the unqualified Stasi would never attain. Recently published facts would back this up. A survey was performed, not by a physician but by an independent lecturer for the IZA in Bonn[f], Dr Amanda Goodall. She studied hospitals in the USA, where most of the chief executives and managers are non-medical. She had found however that *all the outstanding hospitals tend to be those run by somebody with a medical degree.* She seemed to be surprised by the finding and said,

---

[f] The *Instituts zur Zukunft der Arbeit* is an internationally reckoned business school in Germany.

It seems that age-old conventions about having doctors in charge – currently an idea that is out of favour around the world – may turn out to have been right all along.[204]

Others did not find it surprising. Lord Darzi, the health minister[g] had already come to this conclusion a few years earlier. His report in 2008, *High Quality Care for All,*[205] strongly advises that clinicians should take on management s rôles at all levels.[206] Professor Le Grand (an economist) at the London School of Economics wholeheartedly agreed, "*I was always rather impressed with the quality of the doctor-managers I met in the NHS,*" he said and then added the obvious: "*They have that great thing that they command the respect of their colleagues, which is a fundamental problem where chief executives come in from outside.*"[207]

Despite this hardly any *NewSchool* hospitals have leaders who are doctors. There are however the Quislings.

THE QUISLINGS

Damned below Judas; more abhorred than he was
William Cowper, *Hatred and Vengeance.* (1774)

"Quisling" is one of the pejorative terms given to the post of medical director in the hospital. This name is of course taken from the Norwegian traitor, Vidkun Quisling, who was an army officer and fascist politician, who became Minister President of Norway during the German occupation from February 1942 to the end of World War II. After the war he was tried for high treason and subsequently executed by firing squad. His surname has become an eponym for "traitor," especially a collaborationist. Medical directors are otherwise sometimes called "Dr Turncoat," "toadies," "lickspittles" or

---

[g] The Rt Hon Professor Lord Darzi of Denham, KBE, PC, MD, FMedSci, HonFREng, FRCS, FRCSI, FRCSEd, FRCPSG, FACS, FCGI, FRCPE FRCP, is one of the world's leading surgeons at Imperial College London robot-assisted surgery, having pioneered many new techniques and technologies. Author's note: The Darzi (Urdu: درزی) are a Muslim community, found in North India and Pakistan. *Darzi* means *tailor* in Urdu. A small number are also found in the Terai region of Nepal. Our Lord Darzi however is an Iraqi of Armenian origin.

sometimes quite vile names not suitable for this book. The Quisling is a medically qualified person, who joins the Stasi, (that is to say, he changes sides). A medical director is supposed "to represent his colleagues" but clearly this can never be the case because the type of consultant, who is interested in taking on this office, is clearly not representative of his colleagues, otherwise he would never apply!

The whole idea of appointing these posts is far too clever for a manager to have conceived (as we have seen, they are invariably dullards); it must have been created by a politician. It is, of course, based on the Machiavellian[h] principle of "Divide and Govern". It is a very sad reflection on a once noble profession that there will always be collaborators willing to put "the love of money" before duty to their patients, and sell their Hippocratic principles for a financial award. Sadly the profession continues to prostitute itself. Never mind your patients; forget about your colleagues; be an obedient party member, toe the political line and you will receive a very substantial monetary reward.

I am delighted to be able to report that the hospital where I worked up to my recent retirement from the NHS (the North Devon District Hospital in Barnstaple) did not have one member of the consultant cadre (neither physician nor surgeon) who was willing to sell his principles in this way. Previously, the Stasi bussed a consultant anaesthetist in from Taunton and then they got somebody from New Zealand! When he left, the job was advertised and I thought I would set the cat amongst the pigeons and upset everybody on the top floor by applying for the job myself! I had no intention of ever actually taking the post, but I thought that my credentials of having been commanding officer of an extremely efficient field hospital and actually having an army management qualification would really embarrass the odious Stasi and make them very worried. As it was, they acted true to form and I never even got a reply to my application.

---

[h] Niccolò Machiavelli (1496-1527) Florentine statesman and political philosopher.

A local GP was eventually found.

What an accolade for the consultants!

They could not even get any of my hospital colleagues to be the assistant medical director to help her. In the end another GP was found, but not even another local one could be recruited for this job and a chap eventually came all the way from Dorchester, which is in a different county and a four hour round trip of nearly 200 miles!

In the days of *Dr Snoddy* and the *Drain Sniffers,* it was always said that only doctors who have never really been any good at clinical work would take on these administrative jobs. It is probably more true now than it was then. In my opinion, a doctor who takes on the odious rôle of medical director, not only loses his own self-respect but also the respect of all his colleagues. The financial reward for this sycophancy[i] is high however. Many have not considered it derogatory to their dignity to exchange their self-respect for a brown nose and the consideration of quite a few thousand pounds per annum (or should it be anum?). An expression which the Irish use for a turncoat, who changes sides for personal gain, is *taking the soup.* This evidently dates to the terrible days of the potato famine, when the main staple crop which supported the population was all destroyed by fungal potato blight. (For some reason, this was blamed entirely on the English!) Soup kitchens were set up to relieve the starving population, but some of them demanded that the recipients of this largesse must sign a declaration, renouncing the Romanist faith and converting to Protestantism. The ones who acceded were said to have *taken the soup* and so this term is nowadays used for changing one's religious or political affiliation for personal reward.

---

[i] An interesting word derived from the Greek for ςυκέα-φαητέα *fig-blabbers* (suko-phanters). The men of Athens passed a law against exportation of figs. Of course this trade went on despite the dead-letter law, and those who blabbed to the government (for their own private ends) were known as *sycophants*. It later came to be a general term for a toady. In Dante's *Divine Comedy*, the deepest pit in hell was reserved for sycophants.

I have heard colleagues use the term *going to the dark side* when a doctor changes sides in this way.

Setting up the post of medical director is a brilliant political ploy and provides ready scapegoats for the Stasi's mistakes. It works something like this: the chief executive appoints a highly-paid puppet "yes man" (he has to be a consensus director - a political animal unlikely ever to be outspoken and very unlikely to upset any of the Stasi); he is not elected by his peers, but chosen by the chief executive. When in post this toady[j] will, for lucre vile, take the side of management and oppose his colleagues (and whom his peers will be marginally less likely to hate). The price of betrayal is now much more than the traditional thirty pieces of silver.

OUTPATIENTS
And what do you think they told me,
Mocking my awful grief?
That the House was open to us,
But they wouldn't give "out-relief."
George R. Sims (1879) *In the Workhouse, Christmas Day.*

When I was a houseman, and arrived with the *OldSchool* boss at an outpatient clinic, the whole of the assembled waiting room would stand up from their chairs as a mark of respect to the doctors and greet the consultant by saying, "Good morning" or whatever. This respect was given to the doctors

---

[j] There are two possible suggestions for the origin of the word *toady* (one who behaves in an officious grovelling manner). Some say that a toady was a con-man who visited country fairs and bet the punters that he could swallow a toad and live! Toads are well known to have a poisonous skin. People would bet heavily on the outcome. He would then put the toad, warmed in his pocket into his mouth and warm it up there before swallowing it. If it got to his stomach without sweating the venomous secretion, it would be digested by the acidic gastric secretions and he would collect his money. The second proposal is that *Toad-eater* comes from the Spanish. After the overthrow of the Moors by El Cid, the Spaniards had Moorish servants, whose manners pleased the haughty Spanish who called them *mi todita (my factotum).* Hence a cringing officious dependent who will do all sorts of dirty work became a toad eater.

because in those days, they had earned it and probably deserved it. *OldSchool* consultants were often pompous individuals, but this was part of their charm and charisma; they were very seldom arrogant. The patients knew that they might have to wait all morning, but in the end they would be seen *by a specialist doctor* and given time to explain what was wrong with them. This respect and courtesy was also mutual. The consultant would always smile politely and reply to the assembled throng, which on a bad day looked a bit like a soup kitchen, but he considered them to be *his* patients (the Stasi remember, did not even exist).

Then he would go into *his* consulting room where he would then organise the morning's work. First he would then look at the pile of letters from his GP colleagues, which of course, would all be addressed personally to him (with a salutation using his Christian name) and signed individually by the doctors who had written them. He would then allocate patients to members of his firm. This triage depended on the clinical picture which had been painted by the GP. If a patient had not managed to see the boss at the first consultation, he would be seen when he came back in a week or so with the results of the X-rays, blood tests and other special investigations, which would have been arranged by the junior staff at that first visit. They would of course have been trained to know which tests the specialist would want doing.

But everyone would be seen by a doctor. They might have to sit around for half a day or more, but they knew that eventually (it might even be next time) they would get to see the Great White Chief.

Unhappily this is no longer the case.

The patients certainly no longer stand up as a mark of respect when the consultant arrives. Some of them would not appear to know what is meant by this strange outdated ethic and will walk in to their consultation with a baseball cap on their head and apparently intending to continue wearing it! One fellow bounced in to see me, apparently having far more interest in the cellphone he was holding than anything so archaic as saying "*good morning*" to the doctor and nurse he had come to see. After fiddling about and pressing little buttons on it, he then placed it on his side of *my* desk. He then appeared to be most indignant, when I stood up, reached over and knocked it off the desk onto the floor. Yet another lad, not old enough yet to join the army addressed me as his *"Mate"*!

In the *NewSchool* system, you might not even get the chance to be so discourteous and rude to your consultant! You do not necessarily get to see one. It is cheaper to employ non-doctors and the Stasi are very aware of this. They are not medically qualified themselves and have a huge chip on their collective shoulder about doctors anyway; they are jealous of them. They will therefore try to replace them where they can – even in a situation where there is no satisfactory replacement. Managers consider both nurses and doctors to be commodities and in commodity terms this would make sound economic sense. They have been doing this for years.

ACTION IN ENT

...such men are dangerous.
Shakespeare, Willliam *(1599) Julius Caesar. I, ii, 194*

A particularly potty idea was dreamed up by someone with no medical background about ten years ago, when there was a shortage of ear, nose and throat surgeons (ENT surgeons or otolaryngologists are alternative terms). His proposal was to replace them with audiologists (the skilled applied scientists who fit hearing aids), speech therapists and good old-fashioned nurses. The plan was to cut out the specialists and save the NHS money. The problem was that it was an inferior service for the patient and in some cases highly dangerous.

Let me explain the pottiest and most dangerous innovation first. Most people know that hoarseness is quite an ominous symptom and can be the first sign of cancer of the voice box (larynx). The present Grandad generation (who are the ones at the greatest risk of getting it) remember an *OldSchool* film star[k] called Jack Hawkins, who rose to the rank of Colonel during the war and starred in lots of war films including *The Cruel Sea, Bridge over the River Kwai* and *Lawrence of*

---

[k] US *movie star.*

Arabia. Jack Hawkins died of laryngeal cancer and because it changed his wonderful baritone acting voice, his public became aware of the sinister nature of hoarseness as a symptom. Because of this famous actor, a lot of the older generation is aware that developing a croaky voice is a serious matter.

ENT is not well taught at medical school, but one fact almost every newly qualified doctor does know is that all recent cases of hoarseness should be referred urgently to a specialist, who has the special skills and instruments to look inside the throat and examine the vocal cords to see whether or not a cancer is present. The only good news about this malignant condition is that if it is diagnosed promptly, it has a good prognosis. The reason for this is that the tumour on the vocal cords starts to produce the symptom of hoarseness before it has grown to a very big size. The voice changes when the growth is smaller than a melon seed. This can be compared to a cancer of the bowel, which might get as big as a plum and still not cause any symptoms. Not only do laryngeal tumours present themselves at a very early stage, but they do not spread quickly because the blood supply of the vocal cords is poor and so any rogue cells are less likely to get into the blood stream. All in all, the outlook for cancer of the voice box is generally better than cancers elsewhere. Having said that, time should certainly not be wasted in getting the poor person with a hoarse voice to a specialist to make the diagnosis so that treatment is started as soon as possible.

What was the highly dangerous suggestion of the unqualified Stasi trying to save money with his "Action on ENT" initiative? Instead of patients with hoarseness going to see a specialist surgeon with the skill to make an almost immediate diagnosis, that the croaky patient go and see a speech therapist for vocal training. Ask yourself, "Whom would you rather go and see?" I would like to bet that even a low IQ Stasi would want to see an ENT surgeon rather than a speech therapist.

The second "good idea" was to send people with hearing loss to the audiologist (hearing aid specialist) rather than seeing an ENT surgeon first. Clearly what the Stasi apparatchik did not know is that every now and then someone who develops deafness might well have what is known as "dangerous" ear disease, which can progress to developing meningitis or brain abscess. Another trap for the unwary is that deafness is sometimes caused by a (not-too-uncommon) form of brain tumour arising from the nerve which connects the ear to the brain. Perhaps we should be kind and say that if the administrator had known this, he would not have proposed such an ill-advised scheme.

Undoubtedly the commonest, and arguably the most useful bit of surgery an ENT Surgeon ever does is take tonsils out (both children's and adults').The tonsils are an important part of the immune system in birds and reptiles and although they are thought to play a minor part in human immunity during the first few months of life, they rapidly have this function overtaken by the lymphatic glands in the body and then the tonsils often become a severe nuisance and sit at the side of the throat as two chronically infected and uncomfortable organs.

Hardly surprisingly ENT surgeons are often asked by GPs whether or not tonsils need to be taken out and consideration for tonsillectomy forms a large part of an ENT outpatient clinic workload. The Stasi have suggested that the clinic appointment could easily be bypassed and GPs might put their patients directly on the surgeon's operating list.

TOMMY'S TONSILS
It out-herods Herod.
William Shakespeare (1601) *Hamlet*, III, 2, 14

Let me give you the hypothetical example of a child, whose family doctor thinks that he[1] would benefit from having his tonsils out. The poor little lad's life is probably being made

---

[1] This is not just a genderist generalisation: more little boys have their tonsils out than little girls. However, far more teenage and adolescent girls have their tonsils removed, evening the overall numbers up. (The boys might well already have had theirs out a few years earlier) My wife, who is a paediatrician, suggests that it might be because mothers are far more protective to their little sons than their little daughters! (see also Oedipus Complex)

miserable from having two festering bags of pus permanently at the back of his mouth. This is not an uncommon problem and a cause of massive concern to mothers throughout the country. Without wanting to get too clinical, most ENT surgeons would reckon that if a child is losing a lot of time from school or has had three or more severe attacks of tonsillitis over the last few years, then he should at least be assessed by a specialist. There are two new frightening Stasi suggestions. Firstly that if the poor child has not in the last twelve months had seven or eight (yes, that's right; this is not an error, *seven or eight*) attacks of *documented tonsillitis requiring attendance at his GP and antibiotic treatment,* then his letter will be intercepted and sent back to the GP. The poor child will never get to see the otolaryngologist. Quite simply, he will not get a hospital out-patient appointment! He can continue to suffer and his mother can remain at her wit's end.

An even more alarming and sinister (and equally potty) proposal has been suggested. Let us continue with the hypothesis of the same poor child, whose life is being made miserable and whose education is being ruined by invalidism from sore throats. Even if he somehow finds time in the year to have eight episodes of severe tonsillitis (and does not as a result of all these infections die from asphyxiation, septicaemia, brain abscess, quinsy, nephritis or any other well known complication of chronic tonsillitis) he still never gets to see the specialist, but his name is simply put by the Stasi on the ENT waiting list for tonsillectomy. This will save the whole cost of the child having to attend hospital outpatients. The Stasi agent will just read the GP letter and put the child straight on the waiting list for operation. The parents will never get the chance to discuss the pros and cons of surgery. They will never be accorded the basic courtesy of meeting the surgeon who has been designated to perform the important and possibly dangerous procedure. They will not be given the chance to ask questions and tell the surgeon that they are Jehovah's witnesses or worse still suffer from a bleeding disorder. No, the administrators hadn't thought of that.

The cunning Stasi plan is that one morning the little lad just turns up at the hospital with his toothbrush and pyjamas and has his tonsils taken out by someone who he has never seen before.

A colleague of your author has just decided to retire four years early precisely because of this erosion of his professionalism. He is a very able otolaryngologist and will be a great loss to the specialty and to the patients in the catchment area of the hospital for which he works. This of course is a vicious circle situation. There will now be fewer experienced surgeons at his hospital and this will mean that the overworked few who remain will be less likely to cut up rough. As *NewSchool* doctors, they might even have spent their entire professional careers working in Stasi-run hospitals, and be unaware that the hospital would not only continue to run without so-called managers; in fact it would run more efficiently!

I have to say I spent over twenty years without ever talking to them. I always considered Hospital Administrators in the same way as Mrs Thatcher used to regard the provisional IRA: I did not *recognise* them. I always thought that this made my life at work much easier. I never negotiated anything with them because I knew they would inevitably get hold of the muddy end of the wand and I would be less frustrated just sailing on my own course regardless, than I would have been if I had spoken to them (and they had inevitably bungled it anyway).

The *NewSchool* ENT specialists who are still left might not even get to know about the children who have been referred to them, because the non-specialist, who does the triage of the referral letters probably does not communicate the numbers to anybody other than other managers. The job is given to a non-specialist doctor. It is often a GP, who it is generally believed cannot be very interested (or good) at their job and take on these administrative s rôles to make more money.

Stasi are obsessed with trying to make the NHS pay. They do not seem to realise that it is by definition a charity (i.e. an organization set up to provide help for those in need) and it cannot possibly be run on commercial lines. In their efforts to be more efficient, they have tried to keep the operating theatres open for as many hours in the day as possible and the results to the patients have unfortunately been lethal. As I have said, I never actually recognised management and so never got caught up in any of their potty schemes, because I never actually really spoke to them. (Apart of course from the two occasions when they tried to get rid of me.)

I always operated on children on Monday mornings. This meant that if anything went wrong, it would be during the working week, when everyone would be around to deal with complications. There were many abortive attempts to alter my operating practices, but I always said that it was not negotiable. I pointed out that I was not willing to sacrifice the safety of children's lives for political expediency and even went on the local television news to say precisely this.[208,209,210] The current chief executive (Head Stasi) went on after me to say that if Mr Riddington Young did not capitulate, "*He will be asked to move on.*"[211] When the interviewer asked if he meant that I would be sacked, he said yes.

I did not capitulate and continued to operate every Monday morning for over thirty years until I recently retired. Ironically he was sacked.[m]

My steadfast refusal to alter my operating practice was recently proved to be a good idea by a survey from Imperial College London, who looked at four million elective operations in NHS hospitals between 2008 and 2011. They found that in the 27,500 patients who died post-operatively, the lowest risk was in those who had been operated on during Monday. It rose after that as the week went on. On Tuesday, the extra risk was minimal, but went up to 15 per cent on Wednesday, 21 per cent for Thursday patients and 44 per cent on Friday (all compared with Monday). It really wasn't a good idea to have non-emergency surgery at the weekend when the increased risk reached 82 per cent.[212]

---

[m] For a full account of the almost unbelievable, totally ignominious way he was sacked (for failing to keep me in line) see *Showdown at the Little Chef* in YOUNG, JR (2008) *The Hospital Revolution, (op.cit) page 79-81.*

Of course there have been suggestions by the Stasi to maximise operating theatre usage by doing elective surgery on Saturday mornings. These were the poor devils who made up the majority of the 27,500 deaths in the above study done by Imperial College. I remember operating on one poor fellow on a Saturday morning and when he arrived home, he started to have a torrential haemorrhage from his nose. He was rushed back to the ward carrying a yellow plastic bucket into which he had bled a large proportion of his total blood volume. The ward sister at that time was a deeply religious non-conformist and not well known for her sense of humour. When I arrived on the ward, she had had the foresight to get an intravenous drip set ready for me to put in his arm. The patient by now was as white as a sheet and semi-conscious. When I complimented the sister for planning ahead, she said, "Well I did wonder whether or not to get you an infusion set or the death certificate book!" Happily the patient survived for many years.

LIVING WITH ARTHRITIS

We may not know, we cannot tell
What pains he had to bear,
Cecil Francis Alexander, *There is a Green Hill Far Away.* (1848)

It's not just children with sore throats. In orthopaedic[n] outpatients, they have tried to substitute consultant surgeons by physiotherapists. Older people with any orthopaedic problem will have the devil's own job to get to hospital to see a specialist. In the past, if their GP thinks that they need to see an orthopaedic surgeon, he would write a letter to one of the orthopods at the local hospital, who after reading the referral letter would prioritise the case and then his patient would be

---

[n] The term orthopaedics has an interesting etymology. It was derived from the Greek words ὀρθός *(orthos)* meaning straight and παιδιός *(paidos)* which means *child*. It was first used in the French. Nicholas Andry coined the word, when he published *Orthopedie* (translated as *Orthopaedia: or the Art of Correcting and Preventing Deformities in Children*) in 1741. It was first applied to the correction of spinal and bony deformities, but later took on "body coachwork" in general. There is a present move to separate orthopaedics from trauma.

seen in an appropriate clinic. Under the *NewSchool* plan, the specialist might not even get to see the letter! It is intercepted by Stasi agents, who send it to a physiotherapist. Yes that's right, they send it to a physiotherapist and the orthopaedic surgeon never hears about the patient. A distant relative of mine with an arthritic hip joint went to her GP, who referred her to the local hospital. She was seen by a physio, who she told me gave her a very good little booklet called "Living with Arthritis"!

Some years after this, she was properly assessed by a surgeon and at the time of writing now has an artificial hip joint.

A patient should be able to be seen if he has a proven broken bone, but now this is not even guaranteed. Some Stasi have employed radiographers rather than radiologists to check X-ray pictures in casualty departments.° The *radiologist* is a medically qualified specialist X-ray doctor (who has done full medical training) and chosen to specialise in both diagnosing and treating diseases visualised inside the human body by X-ray and similar techniques. The *radiographers* are the highly skilled technicians, who provide such beautiful and detailed images for the radiologists to do a proper job. The Stasi have quickly jumped in here and tried to employ the technicians instead of doctors. Of course it will save money, and to be fair, in some cases it has been useful.[213] The NewSpeak word for this is *Skill-mix*.

TOM, DICK OR HARRY
Banish him not thy Harry's company.
William Shakespeare, (Falstaff) *Henry IV part 2*. IV, 1,532. (1597)

Let us suppose that a hospital had, for the sake of argument, three general surgeons, Mr Tom FRCS, Mr Dick FRCS and Mr Harry FRCS. Let us now presume that a GP specifically wanted his patient to see Mr Tom, who might have

---

° They have in fact, if carefully trained, provided help in limited situations, such as diagnosis of extremity bone fractures in these situations.

a particular interest in whatever ailment that patient was suffering from, then he would write a letter addressed to Mr Tom. In an attempt to stop the most experienced surgeons getting all the work, the management have allocated the workload equally between the three. You would be forgiven for considering this a most equitable solution, but the Stasi have also introduced a mutually contradictory "Choose and Book" system, of which they appear to be inordinately proud. I can quite honestly say that I have never heard one of my consultant colleagues share this enthusiasm.

The NHS Constitution was published in 2009.[214] It made high sounding promises to the public. There was a Charter of Patients Rights, among which was the right to choose which consultant they wanted (although to be fair, it did say, *consultant-led team.*) Unfortunately it does not seem to be implemented at a local level. The "Choose and Book" system entirely contradicts the guidelines which the GPs have been given *not* to refer to a specific named specialist, but to address their letters "Dear Team". (Some of the more gutless GPs show such dog-like obedience to the Stasi that they still address their letters to a "Team," when there is only one consultant!).

Anyway this wonderful new system is available on line where the patient is given a password by his GP. When they log in they are told: *When you and your GP agree that you need an appointment, you can choose which hospital or clinic you go to. You will also be able to choose the date and time of your appointment.* That is of course if the letter is not intercepted by a physiotherapist or turncoat GP collaborator.

WASTING NHS FUNDS
Is wasteful and ridiculous excess.
William Shakespeare. (1596) *King John. IV,2,11.*

I would not wish to fail to give credit where credit is due and what the NHS administrators do wonderfully well is get hold of the wrong end of the stick and waste enormous amounts of money. Let me give just two examples which occurred in two top British teaching hospitals in 2013. The first took place in a well-known *"Centre of Excellence"* in the Midlands. This very term, Centre of Excellence is embraced by the Stasi, (perhaps because it makes the majority of surgeons in the country feel undervalued) but is frowned upon by the Royal College of Surgeons who like to think that all surgeons in the UK provide an excellent service whether or not they are attached to a university. The term "Centre of Special Experience" is therefore preferred.

Anyway perhaps owing to understaffing or for whatever other reason, this People's Palace of Medicine found that with regard to ENT, it had a "black hole" of 4,000 patients waiting to be followed up after their first appointment. Nowadays because of the Patients' Charter this is unacceptable if it persists for over 52 weeks, and the hospital will be liable to a fine. The managers were getting worried and all the time more and more new patients kept being referred by their GPs. The ENT surgeons were told that they must see them, but that the Trust was not willing to pay them the going rate of £45 per patient. (For comparison, BUPA are willing to pay out £250 per new patient consultation.) The Trust was adamant that it would not pay £45 per follow-up to the surgeons and told them that it could not afford it. Then to their horror, the CQC commissioners picked up on the fact that the Trust had "breached" on the deadline required to fulfill the terms of the Patients' Charter and started to fine them £5,000 for every patient that had waited too long. They therefore finished up shelling out over one hundred times more than if they had listened to the doctors.[215]

Another amazing example of the overwhelming incompetence of the Stasi and their total abuse of NHS funds happened in the north of England, where a professor of surgery recently retired. That university Trust is also apparently understaffed, because they were in a bit of a pickle and wanted a locum to fill in for a consultant's holiday leave. If they did not manage to get one, they too would be in trouble with the CQC commissioners and so in the end, offered quite an attractive sum of £18,000 for the fortnight. The retired professor (who is a canny Scot) said that he would do it for £20,000 and they accepted.[216]

He is a bit of a workaholic and said that he would be willing to do five major operations every day for the fortnight period (three in the morning and two in the afternoon). This wasn't a bad deal for either of them; he would get well paid for doing what he loved best – operating, and the Trust would be paying £1,000 per case in addition to having him there to advise and teach the juniors from his vast experience, That of course was assuming that the managers could administrate the operating theatre times and provide all the necessary logistic support (which is what after all they should really do best). The week before he was due to start, he was contacted by the Stasi to say that they had been unable to sort things out, but they still wanted him to come and do three, yes that's right three outpatient clinics. And they still had to pay him the £20,000 they had contracted to do (working out at over £7,000 per clinic.

SATAN FINDS

For Satan finds some mischief still
For idle hands to do.
Isaac Watts, *Against Idleness.* (1715) *Divine Songs for Children.*

Other potty ideas have been dreamed up by Stasi and although it seems that they have done it just to irritate their betters, this cannot really be the reason. The real reason is ignorance of how a hospital works at grass roots level[p] coupled with inherent managerial incompetence (which is of course what they have always done best). One politically correct way of pointlessly increasing the time spent during a consultation is to demand that the doctor fills in myriads of useless forms.

One of the first of these was a mandatory statement in the hospital notes confirming that the patient had been offered his very own copy of the letter written by the Consultant to the GP. Since most specialists dictate the letter whilst the patient is

---

[p] This term "*grass roots*" means *basic*. It is the only bit of journalese in the whole book. I nearly omitted it since I considered it to be somewhat Newspeak, but I left it in when I learned that it was first used by USA politicians as long ago as the beginning of the 20th Century (Salt Lake Herald 1903).

still in the consulting room and presumably still listening, this does seem superfluous to say the least. If the patient is not offered his own "hard" copy of the letter, then the reason as to why this has not been done must be entered in the notes. This, although I am sure incredible to my lay readers, is quite true. Indeed, when this proforma has not been fully filled in, a reason was required to be given as to why not! I always used to fill this section in, "*forgot*," which of course was quite true and has never been questioned.

Of course the manner in which a copy of the GP's letter is offered to the patient is crucial. If you ask, "Would you like a copy of the letter to the GP?" the answer is invariably, "Oh, yes please." If however you say, "You surely do not want a copy of the letter you have just heard me dictate, do you?" the answer is almost always in the negative.[q]

Some patients therefore receive a letter, whether they want one or not since this saves all this waste of time in clinic asking them (what it does not save is the secretarial time and the massive cost of postage).

Probably the pottiest idea was dreamed up in a large teaching hospital in the Midlands. Each and every out-patient attending the ENT Department was asked to sign a form saying that they were fully aware that by merely attending the ENT clinic they were increasing their risk to variant CJD[r] (a particularly horrible incurable and invariably fatal disease, in which the poor sufferer dies both demented and paralyzed). There is little or no type 1 evidence to support this outrageous supposition and I do not know of any other hospital where the poor patients are put to this unnecessary anxiety and stress.

HOSPITAL NOTES

Thou tellest my flittings, put my tears into thy bottle
Are not these things noted in thy book?
Book of Common Prayer (1662) *Psalm 56,* verse 8.

---

[q] Those of my readers fortunate enough to have studied Latin at school will doubtless remember *num* and ve*lle*. If a question was asked expecting the answer, "no" then *num* is used: *velle* is reserved for expected affirmative answers.
[r] Creutzfeldt-Jakob Disease.

In *OldSchool* hospitals, the notes were a very important and useful record of the patient's progress. They were invaluable to the doctor seeing the patient. Those notes often contained important facts about the patient's past medical history. The word, *history* has an interesting derivation. *Historia* is Latin but comes from the Greek, ιστορία *(istoria),* which really means *knowledge gained by enquiry* and is derived from the word ιστορ *(istor)* meaning *judge*. A well-taken history is not just a list of facts but also should be a carefully judged interpretation of them. This is still essential to making a reliable diagnosis and I have worked with a number of *OldSchool* consultants who were quite adamant that they would never see a non-emergency without a full set of the patient's clinical notes in front of them.

Strictly speaking, they were always *medical* notes and the nurses were not really supposed to look in them. Most doctors however (far from enforcing this) encouraged the nurses to read the notes to learn as much as possible about the patients they were nursing. The nurses themselves had their own sets of notes, known as the Kardex[s]: this was kept at the nurses' station and often filled in pencil so that it could be altered as and when necessary. Sadly hardly any *OldSchool* nurses now remain. They have all been either hounded out by the Stasi or have themselves chosen to resign from a nursing world, which they view with broken hearts as a shadow of its former self. The few who are still around bewail the passing of the Kardex. At least in those days, the nurses knew where they could find exactly what they wanted to know.

Nowadays, the patient's notes have become so big and unwieldy that they are actually too big to be of any practical use. Because only the doctors were allowed to write in them, *OldSchool* notes were usually not very thick, but they contained all the necessary details of the patient's previous admissions and medical particulars. It never took very long to

---

[s] Mosby's (US) Medical Dictionary (8th Edition, Elsevier) defines *Kardex* as a trademark for a card-filing system that allows quick reference to the particular needs of each patient for certain aspects of nursing care.

find the important section. Because you wrote in them in longhand, you could often find your own significant entries by flicking through and looking for recognisable handwriting styles. I quickly learned that by using green ink, I would always easily be able to find my own annotations fairly quickly.

In *NewSchool* notes, everybody is encouraged to write what they want and so it is now usual for them to be so full of useless and supernumerary pieces of paper, that they are almost three inches thick. Believe it or not, they sometimes have to make a second volume. Even if they are available on the ward at the same time as the patient, it is difficult to find the relevant section, in which the doctor had actually written, because this entails ploughing through all the other surplus inclusions. The Stasi must have been aware of this since they hit on the brilliant idea of burning quite a lot of the old notes. Yes that's right, they burned them. If a patient's notes had not been used for seven years, they were destroyed. That's not really a very clever scheme: it is usually in the best interests of the patient for his doctor to know details of previous surgery or medication. Once again, the problem has arisen because the person who makes the decision to burn the notes is not even medically qualified (and does not even trouble to consult someone who is).

Because of all this extra documentation, the bulky notes are now substituted with a small empty folder of what are euphemistically called *current*[t] notes, which arrive on the ward at the same time as the patient and contain precisely nothing except the patient's name and address. The history is completely missing.

The Stasi at a major hospital in a large British city has recently had another one of their catastrophic good ideas. As we move towards the promised "paperless society", they have decided to burn all the notes (including even the new ones) and replace them electronically. Needless to say this has all been

---

[t] A senior orthopaedic colleague of mine reckons the current notes are so completely fatuous, that it stands for Completely Useless Ridiculous Redundant Extra Note Trash.

done with a total lack of consultation with the consultants. Unfortunately (but are we really surprised?), it so far has been an unmitigated disaster. A small pilot study was carried out which proved the plan to be unworkable and potty, but the Stasi have insisted that it must proceed. The greatest problem is that it takes even longer to find the relevant part of the computerised notes than it ever did when they were on paper, but full of non-medical trivia. They are still full of rubbish, but on an average it takes about twenty minutes to navigate to the correct part of the electronic folder.

One of the senior consultants (who was once the medical director of the place) has had to cut his usual out-patient clinic quota down from fifteen patients to a mere six to allow him enough time to find the right place in the e-notes.

Even the hospital IT department admits that it doesn't work. The Stasi have been informed by a significant number of consultants that this system is fundamentally unsafe and might well harm patient care. The bully boy Stasi however, still insist that it must take place. The reason is thought by some to be that the Stasi have already paid out hundreds of thousands of pounds of the taxpayer's money on a computerised system and they do not wish to be seen with egg on their face.

REFERENCES

[200]. BORLAND, Sophie and DAVIDSON, Lynn (2011) *Surgeon Quits NHS hospital over poor care.* Daily Mail Saturday, December 3, page 28.
[201]. TIMMS, Michael (2012) Personal communication.
[202]. NAPOLEON (1808) *Observations sur les affaires d'Espagne, St. Cloud 27 août*
[203]. BERKSHIRE LIFE (2011) *For Queen and Country – Royal Military Academy Sandhurst* September 26.
[204]. BRINDLE, David (2011) *Doctors are the best hospital managers, study reveals.* Guardian. 19 July.
[205]. DARZI. Ara (2008) *High-quality care for all: NHS next stage review final report,* June 2008. www .dh.gov.uk/en/Publicationsandstatistics //Publications/ PublicationsPolicy and Guidance/ DH_085825).
[206]. DARZI, A. (2009) A Time for revolutions, The role of clinicians in health care reform. N Engl J Med; 361:e8.
[207]. BRINDLE, David (2011) op.cit.

[208]. TANNER, David (1987), *Consultant in Child Ops Row*.North Devon Gazette. 16th Oct. p1.

[209]. TANNER, David (1987) *Now hospital slaps ban on consultant*. North Devon Gazette. 23rd Oct. p1.

[210]. CLOUGH, Mark (1988) *Tonsil Row Surgeon in Peace Bid*.North Devon Gazette. 19th Aug. p1.

[211]. PARKER, George (1989*) Surgeon's Job on Line in Tonsils dispute.* North Devon Journal. 23rd Mar.

[212]. HOPE, Jenny (2013) *You have 82% more chance of DYING after surgery at the weekend: Shocking death toll following routine NHS operations.* Daily Mail 31 May.

[213]. PERSONAL COMMUNICATION (2013) Paul Treweeke, Consultant Radiologist, North Devon DGH.

[214]. nhsconstitution@dh.gsi.gov.uk

[215]. PERSONAL COMMUNICATION (2013) JRY/~~EJF~~ EWF

[216] PERSONAL COMMUNICATION (2013) JRY/WTF 6 July.

CHAPTER 9

A CANCER IN THE NHS

Suppression by NHS Stasi tries desperately to hide
The malignant mass of management, which lies festering
inside.
It spreads, and grows and infiltrates, yet serves no useful end;
It kills itself by self-abuse, misuse and overspend;
It gives no effective leadership; Morale comes to an end.

IN A NUTSHELL; OldSchool vs. NewSchool:

OldSchool: In the past the hospital administrators didn't really figure much in the grand scheme of the hospital. The hospital secretary was archetypically an amiable cove in a battered suit who smoked heavily. He was decent and well-meaning and seemed truly interested in making the hospital work smoothly, with his first consideration being the patient. He tried to be as helpful as he could in administrating the wishes of the senior medical and nursing staff. His salary was considerably less than that of the senior consultant and he would play in the hospital games teams.

New School: The hospital managers (Stasi) have replaced the hospital secretary. They have no medical qualifications at all which gives them a huge chip on their collective shoulder. They are trying to control highly qualified and intelligent doctors but have no leadership abilities and get little or no respect from them. They are often hated. The archetype is an overweight bossy woman who power dresses (but wears cheap shoes). Their salaries are invariably more than the senior consultant. Their main considerations do not appear to be patient care. They are more concerned with meeting targets. They never come to the hospital pantomime and do not play in the cricket team.

ARMED ROBBERS

The proper solution to armed robbery is a dead robber, on the scene
Jeff Cooper[a]

During almost fifty years working for the National Health Service, I have never even met one Stasi whom I would personally consider to have "officer calibre". I have only personally worked with two whom I have thought to be reasonably intelligent (both over ten years ago) and over the years, I have met more than one who has been seriously mentally unstable.

A few years ago the type of persons appointed to senior NHS executive positions were becoming worse and worse. They were so very inappropriate academically that doctors were reassured by government that future appointments would be restricted to candidates who had at least a university degree of some kind (and goodness knows, they are not exactly difficult to come by nowadays). When this promise was never kept, nobody was particularly surprised.

I have known one senior hospital executive (who did not even have a St John First Aid Certificate, let alone any proper qualifications to be a chief executive) and probably did not even know what the word nepotism meant, but nonetheless she appointed her own son to a job in the hospital records department without any interview! When I approached the hospital chairman about this, he told me that he did not intend to take any action about it, although he said that he believed the story to be quite true. He did not want to rock the boat and

---

[a] John Dean Cooper has developed a method of shooting handguns and is an expert on the use and history of small arms.

pointed out that her appointment was only an interim one. It went on however, to last for several years after that.

Amazingly, I was once lobbied by a group of outraged hospital cleaners about what they considered to be the improper behaviour of another very senior hospital executive (who did have a decent university degree) but who was evidently having sexual relationships with a very young hospital porter. I don't think they had heard of the Trust's Dignity at Work policy, but they certainly thought that this conduct was inappropriate and somewhat beyond the pale[b] for the senior executive. How ironic that the cleaners were disconcerted enough by this indiscretion that they brought it to the attention of one of the consultants! Being a firm believer in the principle about people who live in glass houses,[c] I told the domestics that there was not much I could do about this shameful situation. A week after this, I was approached and questioned by the current Chairman of the hospital (a retired senior police officer), who asked me if I could apprise him of this disgraceful liaison and in particular about any possible indiscretions happening during the working day (either on- or off-site). Goodness only knows why they both chose to ask me about it. I suppose my antagonism to this particular Stasi was fairly well-known at the time throughout the town, so perhaps they thought that I would be anxious to join in the attack. I did not however think that it was appropriate for me to get involved.

When all the hospital gardeners were sacked and the job was put out to private tender, one of them came round to my home to help me one day a week in my garden. He too was a

---

[b] The phrase "beyond the pale" dates back to the 14th century, when the part of Ireland that was under English rule was delineated by a boundary made of such stakes or fences, and known as the English Pale. To travel outside of that boundary, beyond the pale, was to leave behind all the rules and institutions of English society, which the English modestly considered synonymous with civilization itself.

[c] Interestingly, this proverb appeared in G. Herbert's wonderful collection, written in 1640 entitled *Outlandish Proverbs* and re-printed in 1651 with the more erudite title, *Jacula Prudentum.* Glass greenhouses had begun to appear in the 17th Century.

young lad and told me that he had also been propositioned at a hospital party by this same randy administrator, who had made somewhat tacky allusions to Mellors and Lady Chatterley.

I honestly believe that if any of the male medical staff had harassed a young nurse and this behaviour was reported to an administrator, they would have been immediately suspended.

I have certainly come across some "rum" chief executives, but I have never yet personally (knowingly!) worked with a senior Stasi operative who was a convicted armed robber. Mark you, I don't think the Brent NHS Stasi knowingly appointed to their ranks a young man who has a previous criminal record for armed robbery!

In 2007, Craig Alexander was jailed by Guildford Crown Court for threatening two cashiers at Tesco's with a gun and stealing £1,140 in cash.[217] He was wearing a stocking mask and pointing a handgun at customers in the shop and the two young girl cashiers. The judge said that this was such a terrifying crime that *a custodial sentence was, therefore, inevitable.*[218] That attack took place in 2001. The villain evaded justice however until six years later, when he was arrested for a different offence. Police took his fingerprints and a DNA sample. The saliva inside the mask found near the Tesco shop and fingerprints on the handgun linked him to the armed robbery. Alexander admitted the crime and was sent down for three and a half years.

If this vicious young thug had only waited, he could lawfully (whether or not morally is open to debate) have earned that amount of money by working for a mere two days with the Stasi. *Colleagues claim that the contracted agency employee earned £1000 a day - or about £250k a year - during his 17 months in the job.*[219]

Can you really call his NHS employment a job, however? He was certainly earning all that money and was definitely employed by the NHS. He was evidently in charge of QIPP budgets for the Brent NHS. This stands for Quality, Innovation, Productivity and Prevention. What on earth sort of Newspeak drivel is that? QIPP is intended to be a resource for everyone in the NHS, public health and social care for making decisions about patient care or the use of resources. I have no doubt at all that if these types of *NewSchool* non jobs were all abolished, that not one patient would suffer as a result. Quite the reverse. More money could be diverted to *OldSchool* priorities such as doctoring and nursing.

Anyway, he was employed by the Brent NHS, where he was evidently extremely unpopular (and could not even write letters in good English). One of his former colleagues said that everyone in the office was scared of him, '*You get in his way and you're sacked.*'[220] His lack of esteem and leadership skills finally drove a co-worker, with whom he had had an altercation at work to Google him. It was only then that his previous prison sentence was discovered.[221] When the senior Stasi were told that they had an armed robber on the staff, he was immediately suspended. The local newspaper the *Brent & Kilburn Times*, made the very insightful comment: '*Be more worried about the idiot execs who took him on board ... despite the complaints from GPs about his terrible grammar and spelling in emails.*[222]

The reporters of this local newspaper have of course, hit the nail right on the head. The question which causes most concern is how come the incompetent buffoons in the NHS appointed this man in the first place.

Why didn't *they* Google him?

How come they did not realise that he had been in trouble with the police not once, but twice for gun offences and on one of these occasions, the judge had found his crime so heinous that he had been sent to gaol for three and a half years. The Mail also asked *Could there be a more alarming example of the shambolic workings of the modern NHS?*

Alarmingly fast off the mark to find a scapegoat, the Stasi said that it wasn't their fault at all but laid the blame firmly and squarely at the door of a company of *leading recruitment specialists* called Hunter Healthcare. Clearly Brent NHS thought that they should have Googled him; they said that the blunder was entirely the responsibility of Hunters and added that checks by the CRB (Criminal Records Bureau) were only necessary *if you are working with children or vulnerable people not under supervision, which was not the case here.* (I have left the Stasi English unaltered). They added (with amazing lack of insight) that in addition, *these might be used for certain positions of trust*. This did make one wonder *how can a man taking home £236,000 a year and who was in charge of multi-million-pound taxpayer-funded budgets did not occupy a position of trust? It beggars belief.* '[223]

Perhaps I should add just here (for comparison as well as sour grapes!) that after 32 years as a consultant surgeon, called in the middle of the night to perform emergency surgery and occasionally save lives, this ex-armed robber's salary was well more than double the one I got on retiring in 2013

TARGETS AND TERROR[d]

Government Targets are now all that count:
All else has been overthrown;
Goodwill has been killed; Trust no longer means trust;
Duty is now unknown.
Now no-one ever feels valued;
The old Ethic of Service is dead.
Respect is unheard of for doctor or nurse;
Decorum is stood on its head.
Dedication now is a thing of the past:
Now we have Targets instead.

A dozen or so specialist surgeons were sitting drinking port after a dinner at the Royal College of Surgeons bemoaning the terrible state into which the Stasi have dragged the NHS, when one of my colleagues came out with a memorable statement in which he compared the present National Health Service to "an archetypal Stalinist System": he pointed out rather eloquently I thought, that it now had all the characteristics which Stalin had introduced to the USSR in 1928. As my friend said,

It is centrally controlled; it has politically appointed masters; it is target driven and finally, it is based on a system

---

[d] This term was first used in relation to the NHS by Hood and Bevan, '*Governance by Targets and Terror: Synecdoche*', Gaming and Audit. Westminster Economics Forum, 2005 Issue 15.

where punishment replaces reward as an incentive to the workers.[224]

I think he has got it bang on. Targets were an important part of Communist policy[e] and indeed very reminiscent of the whole of the old Soviet philosophy. Of course, it makes the term *Stasi* even more appropriate. The USSR had *apparatchiks*[f], who were moved about from one department to another (e.g. from transport to electricity with no training in either); they often had absolutely no idea of what they were supposed to do, but just got on and did it. They were purely political appointments (just as NIIS posts are today). The apparatchik just had to get on with his task, even if he did not understand it just as long as he met his targets.

Perhaps it is not just by chance that the chief executive of the NHS (in 2013) was a former member of the British Communist Party and *on the hardline, so called "Tankie" wing of the party which backed the Kremlin using military action to crush dissident uprisings*[225] He evidently once boasted *to have a 'Stalin-like' control over the NHS.*[226]

In over forty years working for the NHS, I only ever came across *one* chief executive, whom I personally considered to have a high intelligence. Unfortunately he had the leadership qualities of an ostrich. Evidently my colleagues share my opinion of Stasi intellect. In the Cheltenham and Gloucester area, they are known as "Woodentops" rather than Stasi. Jokes about the stereotypical "Hospital Bosses" in hospitals are a bit like the rather unkind jokes about the Irish.[g] There was a particularly dull person in one hospital where I worked, who was considered by her political masters to be highly successful. She was so monoptic in her outlook that she would not listen to logical or reasonable arguments about considerations such as patient safety or increased dangers, but

---

[e] Soviet Five Year Plans were instituted by *Gosplan* (Gosudarstvenniy Komitet po Planirovaniyu Государственный комитет по планированию, State Committee for Planning).

[f] Actually the proper (transliterated) plural of the Russian word, аппара́тчик is *apparatchiki.*

[g] The Finns make similar jokes about the Estonians and in USA, the jokes are about *Polaks.*

just blinkeredly bulldozered her way to attain the government targets. She might have been well thought of by Sir *Somebody or Other* at the Regional Health Authority, but she was despised locally for her bullying by the consultants and nurses. She just followed the party line.

The aggressive policy of *targets and terror* [227] (copied by New Labour from their Russian antecedents) was introduced to the NHS in 2000. If the targets were not reached by a particular hospital, the poorly performing hospital manager would be publicly named and shamed in lists of waiting times data. Strong sanctions would be taken against the offender, which could even mean being sacked. Small wonder that the apparatchiks lost sight of everything else. In fact, with respect to actual figures, the terror policy (it must be grudgingly admitted) did definitely work. The price paid however in terms of morale was too high. Punishment took the place of reward and the real professionals (the life blood of the NHS) started to become demoralised, disillusioned and then take early retirement and leave. The Labour party did a very rapid backpedalling in 2013 with respects to their targets policy. When it was cited as the main cause for the Mid Staffs Hospital disaster, the party leader, Ed "the millipede" Milliband said that *they* (targets) *had improved care for millions*, but *they must be kept in their place.* [228]

Targets are a prime example of making the important people in the hospital feel unvalued. The King's Fund is a notable healthcare charity started as long ago as 1897[h]. It is completely independent and as such highly respected by everyone except the Stasi (who are probably so thick that they don't even know of its existence). Its raison d'être is *to understand how the health system in England can be improved and using that insight, working with individuals and*

---

[h] The King's Fund was formed in 1897 as an initiative of the then Prince of Wales to allow for the collection and distribution of funds in support of the hospitals of London. Its initial purpose was to raise money for London's voluntary hospitals, which at that time offered the only health services available to poor people in the capital. It also ensured that the contributions raised flowed towards those hospitals in greatest need. It was granted a Royal Charter by HM in July 2008.

organisations to shape policy, transform services and bring about behaviour change. The King's Fund consider targets to be an example of *"overadministration"* and point out *that health service professionals who traditionally felt that they controlled clinical services now feel they have to carry out instructions in which they have little personal investment and hence ownership.*

Targets were introduced in the year 2000. Since then morale has continued to plummet. The British Medical Journal summed up by saying that *telling people that "the floggings will continue until morale improves" is not sustainable in the longer term.*[229]

MISSING THE TARGETS
You need to meet targets whatever the demand.[i]
Dame Barbara Hakin. (2008)

One should never underestimate the enemy.

Occasionally the Stasi show unexpected flashes of intelligence (!) in their ingenuity at meeting government targets. The "Hello Nurse"[j] in accident and emergency departments was an outrageous Stasi response to ensure that patients were treated within NHS guidelines and did not miss the targets. In order for casualty departments to achieve good ratings, patients coming through the door had to be seen by a nurse within ten minutes of arrival at the hospital. Rather than sack one or two senior Stasi and use all the hundreds of thousands saved to employ ten more nurses to speed up work in the emergency department, some trusts gave a single nurse the task of going round and doing little more than say, "*Hello!*" to patients who had just come through the door and

---

[i] Dame Barbara Hakin, Managing Director of Commissioning Development at the Department of Health Internal e-mail sent to Hospital CEO. (see *Private Eye* endnote)

[j] Here our American readers might get somewhat confused since "Hello, Nurse!" has become somewhat of a trope in the US. Used above, it has nothing to do with a New York rock band, a fictional character from the Spielberg animated series *Animaniacs* or the evidently once popular catcall used during the heyday of vaudeville.

then recording this on the front of the patient's casualty card. At least then the target of the patient having been seen by a nurse within ten minutes of arrival was being met. She was known as the "Hello Nurse".

The (Socialist) Health Secretary, Frank Dobson[k] put a stop to this absurd practice in 1997,[230] but the same Stasi spirit of sticking doggedly to the letter of the law (but not the spirit) lives on. A leopard after all cannot change his spots[1] and so they continue to do what they do best.

One canny Trust in Scotland came up with another brilliant idea in order to keep their waiting lists down. So much so that their Health Secretary was able to claim they had the shortest waiting lists on record.[231] Lothian NHS Stasi hit on a really novel way of meeting their waiting list targets. They gave their patients out-patient appointments in a different country! Poorly folk in Lothian, Scotland were given clinic appointments in Harrogate, (which for the benefit of any Americans or other colonials, who might have just picked this book up, is in North Yorkshire, which is in England) some 200 miles away from Lothian.

You will not be too surprised to learn that quite a lot of the sick and ailing people, the majority of whom are old, declined to travel all the way to England to get their piles, varicose veins and hernias sorted out. This is of course what the Stasi are banking on. The patients who demur are then marked as declining the offered appointment and are therefore no longer counted against the waiting list targets. Both the Stasi and the Government think that it is acceptable practice . A representative of NHS Lothian assured us that this was *standard policy in Scotland,*[232] whilst a Scottish Government

---

[k] A fact which is not generally known about this Minister of Health but which has been confided to your author on two separate occasions by disenchanted London cabbies is that, on entering a black London taxi, he always pulls down the dickie seat and sits with his back to the engine (he is the son of a railwayman). He does this, even if he is alone. To my good knowledge, this fact does not appear in any book by another author!

[1] This proverb is from a Biblical quote in Jeremiah (ch.13,v.23) *Can the Ethiopian change his skin?*
Or the cat of the mountain, his spots?

spokesman insisted, *"Patients across Scotland are benefiting* (sic) *from the lowest-ever waiting times in years. Those offered treatment further from home, but who choose to be treated locally, remain on the waiting list and are treated within NHS guidelines.*[233]

An investigation was carried out into the whole ethos which evidently assumed that this massage (i.e. *fiddling*) of waiting time figures is acceptable.[234] This inquiry elicited very clearly how *terror* is usually associated with *targets* in the Stalinist culture which is now our National Health Service. *There were numerous reports from staff of both overt and covert bullying.*[235] Threats were made such as *"Those of you with mortgages and career aspirations had better be afraid."*[236]

Another way to get over the problem was conceived in England, The numbers on the waiting time for a first appointment for a child with suspected autism in North Devon kept going up and up. When it reached thirty months, (yes, that's right two and a half years), the Stasi did not make any attempt to massage this waiting list - instead they just *closed it*! That's alright evidently.[237]

MASSAGE AND THE NATIONAL AUDIT

...such blind obedience to something they know to be
wrong is worse than folly to us; it is slavery in the extreme;
and the man who would thus willingly degrade himself,
should not claim a rank among intelligent beings.
Brigham Young, *Priesthood.* (1852).

The Stasi have their own pseudo-language (a sort of pidgin). It is tied up inextricably with political correctness and euphemism[m] They call inappropriate adjustments of waiting lists, *massage*. It doesn't sound quite as bad as *lying through your teeth*. The National Audit Office (known to journalists as

---

[m] For a full investigation into *The New Language* in the NHS, an entire chapter has been dedicated to this in YOUNG, JR, (2008) *The Hospital Revolution, Doctors Reveal the Crisis Engulfing Britain's Health Service.* Metro. London.

the Parliamentary Watchdog) made an official report in which they found that:

Nine NHS trusts inappropriately adjusted their waiting lists, three of them for some three years or more, affecting nearly 6,000 patient records. For the patients concerned this constituted a major breach of public trust and was inconsistent with the proper conduct of public business.[238]

The report makes fascinating reading. Of course, the Audit Office can actually "blow the whistle" on the Stasi without any fear that blistering reprisals will be taken against them. It must be very reassuring to know one can make a valid criticism of the NHS and not be immediately out of work and not likely to find further work in the monopolistic system which the NHS runs in the UK. The NAO report tells how these nine trusts (viz. Barts and the London, Plymouth, Stoke Mandeville, Guy's and St Thomas's, Salford Royal, Redbridge, South Warwickshire, University College and finally Surrey and Sussex) had been given a very strong message by their respective Stasi that *delivery to achieve waiting list and waiting time targets were key priorities.* Because of this, patients with life-threatening illnesses had had their treatment delayed because in order to achieve targets, priority had been given to those with minor ailments (who had been waiting longer).

The report investigated fifty NHS Trusts in detail and gave questionnaires to 558 consultants. More than half admitted treating less complex medical problems before more needy patients. The investigation found that consultants themselves had complained of heavy pressure from the Stasi to distort clinical priorities. Non-emergency operations to reverse vasectomies had been performed at the expense of patients waiting for bladder tumour surgery. Patients had received hip and knee replacement before those needing urgent surgery to repair artificial joints. Those approaching the target deadline of an 18-month maximum wait set by the Government would frequently be given priority. Also greater numbers of shorter, easier operations were preferred to more complex surgery as this would reduce numbers on the lists more quickly.

NAO Deputy Auditor General Martin Pfleger, did not excuse the illicit "adjustments" but admitted, *'It is understandable that occasionally a small case can be slotted into operating theatre schedules to make best use of the time but the scale we found raises more serious issues.'*[239] The British Medical Association said:

'This confirms what the BMA has been saying for a long time, that waiting lists need to be managed from a patient's point of view, with the most urgent treated first. If patients know they are waiting because someone with a greater clinical need is having surgery before them they may not mind waiting slightly longer. We need to get away from blind adherence to rigid targets which does not acknowledge how serious a patient's condition is and which is used to pillory the medical profession.'

They added that it was impossible to state whether these practices had led to avoidable deaths, but that it had certainly increased the suffering of some patients.

After the Francis Report, a whistleblower claimed that she had been specifically headhunted by the Stasi and asked to "*fix the mortality figures*" at the Royal Wolverhampton Hospital.[240] Mrs Sandra Haynes Kirkbright was sought for employment as a health coder: this is a non-medical post responsible for health statistics. She says that because the Trust believed that she had cooked the books for her previous employers (at the Mid Staffs Hospital!) they offered to almost double her salary to £54,000 a year to distort the mortality figures for them too! She said that when she realised what the Stasi wanted her to do, she refused. *'They wanted me to fix it. But they didn't want me to fix it properly,'* she said. However, she claimed others at the Trust were '*breaking every rule in the book*'.[241]One of the ways in which mortality figures can be *massaged* is to record more fatalities as unavoidable. An example of an unavoidable death would be a patient known to have terminal cancer who comes into hospital for "end of life care" or as it is more properly called palliative[n] care. If a patient is recorded as being treated by the palliative care team, this would mean that their unavoidable death does not alter the hospital's mortality rate. Mrs Kirkbright has averred that the Trust would use any excuse to code any patients' deaths as unavoidable, even if they had never been seen by palliative care doctors. Hardly surprisingly the Trust vigorously denies this claim. The facts remain however that between 2009 and 2011, the death rate in Wolverhampton dropped by 13% from quite unacceptable levels to reach the national average. It is also irrefutable that this excellent improvement coincided with a concomitant increase in the recorded number of *unavoidable* 'palliative care' deaths, which rocketed from 2.19% to 20.3% (which is roughly double the national average). Mrs Kirkbright is understandably very bitter about her suspension from the hospital, which she claims is wholly and exclusively because she has not only refused to fiddle the figures in an immoral manner, but that she has had the temerity to talk to the media. She said that *she wouldn't even send a dog to Wolverhampton because staff didn't really care.*[242] The Trust however claims her suspension is for alleged bullying of colleagues.

The massage (i.e. falsification) of death rates was said by Professor Jarman to be more widespread. He reckoned in 2013 that *within the last five years other hospitals have lowered their mortality rates by wrongly labelling deaths.* He says that *The whole thing is appalling*[243] and cited Bolton as an example. It had one of the highest mortality rates in the country. Then in 2011, the figures suddenly plummeted. Overnight Bolton became one of only about 50 in the country with 'lower than expected' death rates. They told Professor Jarman that it was a happy coincidence *but there are now concerns it was merely a statistical trick. In fact, it is feared that since 2001, an estimated 2,000-plus patients may have died there unnecessarily.* There was concern that preventable deaths from hip fractures or urine infections had been

---

[n] The origin of this word is interesting. A *pallium* was a large *cloak* (in Roman times favoured by the Greeks). To *palliate* therefore became to mean *effecting some temporary relief, but not to cure an illness.*

intentionally (and dishonestly) re labelled as septicaemia to lower the mortality rate. A death from such a serious disease as septicaemia would not be unexpected. Such a death would not affect the mortality figure in the same way as so-called preventable deaths from a hip fractures and cystitis. It certainly looked very suspicious, when at the same time Bolton's mortality rate dropped, 800 cases of septicaemia were recorded (which is four times what should be expected in a hospital of this size. Other hospitals under investigation for this sort of mendacity were Medway in Kent, George Eliot in Nuneaton, Walsall and Mid Staffs. In all these Trusts, mortality rates have been slashed by up to quarter in a single year.

A PERVASIVE CULTURE OF FEAR
Blind obedience to authority is the greatest enemy of truth.
Albert Einstein. Autoritätsdusel.°

Blind obedience to achieving targets was the main reason cited for the terrible tragedy and almost genocidal neglect at the Mid Staffordshire Hospital (in Stafford, the county town of Staffordshire), where it was estimated that because of the substandard care between 400 and 1200 more patients died from 2005 to 2008 than would be expected for the type of hospital.[244] Certainly nobody would suggest that there is no risk to going into hospital and having surgery, but these figures are impossible to justify. The actual risk, calculated in 2012 and published in *The Lancet* was described by the researcher as *very worrying.* He found that the risk of dying within two months of surgery is one in 28 (3.6 per cent), which was evidently *twice as high as thought.*[245]

One of the theatre sisters at the hospital where I work told me that she thought this was the worst example of NHS management failure in recent years. She said that the Mid Staffs Hospital did for nursing what Dr Shipman did for medicine. Personally I think her argument is basically flawed. Shipman was a one-off serial killer. He was a rare psychopath,

---

° What he actually said was, *"Autoritätsdusel ist der größte Feind der Wahrheit"*

who happened to be in a profession where he had every opportunity to gratify his homicidal need. This does not really compare with the Mid Staffs tragedy. The sad truth is that the institutionalised neglect at Stafford Hospital is probably commonplace throughout the United Kingdom, but just not to the same degree. Mid Staffs is at one end of a spectrum. Unfortunately the balance of probabilities favours that unlike Dr Shipman, it is not just a one-off hospital, but that the same pervasive culture which was thought to be the basic cause for the disaster is the rule rather than the exception in the greater NHS.

Although it took nearly seven years for the final report to see light in 2013, the whole sorry business started as long ago as the summer of 2006. A retired government advisor was called to the Mid Staffordshire Hospital and spent three hours inspecting the accident and emergency department with a retired matron. They were evidently shocked and disgusted by the filthy state of the place. They promptly submitted his three page report to the hospital's Patient and Public Involvement in Health Forum (PPI), who chose to completely ignore it! The author, Mr Terence Deighton said, *"They refused to pass my report to the hospital. They didn't want to upset the new chief executive and didn't want to rock the boat."*[246] Alarmed at this flagrant disregard for safety and hygiene, Mr Deighton, a former member of the Institute of Risk and Safety Management, decided to blow the whistle and contacted the local newspaper. They of course showed a lot more interest and published the report under the headline, *"Town Hospital in 'a squalid state'."*

Hospital staff and patients' relatives worried about the standard of care their loved ones were receiving, began contacting Mr Deighton with frightening stories. The Stasi refused to take any action to ameliorate matters and tried and shut Mr Deighton up. Since he was not an NHS employee, they could not suspend him or threaten him that if he didn't keep his mouth shut, he would never work in the United Kingdom again (like they do with doctors and nurses). This is of course what the Stasi do best. The most spiteful thing they could think of was to ban him from the hospital premises and threaten to have him removed if he visited again.

Things then took a very sinister turn for the worse.

In September 2006, an 86-year-old lady was admitted to Stafford Hospital for a routine hernia operation. Just before being discharged, Mrs Bella Bailey suffered a fall and over the next two weeks her condition deteriorated rapidly until she died in what her daughter described as terrible conditions on the ward during her final days. She said, *"My mum was supposed to come out after six weeks but she was dropped by one of the nurses and she never recovered. My mum would not let go of my hand after that because she was so afraid of the staff."* Julie Bailey, the daughter mounted a 24-hour vigil by her mother's bedside and was horrified by what she witnessed. *"Poorly trained health care assistants brought meals to patients without helping them feed themselves, elderly men were left to wander the ward in a confused state, vulnerable patients were left hungry, dirty and frequently in pain. Some patients were so thirsty they were reduced to drinking from the flower vases scattered around the ward. Patients were screaming out in pain because they could not get pain relief. Patients would fall out of bed and we would have to go hunting for staff."* She described Stafford Hospital as, *"like a Third World hospital."*

Things got even worse!

The evident death toll in the hospital became apparent and was frightening. More and more people were coming forward with stories of dead relatives. Miss Julie Bailey runs a café close to the hospital. She and her supporters plastered the walls with photographs of dozens of elderly men and women – husbands and wives, fathers and mothers, brothers and sisters they claimed had died unnecessarily at Stafford Hospital because of neglect. Breaks Café and the memorial photographs became the epicentre of a Cure the NHS Campaign.[p] It couldn't have done much for customers who called in for a nice cup of tea, but more and more photos went up on the

---

[p] Cure the NHS Campaign, 5b Lichfield Road, Stafford, Staffordshire, ST17 4XJ; Telephone:07708469513; Email:curethenhs@hotmail.co.uk

walls of the café, a constant reminder of the appalling conditions being endured by hundreds of vulnerable patients inside the hospital, which should have devoted itself to their care. The residents of Stafford lived in mortal fear of being admitted and would try to bribe ambulance men to take them elsewhere.

Among the macabre rows of photographs of the dead staring out from the walls of Breaks Café was Irene Guest, enjoying a family function with her 79-year-old husband Jeff. He said his 73 year old wife had received appalling care during her five-week stay at the hospital. She was known to have dementia, but had been admitted with a urinary infection. Her condition deteriorated rapidly during her stay. Mr Guest, a former builder, said his wife never received a bath in five weeks: worse still, she was left to lie in soiled sheets, was given no proper medication and although she was given food, was never helped to eat it. *"Irene had early Alzheimer's but in my opinion some of the staff did not know how to deal with her,"* he said. *"I also noticed they didn't wash their hands between patients."* Mrs Guest was discharged and died two weeks later. *"Her official cause of death was listed as dementia and respiratory problems, but she never had any problems with breathing before she went there."* said Mr Guest. *"Sometimes I blame myself, thinking I shouldn't have taken her there, but at the time I thought it was the one place she'd be safe."*

It was not only geriatric cases who were killed. In one of the worst tragedies in the hospital's appalling catalogue of failure, four members of the same family were lost within 18 months.[247] Thirty-six year old Kelly Linten lost her grandmother, uncle, sister and six-day-old baby. She then almost became a fifth victim herself, when a nurse from the hospital was about to give her pethidine, while she was in labour, despite her wristband and an entry on the front of her medical notes both clearly stating she was allergic to the drug!

The appalling concatenation of disasters started in January 2007. Almost unbelievably, Kelly's baby daughter, Nyah had to be delivered by her own grandmother, because a distracted midwife was not paying attention! The baby was not breathing but was resuscitated, then discharged home by a junior paediatrician just two days later, despite the family's fears that something was seriously wrong with her. The new born daughter still appeared the same blue colour, which she had been when she was born and in addition to this, she was not taking her feeds properly. She died four days later. A post-mortem examination revealed four holes in her heart. Although the mother accepts that Nyah's death might well have been inevitable, she feels that the hospital should at least have *realised there was a problem'*. It was during the labour with Nyah that a nurse came to inject Kelly with a syringe containing pethidine, unaware that her patient was allergic to it. If this had been given, it would probably have killed her too.

A few months later in April, Kelly's sister Laurie, 37, died of lung, bone and lymph cancer. Particularly distressing for the family was finding the body of Laurie, with her dead eyes still staring wide open, lying on her blood-splattered sheets in full view of the other patients on the ward. Even though she had displayed all the tell-tale symptoms early in her illness and the markers were present in her blood, it was 18 months later, when she had been sent for a scan at another hospital that the diagnosis was eventually made.

It was Oscar Wilde's Lady Bracknell who said that, "*to lose one parent may be regarded as a misfortune; to lose both looks like carelessness.*"[q] Sadly, there were to be more tragedies for Kelly to contend with. Her 48 year old uncle died in January 2008 after his intestine was accidentally pierced during an operation for bowel cancer. Her Majesty's Coroner ruled the death to be accidental. Later that summer, Kelly's 80-year-old grandmother also died in Stafford Hospital, hungry and dehydrated after suffering a stroke. The family said the dehydration was caused by the nursing staff failing to give her enough to drink. They also said that the poor old lady was abandoned in her own excrement during her final days and it

---

[q] Oscar Wilde. (1895) *The Importance of Being Earnest* . Act 1. To lose one parent, Mr Worthing, may be regarded as a misfortune; to lose both looks like carelessness.

was left up to the relatives to change the incontinence pads in her bed.

One of her dying wishes had been to see Kelly's new baby, Khalen. Anxious to comply, Kelly checked with staff before taking the newborn baby into the ward. Then as the frail old lady held her great-grandchild, another nurse appeared and said: '*What on earth is a baby doing here? You do know we've got MRSA and C-Diff on this ward?*'

THE FRANCIS REPORT[r]

So great was the outcry in England,
Darts players neglected their beer!
Marriott Edgar. *The Channel Swimmer.* (1933)

The Government (of whatever colour) always tries to avoid "getting involved" with controversial health issues,[s] but it could hardly ignore this one. The first report into the care provided by Mid Staffordshire NHS Foundation Trust was published in 2010, but the Inquiry Chairman, Robert Francis QC, criticised the narrow remit he had been given. He concluded that patients were routinely neglected by a Trust that was preoccupied with cost cutting and targets, and which lost sight of its fundamental responsibility to provide safe care.

What's new?

In his initial report, one section entitled "bullying" referred to *a forceful style of management* as part of the culture of the Trust.[248] He also said that a *pervasive culture of fear* existed in the hospital. He said that this was not conducive to providing good care for patients or making available a supportive working environment for staff. Any senior consultant or experienced nursing sister at almost any hospital in the UK could, I think have told him this. Robert Francis singled out the target-driven philosophy:

---

[r] There were in fact three Francis Reports. The final definitive one came out in 2013.

[s] A very senior (now retired) orthopaedic surgeon told me many years ago, "they try to adopt a DIY approach – don't involve yourself!"

A high priority was placed on the achievement of targets...
The pressure to meet this generated a fear, whether justified or
not, that failure to meet targets could lead to the sack.[249]

He reported that the consultant body had largely dissociated itself from management, for whom they had a lack of trust. He cited one particular incident concerning an attempt to persuade a consultant to alter an adverse report to Her Majesty's Coroner. A 20-year-old lad had gone over the handlebars of his mountain bike on Cannock Chase in 2006 and had been taken to the Stafford Accident and Emergency Department. He had in fact ruptured his spleen[†] but this had not been diagnosed and the young man was sent home. His friends were protesting about his dismissal from the Mid Staffs Hospital, because he was evidently too weak to walk and was still actively vomiting. But he was discharged from the department in a wheelchair. He died two days later in another hospital.

The Head of Legal Services at the Stafford Hospital, Kate Levy had asked consultant surgeon, Mr Ivan Phair FRCS to give a second opinion on the death. His report was certainly not what the Stasi wanted to hear. He opined that the death of the young lad was *avoidable* and further *that there was a high probability that the level of care delivered was negligent.* When I recounted this terrible story to one of the unqualified health care assistants in the hospital where I work, I was delighted to hear her say that she thought that a ruptured spleen might have been the cause of death. It's even the sort of thing that the better St John Ambulance men know about. It is also a very common injury, after going over the handlebars of a bike. It could have been diagnosed by a scan of the abdomen, which was certainly available in the Stafford Hospital, but not performed.

The Francis Inquiry heard that Miss Levy had asked Mr Phair to delete his pejorative criticisms from his report *to spare distress to the family and avoid adverse publicity.*[250] As it

---

[†] This injury occurs in both rural and urban environments and results from motor vehicle crashes, domestic violence, sporting events, and accidents involving bicycle handlebars.

happened, she sent neither the original nor the altered report of Mr Phair to the coroner, but when details of the cover-up were published two years ago in a Sunday newspaper, she was sacked by the Trust. She appealed against her dismissal. The lawyer pointed out that her duty was not a Hippocratic ethic to her patient, but that she was employed by the Trust and that she was acting in her employers' best interests by omitting to inform the coroner of Mr Phair's report. The appeal was unsuccessful, so she then started tribunal proceedings against the Mid Staffordshire NHS Foundation Trust. They eventually conceded that Miss Levy had been '*wrongfully and unfairly dismissed*', and authorised a settlement to her of £103,000. I leave it for my reader to decide the moral (rather than legal) issue here, when comparing this sum with the £13,000 which the boy's father received from the Trust to cover funeral and legal expenses.

Francis said that this caused him serious concern and called into question how candid the Trust was prepared to be about things that went wrong. He once again reiterated the devastatingly low level of morale among the working staff.

The inquiry report, which was fairly damning was first published in early 2010. Although it was described as *the worst-ever NHS hospital scandal*, not a single Stasi was disciplined. Public outrage was inflamed, when the press announced that the chief executive of the hospital, one Martin Yeates, had resigned with a pay-off of more than £400,000 and a £1 million pension pot from Mid Staffordshire Foundation Trust, which runs the hospital. Was this his reward for running a hospital in which 1,200 people more than expected had lost their lives, because of putting government targets and cost-cutting before patient care?

Sir Bruce Keogh, Medical Director to the Department of Health was called to give evidence and he summed up the issue neatly. He said poor care *"was inescapably"* the fault of *"incompetent management."*[251] It had been hoped by many that the person in charge of that incompetent team, Martin Yeates would be taken to task, but he sent a message to the inquiry that he was too ill to appear in person and even said that he was so distressed he had considered suicide.[252] He was evidently not feeling too suicidal earlier in the year. The local newspaper angrily pointed out that he had been *on a luxury skiing holiday to France earlier this year with a group of medical pals*.[253] What absolutely amazes your author is that hospital doctors would even contemplate socialising in any way with a Stasi official. I do not think that any of my consultant colleagues know (or even care) where the chief executives of their respective hospitals live. I personally would avoid any form of intercourse with the Stasi like the plague. I would avoid having a drink with one of them, let alone go on holiday with a chief executive. Then the irate newspaper article went on to say that it was a medical director with whom the suicidal administrator had gone skiing. (see also *The Quislings* – section on medical directors in chapter 8)

Inevitably with the change of government, Robert Francis was asked to provide the much demanded follow up inquiry. This started in June 2010 and took another thirteen months. It involved 139 days of hearings, 181 witnesses and over a million pages of evidence, and cost over £10m.[254] This was not the last of it however; Francis was still not satisfied with his remit until his final report in 2013 which cost another £13million pounds and was evidently nobbled in the same way that Miss Levy had stifled the truth about the poor boy with the ruptured spleen.

Professor Sir Brian Jarman,[u] whose work helped highlight high death rates at Stafford, said the final version of the Francis report was "muted". In a lecture to the Birmingham Medico-Legal Society in early 2013, Robert Francis himself said that the report when finally published was certainly not the report he had written.[255] It had been heavily edited by the NHS apparatchiki. In this case it was Civil Servants (Department of Health Officials) who "neutered" the final version of the Francis report into the Stafford hospital scandal. As a result of this, groups of management Stasi and some Quisling physicians were shielded from exposure and the main

---

[u] Professor Sir Brian Jarman OBE, PhD, FRCP, FRCGP, FFPH, FMedSci is the past president of the British Medical Association and Emeritus Professor of the Faculty of Medicine at Imperial College, London.

blame was put once again on the most vulnerable faction – the poor nurses. Not enough emphasis was given to the Stasi's cutting of nursing manpower down to almost unmanageable levels. There were great differences for example, between the nursing on the same ward but on different shifts. The main reason for the rewriting of the final Francis Report however, was thought to be for the protection of the chief executive of the NHS, a man called David Nicholson, who nobody in the NHS had ever heard of until then. When they did hear of him they wished they never had. It is suggested[256] that he did not want anybody to hear of him with respect to the Francis Report either.

THE MAN WITH NO SHAME[v]
The smaller the lizard, the greater its hopes of becoming a crocodile.
Ethiopian Proverb.

Sir David Nicholson, who had overseen some of the catastrophe at Mid Staffs as Chief Exec of the Health Authority, then went on to over-see an era of whistle-blower stifling, suppression of mortality data, and a burying of vital warning reports about the state of the NHS as its over-all Chief Executive...
Charlotte Leslie, (2013) *Parliamentary Debate on NHS Accountability.*[257]

The chief executive of the NHS at the time of the Mid Staffs Scandal was called Sir David Nicholson. Perhaps surprisingly (and perhaps not), he was a former hard-line communist. Hardly anybody had ever heard of him until just before the publication of the long awaited Francis Report in early 2013. But it was just a few days prior to the Francis Report when Nicholson really hit the tabloids. Ironically it was not initially for his responsibility for the tragic effects of the 'target culture' he ruthlessly enforced which undoubtedly

---

[v] Front page Banner headline name for Sir David Nicholson in the Daily Mail, 7th Feb. 2013

contributed to the deaths at Stafford, but his censure by a committee of MPs for using taxpayers' money to furnish his luxurious lifestyle.

David Nicholson went to grammar school in Nottingham. He then went on to a Polytechnic, where he got a 2:1 in History and Politics. Immediately after his graduation, he joined the Communist Party of Great Britain and remained a party member until 1983. As a NHS management trainee (whatever that is!) at the height of the Cold War, David Nicholson apparently idolised Soviet leader Leonid Brezhnev (the 'Russian Bear') and perhaps modeled himself on him. He later became known as the 'Big Beast' of the NHS (not because of any ugly physical appearance, but because of his abrasive management style) and evidently boasted of having Stalin like control over it. One senior official said, *No one crosses him! He's like a ruthless omnipotent medieval Pope*. As a card carrying communist to the left of the party, he must have regarded political honours as élitist symbols of bourgeoisie government, but these principles had clearly changed by 2010, when he was happy to receive a knighthood from Her Gracious Majesty, the Queen.

A few days before the Francis Report in early 2013, the *Daily Mail* announced that he had *spent thousands of the taxpayers money on weekly trips to Birmingham – where coincidentally his new wife lives.*[258] He evidently had an annual expense account of £48,900 and kept travelling to Birmingham (in first class railway seats) at weekends to attend video conferences (even though the *raison d'être* of video conferences is that they can be attended from anywhere in the country). I have little doubt that if Nicholson had been an NHS doctor, he would have been immediately suspended for this.

He was evidently spotted travelling in his first class accommodation by the Rt Hon Andrew Lansley MP, the Secretary of State for Health, whilst the Tory cabinet minister was himself (Bless him!) travelling second class. They were evidently going to the same meeting. Those one time Socialist principles seemed now to be definitely lacking. In fact Nicholson's own personal spending budget included £155,000 worth of expenses in four years. His annual expenses for his plush London flat was triple the MPs' second homes allowance and of course, he had a taxpayer funded chauffeur.[259]

My old boss always told me somewhat didactically that *all* politicians are corrupt: left wing ones with money and right wing ones with sex.[260] I am beginning to think he was right!

Mind you, one of these does not necessarily exclude the other.

When the name of David Nicholson was mentioned at a dinner at the Birmingham Medical Institute a few years ago, my medical colleagues there linked it with that of the chief executive of Birmingham Children's Hospital, Sarah-Jane Marsh, who had just married him. They were not particularly interested in the 22-year age gap, but did find it fascinating that Nicholson had met her whilst she was seconded to his office as a junior. He was then working in Birmingham as the director of Health and Social Care for the Midlands and East of England and had clearly taken a shine to the attractive graduate trainee working with him. He later gave her a job reference, which led to her appointment as the CEO at Birmingham Children's Hospital on a £155,000 salary, and at the relatively youthful age of 32. By this time she was engaged to Nicholson – the all-powerful head of the NHS (the one, you will remember, who *no one dared to cross*).

I can see why they found this such an intriguing tale.

Then the following week he was front page news in the Telegraph[261] and the Times[262] with his picture plastered on the front page of not only the Mail[263], but also the Mirror.[264] They all held him personally responsible for the Mid Staffs catastrophe.

Shortly afterwards forty two MPs (including *several cabinet ministers*) called for his resignation. This smooth tongued political animal steadfastly refused to stand down, claiming that the tragedy in Stafford was not really his responsibility at all, but a mere "system failure". Remember that this so-called failure of the system (for which he was responsible) led to 1,200 people needlessly dying following appalling hospital care between 2005 and 2008. One MP demanded that he *resign and take responsibility for the "diabolical" situation at Mid Staffs that developed under his watch. What we all value and love about the NHS is not a system, it is the great professionals who work in it - who go the extra mile, and who are desperate to speak out when things are wrong. We must put those people at the heart of our NHS, not a system of stifling the truth.*[265]

The Prime Minister however continued to support him: he had been advised by the head of the Civil Service that the NHS would be destabilised by his removal. Ironically the truth is that the NHS would be more stable than it has ever been for years if all the NHS managers were removed! Of course the PM has a complete lack of insight into what is going on in the Health Service and takes his advice from another manager. Pure *Yes Minister.*[w] I sincerely believe that the majority of my colleagues would have been absolutely delighted to see him go and experienced a much needed upward surge of morale if he had been actually kicked out. They might even have whooped with delight to hear that he had been gaoled under the Corporate Manslaughter Act of 2007.

Nicholson might have had the leadership qualities of a lemming, but he had the sticking ability of a limpet. He hung on for months and only eventually resigned (with a £2million pension pot) in May 2013. This was greeted with mixed feelings. Julie Bailey said she thought that it was *fantastic news. This is the start of the cure for the NHS,* she said. *We can start to look to the future now. He was part of the problem, not part of the solution. We now need a leader who will galvanise and inspire the front line, not bully them.* Sadly most NHS employees are not likely to share her optimism.

Many were *absolutely sickened* that he had hung on so long and was now leaving on his own terms, with a massive pension that will pay him a six-figure annual sum for life. Charlotte Leslie, a Tory MP, thought that it was a *terrible insult* to the surviving families of Mid Staffs victims and *a terrible indictment of our political system that he has not already been fired.* She opined: *It is an even worse indictment*

---

[w] A satirical and highly successful British television sitcom (1980 – 1984), which pointed out that it is not the MPs but the civil service who really pull the strings in government.

that in an era where we talk about accountability, he should walk away to an enormous pension, funded by the public.

I have to admit that I too found his resignation letter particularly nauseating. Nowhere did he apologise for the Mid Staffordshire tragedy. The nearest he came to it was to say: *Whilst I believe we have made significant progress together under my leadership, recent events continue to show that on occasion the NHS can still sometimes fail patients, their families and carers.*

What a masterpiece of understatement from the man who was dubbed the Man with No Shame.

He can have absolutely no insight whatsoever to what people think of him. Instead of just keeping quiet and going off with his girlfriend to enjoy their massive pay-outs, he whined about how difficult the job was six months after he had left. He had the absolute gall to say that *people should not denigrate and criticise the salaries of NHS managers because they do incredibly difficult jobs.* He moaned on that *the complexity of those are on a scale managerially that most of us would have difficulty to understand.*

Who is he trying to kid?

Having worked in the NHS for almost 50 years and actually having run an (army) hospital myself, I think I can start to understand what a sinecure moneyspinner he and his cronies are on. *Executives running hospital trusts can earn up to £260,000, with an average salary of about £164,000.*[266]

It was even more sickening to hear that not only had the Prime Minister backed him, but he had then somehow achieved the support of the chief Drain Sniffer, Sir Bruce Keogh, who as a surgeon (before he *took the soup*) should have known better. He actually said that NHS managers *deserve very significant salaries*, so that managers of *the right calibre* are brought into the health service. Judging on recent events, wholesale bullying of staff and lying through their teeth to cover up their own incompetence, it certainly has not happened so far.

WHAT THE NHS NEEDS

What the NHS needs are more unemployed Chief Executives.[x]

It was related above how the main player for the Mid Staffs scandal had resigned with a pay-off of more than £400,000 and a £2 million pension pot from Mid Staffordshire Foundation. At the end of 2011, the *Daily Telegraph* printed an amazing exposé on just how much the top Stasi "fat cats" are fleecing the taxpayer for.[267]

Collectively we are paying them millions for the privilege of watching them slowly destroy the wonderful NHS that we once had. Their basic salaries (for people who are often totally unqualified) are exorbitant.[268] I was told that one chief executive, who retired in 2014 earned far more than the senior surgeon at the hospital where she worked, "*does not even have a Saint John Ambulance First Aid Certificate.*" I had always refused to use the word "obscene" in the context of large salaries, but I now find that the OED defines the adjective as *offensive or disgusting by accepted standards of morality and decency* and I therefore think that in the case of Stasi salary, it is quite appropriate.

One particular little ploy they use is "the revolving door". There is a pool of top Stasi, who quit their posts with massive backhanders and then get re-employed on temporary contracts worth thousands of pounds a day. In one case a Stasi was paid off with £300,000 was then re-employed on a daily rate of £3,400. The *Telegraph* cited thirteen other "interim" executives on more than £1,000 a day, most of whom had worked elsewhere in the health service.

Let's just single one out for examination. Derek Smith was cited *as the NHS' most expensive Chief Executive, picking up a salary in excess of £200,000 in 2003/04.*[269] More recently, NHS accounts for 2010/2011 show that he received £150,000 for 44 days work in charge of Dorset County Hospital Foundation Trust. This sum, which includes expenses,

---

[x] The quote, *What this country needs are more unemployed politicians* is usually attributed to Edward Langley, Artist (1928-1995), but he evidently never existed.

amounts to a daily rate of £3,400 which is twice as much as a nurse takes home in a month, and five times the salary of the chap who did the job before him. During the previous year he was paid £268,000 by the same trust for 97 days in charge. Whilst working at the Dorchester Hospital, he proposed 200 job losses and a pay freeze for everybody else apart from him. He even said that these "tough but necessary" measures would boost morale. After he was made redundant as chief executive of Hammersmith Hospitals trust in 2007, where it is thought he raked in more than £300,000, he started to call himself a "management consultant" and went to Leicester (as of course a lucrative "interim" post). The University Hospitals of Leicester Trust paid him more than £205,000 for six months work. He took a bit of a drop in salary from April 2011, when he went to work for Hertfordshire Community Trust, on paltry daily rates of £900.[270]

Bear in mind that this man never gets called in the middle of the night to save a life, never gets blood, shit, urine or pus on his hands and yet he gets far more than those who do. On the contrary, *the "revolving door" of managers includes one who had to leave a previous job in disgrace after he presided over a hospital whose own doctors said some of its services were worse than the Third World.*[271]

In January 2011, The (tory) Minister of State for Health, the Right Honourable Andrew Lansley published his completely potty and totally unintelligible Health and Social Care Bill. Although this was based on the excellent premise to rid the NHS of hundreds of Stasi, it all went disastrously wrong. I remember being asked at a public meeting in the summer of that year if I was optimistic about Lansley's plan to get rid of thousands of NHS managers, I answered that I would only believe it, when I saw it. I pointed out that the only people who could sack managers were the managers themselves and quoted the Arabic proverb, *a man does not cut off his own head.* As it happened, initially thousands of hospital administrators took voluntary or compulsory redundancy. Why were they so quick to lose their jobs? Because they themselves had legislated a rule by which NHS managers who are made redundant receive one month's pay for every year served. The average payout has been calculated at £48,000 each, whilst some staff received hundreds of thousands. The total paid out ran into tens of millions.[272]

And what did they do then?

At least 2,200 Stasi walked straight back into new NHS jobs just weeks after pocketing their huge redundancy payoffs. The Stasi had also made rules safeguarding their own jobs saying that managers do not forfeit their redundancy payments if they wait four weeks before taking another NHS job. The Public Accounts Committee chairman Margaret Hodge said she was *'livid'* about the jobs merry-go-round and added, *'It is clearly absurd that when NHS finances are so fragile and under so much stress that money should be wasted like this; It's mad. We've seen the first sign of rationing of operations like cataracts and knee operations. With these pressures, it is a betrayal of patients to use public money to fund redundancies for staff only to then re-employ them.*[273]

David Nicholson really came up trumps: he urged them to wait six months rather than four weeks (yes, it's true; I haven't made it up) and added (in really typical StasiSpeak) *these individuals must be mindful of the possible reputational damage to themselves and to the NHS*. How ironic coming from the Man with No Shame.

The average salary for a fully registered nurse in the UK is £24,826 (with a range from £15,109 to £34,543). An understandably embittered hospital porter (employed with the hospital for 34 years) showed me his wage packet. The magnanimous Stasi intended to cut his hardly exorbitant remunerations from £18,687 to £17,248 per annum.[274] Clearly he feels undervalued. That is because he obviously *is* undervalued. In my opinion, he is far more integral to the effective running of the hospital than the chief executive; if she left, things would undoubtedly improve! At least nurses and porters are necessary for the hospital to function. If they walked out, the place could not work effectively and everything would be more difficult. In fact I honestly believe that if *all* the Stasi left, things would undoubtedly improve.

Dr Albert Schweitzer, the famous African missionary physician and Nobel Peace Prize winner was also a brilliant theologian, gifted musician and dedicated doctor. He should be a shining example to us all. This great genius wrote many scholarly tracts and set up hospitals and leper colonies in Equatorial Africa. He once said that:

You can easily run hospitals without administrators; it is easy and I have done it many times. You can also run hospitals without laboratories and X-rays; it is not so easy, but I have done it occasionally. You can even run hospitals without qualified nurses; it is extremely difficult, but I have done it on a few occasions. But you cannot run hospitals without doctors!

Consultants' salaries vary massively, depending usually on how sycophantic and brown-nosed the surgeon or physician is willing to be to the Stasi. I cannot find an average figure, but can cite the annual salary of the senior surgeon at one district general hospital as being £90,530 (2013). This dedicated chap is exceptionally well qualified, has spent most of his long working life being on call every other night and has doubtless saved quite a few lives. He has lost count of how many times he has been called to emergencies in the middle of the night. He certainly felt very aggrieved and used some choice language, when he learned of the Stasi salaries above.

WHISTLEBLOWERS

He who does not bellow the truth when he knows the truth makes himself the accomplice of liars and forgers.[275]
Charles Péguy, French philosopher (1899)

All that is necessary for the triumph of evil is that good men do nothing.[y]
Edmund Burke (attributed)

---

[y] This quotation (in various forms) is attributed (although no written work exists to support it) to the brilliant Irish orator, philosopher, & Whig politician, Edmund Burke (1729 – 1797), who, I like to think would approve of my *OldSchool* and *NewSchool* categories. Burke was a staunch supporter of the American Revolution and dubbed those other similarly minded members of his party, "Old Whigs." He was however vociferously averse to the French Revolution; not all Whigs agreed with him in this respect and some liberal minded politicians supported the French cause. These he dubbed, "New Whigs." The Whig Party was succeeded by the Liberal Party in 1868.

*Le monde souffre beaucoup. Pas à cause de la violence de
mauvaises personnes, mais en raison du silence des bonnes
gens.*[z]
Napoléon BONAPARTE

When the Reverend Cobham Brewer first published his
Dictionary of Phrase and Fable in 1870, he said that *to blow*
(or *peach*) meant *to inform against* and made no reference to
whistleblowers, which evidently only came into usage during
the 1950s.[aa] Presumably it then derived from a policeman
blowing his whistle to raise a hue and cry, when chasing a
villain, although I am reliably informed that the constabulary
no longer carry whistles on the end of the silver chain which
went into the top pocket of the *OldSchool* police tunic. Any
younger readers will not know what I am talking about and can
perhaps console themselves by equating it to an Association
Football referee blowing the whistle when a misdemeanour has
been committed on the games field.

Perhaps the best treatise on whistleblowers was the eight-
page special report which appeared in *Private Eye* in 2011.[276]
It is brilliant but makes most depressing reading.

Aneurin Bevan was the Welsh Labour M.P.[bb] who started
the National Health Service in 1948. He promised all workers
in the new NHS:

---

[z] The world sorrows not for violence by bad men, but for the silence of
good people

[aa] The *Cassell Dictionary of Slang* on the other hand has no less than 219
references to *blow*, (many of which are sexual) of which *blow the whistle*
is number 200. My favourite was undoubtedly *to blow with a French
faggot stick*, which was listed as *the loss of ones nose through syphilis*!
(GREEN, Jonathon [1998] London.)

[bb] Is *Welsh Labour M.P.* a tautology cf. *dour Scotsman*? Would it not
convey exactly the same meaning with economy of words to say *Welsh
M.P.* and *Scotsman*? John Braine was thinking along similar lines when
he described one of his characters as *"The meanest man in Yorkshire -
which meant the meanest man in the world"*. Your author comes from
Yorkshire, and considers more correct adjectives would be *careful* or
frugal rather than *"mean"*.

You will be fully free to conduct agitation and vote against the Ministry of Health at any time you care. There will be no limitation at all upon the civil liberties of the persons working in the NHS.

The Nolan Report of 1995[277] ostensibly encouraged *whistleblowing* (and coined the term). Later in the year *Whistleblowing in the Health Service*[278] added its support and the following year the *BMA News Review* reported the overwhelming wave of magnanimity which was overtaking the NHS: 83 out of the 120 doctors who had been suspended over the past ten years had been re-instated! The Nolan Proposal, however, was far from being universally implemented, particularly in Trusts in Trent, North West Thames and West Midlands regions, and *Stalinism in the Health Service* (a term used in the British Medical Journal in December 1994)[279] continued to be practised. We have seen how the Stasi alter the meaning of words for their own expedient ends and those Stalinist Trusts chose to interpret the term *whistleblowing* in a highly specific manner: indeed they appeared to welcome the practise insofar as it only ever applied to a doctor blowing the whistle on one of his colleagues (the so-called "shop a doc" principle) but it should certainly never be used to criticise an authority!

One poor senior community paediatrician (the *OldSchool* term for this would have been "school doctor") found out to her own detriment that very senior Stasi indeed do not live up to Nye Bevan's pledge and tried to crucify her when she quite rightly blew the whistle in 2007 and then refused to take a backhander to keep quiet about it. She and her family were pilloried and suffered terribly for the next four years until she was eventually exonerated and indeed praised for what she had done. I refer to the terrible story of the persecution of Dr Kim Holt. They had chosen the wrong doctor to persecute, however. Her *gentle, quiet manner masks a fierce determination to do the right thing.* She became a whistleblower, she says, *because she feared something terrible would happen to a child and was devastated when the warnings went unheeded.*[280]

The tragic thing is that something terrible did happen. If Great Ormond Street Hospital had acted vigorously on her advice, she believes that the sad and well-publicized death of "Baby P," the 17 month old toddler who, despite being covered by bruises was sent home to be killed by his parents, might well have been averted. Dr Holt was suspended from her job. She believes that this was a punishment for blowing the whistle in this case. The Great Ormond Street Trust then offered her £80,000 with a gagging clause, as compensation if she left quietly and promised not to talk to the media, but she was not going to be bought off and refused.

When there was a public outcry about the death of Baby Peter, the offer (one might well ask if this should be called a blackmail pay-off?) went up to £120,000. Was this the action of an innocent party? Again, Dr Holt did the honourable thing and refused, but not without considerable cost to her health. She said,

The whole thing has been like a nightmare and caused a huge strain on my family. For a long while I struggled with depression – I was crying all the time, I couldn't sleep and lost interest in all the things I used to enjoy. My family also suffered – my husband had to watch helplessly as I changed, for the worse, before his eyes.

Happily, her plight received public attention and the Stasi hate this more than anything. Three thousand medical professionals and supporters up and down the country signed a petition calling for her reinstatement. In June 2011, Kim eventually received *a grovelling apology* from executives at the world-famous Great Ormond Street Hospital, London for 'the distress' they have caused her over the past four years.

"It is worth its weight in gold," she says.

The *"Teflon-coated Chief Executive[cc]"* Dr Jane Collins remained in post for another year, however. The editors of *The Lancet* made the interesting comment that "*If Great Ormond Street's management team had been in Wigan, they would almost certainly have departed by now*[281]" Dr Collins is

---

[cc] I love this expression but can't claim credit for this; it is what *Private Eye* always call her!

medically qualified,[dd] but during the furore about Baby P, she came off the Medical Register. Some[282] scurrilously suggest only to avoid a General Medical Council investigation into her behaviour in this matter – the very thought! It is true however that in 2010, around half GOSH consultants signed a letter of no confidence in its senior management. However most of those Stasi are still there.

After the Francis Report, and the promise that the climate would change and the bullying would stop, there has been some improvement. In November 2013, a report by the CQC praised whistleblowers in Colchester Hospital, who had reported the duplicity of senior managers at that hospital in regard to cancer care. Evidently, nursing staff had *told inspectors they had been pressured or bullied to change data.* The problem there had evidently been that the Trust had had difficulty in meeting the exacting national timescales appointments, diagnoses and treatments for Colchester cancer patients. The Care Quality Commissioners said that *of the 61 care records examined, 22 showed people had been put at risk of receiving care that was unsafe or not effective, due to delays in receiving appointments or treatment.*[283] It is one thing to be unable to meet deadlines and somewhat stringent timeframes quite rightly expected for cancer patients. It is quite another to lie about them and even worse still to bully sincere subordinates into lying about them to cover up your own ineptitude.

Unfortunately this is just the sort of people the Stasi are.

Because this of this dishonesty, the Essex police were called in by the CQC who said that *criminal investigation could be launched* against those who *bullied and pressured* staff into *falsifying information about patients' cancer care, potentially putting lives at risk.*[284]

[dd] This reminds me of when I once asked an army surgeon in a field hospital if the Commanding Officer was medically qualified. "*Yes,*" he replied with a smile, "*but he is not a doctor.*"

THE LEGALITY OF IT ALL

"I'll be the Judge and I'll be the Jury" said cunning Old Fury.
"I'll try the whole case and condemn you to death!"
Lewis Carroll. *Alice in Wonderland.* (1865)[ee]

Should public money ever be used to offer bribes to doctors to keep quiet about information which is in the public interest? This after all is what "gagging clauses" amount to. In a previous book, more than a dozen examples were cited of how the Stasi have scant respect for natural justice and trample roughshod over Public Interest Disclosure Act the Law of the Land.[285]

Gagging clauses were made illegal by the Public Interest Disclosure Act (1998), which is an Act of Parliament made specifically to protect whistleblowers from spite and malice from their employer. Despite this, a Channel 4 investigation thirteen years later showed that out of the 64 NHS "compromise agreements" it had examined, that 55 of them contained gagging clauses.

The General Medical Council regularly send patronizing booklets to their members, who by definition must be doctors. (See also *Janet and John* book, chapter on general practice). Perhaps the worst thing about these demeaning little pamphlets is that the contents are so vague and woolly they sometimes allow the Stasi to concoct complaints against doctors. I was surprized therefore to receive in early 2012 another condescending booklet (always entitled *The Duties of a Doctor*) with a letter from the Registrar of the GMC urging me to be a whistleblower. Of "gagging clauses", Dr Niall Dickson[ff] said, *These clauses are totally unacceptable. Doctors who sign such contracts are breaking their professional obligations and are putting patients, and their careers, at risk.*[286] I wish that I could be a little more optimistic that this would be the end of it.

[ee] One often gets the feeling that the whole NHS is based on Carroll (or perhaps, Kafka)!
[ff] Head of the GMC

I would love to think that the time is now here, when anyone in the NHS who has a genuine concern about their work can freely speak out about this against the odious Stasi. The Francis Inquiry into the Stafford Hospital *revealed the unflattering truth that nurses, doctors and frontline staff allowed poor care to go unchallenged. And the few who did speak up found themselves sidelined, bullied, and even threatened.*[287] One whistleblower, Helene Donnelly broke down in tears when she told the inquiry she was frightened to walk to her car at night after threats from other hospital workers, who thought that she was rocking the boat.[288] She said that two casualty *sisters ruled the Accident and Emergency unit with fear. The staff were scared of the sisters and afraid to speak out about the poor standards of care patients were receiving.*[289]

It always comes hard to admit that the Americans ever manage anything better than us, but with respect to whistleblowing, they certainly have. They have a massive and effective National Whistleblower Support Centre, which really does support people. The reason they give is because there is sound evidence that whistleblowing is cheaper and more efficient than any secret police type of organisation (Stasi) and therefore much more likely to save lives and money. It goes without saying that they too effect to cherish such honourable concepts as liberty and freedom of speech.

Whistleblowers can also find that one's principles can work out to be very expensive. Mr Ramon Niekrash, FRCS blew the whistle on the Stasi at the Queen Elizabeth Hospital in Woolwich[gg], where he had worked as a urological surgeon since 2000. When the Stasi closed the urology ward down, he kept writing complaining letters to the Stasi, who obviously could not handle it and so suspended him for ten weeks. I can understand that a lay person might find it a bit over the top to

---

[gg] This hospital's name originates from the Queen Elizabeth Military Hospital, which occupied the site from 1977 until its closure in 1995 and was named after Queen Elizabeth the Queen Mother. The military hospital was built on the site of the former Shrapnel Barracks, which was named after Lieutenant-general Sir Henry Shrapnel (1761 - 1842) inventor of the "shrapnel shell".

stop a consultant surgeon from working for the NHS (but keep him on full pay) for ten weeks, just because he had written some vexatious letters to the Stasi complaining about a ward closure. Ramon, who qualified in the Antipodes alleges that he was subjected to a campaign of bullying and harassment and claimed that one of the doctors collaborating with the Stasi, had said that she would,

...just like him not to come back, I'd just like him to be in chains on a plane in Heathrow back to Australia, if you really want to know.[290]

Mr Niekrash took his employers to a tribunal, which ruled in his favour in February 2010, but by 2012, he had still not been reimbursed for his legal bills amounting to £180,000.[291]

What about the doctors' trade union, the British Medical Association? Always a veritable tower of strength in times of crisis, they claim to support whistleblowers, but there is no prize for guessing who negotiates the majority of the compromise agreements containing gagging clauses. They develop cosy little relationships with the local Stasi, with whom they are usually (nauseatingly) on first name terms! Their collaboration in negotiating these illegal clauses is because they realise that sacrificing one of their own members (and one who will, no doubt in three more months no longer pay their exorbitant membership fee) will be much more comfortable than losing their stress-free first-name relationship with their local Stasi. Surely it would be better for the doctor if the BMA were to provide him with a confrontational medico-legal expert who would be willing to travel around the country and take on a gladiatorial attitude towards the troublesome Stasi. It almost goes without saying that they will have absolutely no intention of being "reasonable". It is hardly difficult to get the intellectual better of them and the balance of probabilities in all such cases is that the doctor is going to be in the right anyway (otherwise he would not have risked everything to take on the juggernaut Stasi[hh]).

[hh] The word *juggernaut* is derived from the Jagannath Temple in India. A huge wagon bearing an image of a Hindu god was reputed to crush devotees under its wheels. In colloquial English usage it usually avers to

NAME AND SHAME

May coward shame distain his name
The wretch that dares not die.
Robert Burns. *McPherson's Farewell.* (1788)

Presumably to take the heat off all the Stasi who were eventually getting all the public exposure they had managed to escape for the previous twenty or so years, the (Tory) Minister of Health, the Right Honourable Jeremy Hunt MP, a former exporter of marmalade to Japan, decided to have a go at the doctors. This led fairly swiftly to them passing a vote of no confidence in him.[292]

He had asked (fairly reasonably) that all individual surgeons make public their own personal "outcome data," including death rates under their care. The spiteful vindictive Stasi rubbed their hands in malicious glee; here was a chance for them to sit back and watch whilst their hated rivals were publicly humiliated! All else being equal of course this would have held no horrors to the majority of my colleagues. The Royal College of Surgeons said somewhat cautiously that this *risked wrongly stigmatising individuals and harming patient confidence.*[293] The big problem is however that the NHS book-keepers are incompetent buffoons.

Let me give you a true example of their bungling attempts at keeping accurate performance data. A colleague of mine at a major teaching hospital in Birmingham was asked to sign a document giving permission for his surgical success rates during the last five years in head and neck cancer surgery to be made available to the public. He quite rightly refused. He once worked for me and I know him to be an excellent surgeon, but the reason why he demurred on this occasion is because he is not a head and neck cancer surgeon and has not performed any operations of this sort in the last fifteen years. The hospital data bank however says that he has. A few years ago, the data base in my own hospital had recorded the fact that I was

---

a literal or metaphorical force, which is mercilessly destructive and unstoppable.

supposed to have done some urological procedures. I have not performed any urological procedures for over forty years and so I realise that similar mistakes are more than likely to have occurred elsewhere. My friend does not know who has done the operations which are down to him but it is certainly not he. He therefore (reasonably) refused to consent to giving access to what needs must be false data. The Rt Hon. Mr Hunt said: "*Subject to proper risk adjustment of the data there can be no valid reason why it should not be published.*[294] and ordered his officials to draw up plans to "name and shame". Our right honourable friend clearly has more confidence in the NHS data bases than those of us who have spent our working lives in NHS hospitals. This heavy-handed political manner would indicate perhaps why his business exporting marmalade to Japan[295] went down the tube.

The thick Stasi at my pal's hospital however were not appeased by his explanations and approached him a second time, on this occasion brandishing a letter signed by the marmalade salesman, threatening to publicise his name if he continues to withhold access to (what must be erroneous) records.

In the end, the jam seller capitulated and the threat of the "Name and Shame" list came to nothing. Unsusually, common sense had prevailed. The Department of Health realised that their managers had been so totally incompetent in collecting individual surgeons' outcome lists, that they had got different surgeons results completely mixed up and finished with an inaccurate set of botched figures. Having read thus far, I feel confident that my reader will have no feeling of great surprise at this. Once again the Stasi did not want to end up with egg on their faces and the deadline passed like a damp squib.

REFERENCES

[217]. BROWN, David (2013) *NHS executive sacked over armed robbery conviction.*
The Times May 31 2013

218. BRACCHI, Paul; STEWART, Tim (2013) *How DID this convicted armed robber get a £236,000-a-year job as an NHS manager?* Daily Mail.7 June.

[219]. *Ibid.*

[220]. *Ibid.*

[221]. DIXON, Hayley (2013) *Armed robber employed as NHS chief on six-figure salary.* Daily Telegraph May 30.

[222]. WALTERS, Max (2013) *NHS Brent to investigate how convicted armed robber was given £1,000-a-day job.* Brent & Kilburn Times June 6,

[223]. BRACCHI, Paul; STEWART, Tim (2013) *op. cit.* (n. 2).

[224]. O'MALLEY, Steven. (2011) Personal Communication.

[225]. PIERCE, Andrew (2013) *The Ex-Commie NHS Chief* Daily Mail Feb 7 page 6

[226]. DOMINICZAK, Peter,.(2013) *Demands grow for Sir David Nicholson to resign over Mid Staffs.* Daily Telegraph. 5 Mar

[227]. PROPPER, C et al. (2007) *Did Targets and Terror Reduce Waiting Times in England for Hospital Care?* pub. (2008) B.E. Journal of EconomicAnalysis & Policy 8 (1).

[228]. PIERCE, Andrew. (2013) *The ex-communist NHS chief, the young wife he fast-tracked and a very lavish lifestyle.* Daily Mail 7 Feb. page 7.

[229]. SHAPIRO, Jonathan. (2011) *Leadership in the NHS.* Editorial 342, 1271.

[230]. WISE, Jacqui (1997) *Goodbye to the "hello nurse" in casualty departments.* Brit.Med.J. 315, 145.

[231]. STURGEON, Nicola (2011) SNP Conference Inverness. *NHS Lothian chiefs deny 'doctoring' waiting lists.* Scotsman 24 October 2011

[232]. SUNDAY TIMES (2011) 23 October .p17.

[233]. GYFORD, Sue, CUMMINGS, Laura (2011) *NHS Lothian chiefs deny 'doctoring' waiting lists.* Edinburgh Evening News. 24 October 201.

[234]. BOWLES, David J (2012) *Investigation into Management Culture in NHS Lothian.*

[235]. PATRICK, Kirsten (2012) *Barriers to Whistleblowing in the NHS.* Editorial Brit.Med.J. 345. p7.

[236]. DEPARTMENT OF HEALTH (2010) Robert Francis Report *Independent Inquiry into care provided by Mid Staffordshire NHS Foundation Trust January 2005 – March 2009*, The Stationery Office, p. 352

[237]. Personal Communication (2013) December. EAB/JRY.

[238]. NATIONAL AUDIT OFFICE (2001) *Inappropriate adjustments to NHS waiting lists.* HC 452. 19 December . p. 1

[239]. HOPE, Jenny http://www.dailymail.co.uk/news/article-62671/NHS-waiting-list scandal revealed.

[240]. BENTLEY Paul (2013) *Hospital hired me to fiddle death figures: Expert claims NHS ordered cover-up.* Daily Mail. 30th October. p.1.

[241]. *Ibid.*

[242]. *Ibid.* page 4.

[243]. BORLAND, Sophie, BENTLEY Paul (2013) *NHS Hit by New Hospital Deaths Cover-Up.* Daily Mail. 28 February. p.1.

[244]. COOK, Emily (2009). *Stafford hospital scandal: Up to 1,200 may have died over "shocking" patient care.* Daily Mirror March 18, 2009

[245]. ADAMS, Stephen (2012) *Surgery death rate 'twice as high as thought'.*

Daily Telegraph. 21 September

[246]. SAWER, Patrick (2009) *Staffordshire hospital scandal: the hidden story.*

Daily Telegraph. 22 March.

[247]. SCHLESINGER, Fay; DOLAN, Andy; SHIPMAN, Tim (2010) *Family who lost four loved ones.* Daily Mail. 25 February

[248]. FRANCIS, Robert (2010) *Independent Inquiry into care provided by Mid Staffordshire NHS Foundation Trust January 2005 – March 2009.* Volume I. HC375-I para 43, p15.

[249]. *Ibid.* p.16.

[250]. DOLAN, Andy, (2012) *£100,000 for NHS lawyer who told doctor to cover up a death.* Daily Mail. 2 Feb p 21.

[251]. LINTERN. Shaun (2011) *Mid Staffordshire was a total system failure.*

The Guardian. 7 December.

[252]. SAWER, Patrick and DONNELLY, Laura (2011): *Boss of scandal-hit hospital escapes cross-examination* Daily Telegraph. *02 Oct*

[253]. ASPINALL, Adam (2011): *'Suicidal' former Stafford Hospital boss enjoyed ski trip abroad.* Sunday Mercury. Nov 27

[254]. CAMPBELL, Denis (2011) *Neglect and indignity: Stafford hospital inquiry damns NHS failings.* Guardian Thursday 1 December

[255]. Personal Communication (2013) ~~EJF~~ EWF /JRY 31 March 2013

[256]. ADAMS, Stephen and DOMINICZAK Peter, (2013) *Sir David Nicholson protected by 'neutered' Francis report.* Daily Telegraph March 4th

[257]. LESLIE, Charlotte (2013) *Charlotte Leslie MP: Sir David Nicholson must not be allowed to appoint 'comrades' to senior NHS positions.* Daily Mail 17 Mar.

[258]. BORLAND, Sophie (2013) *NHS Chief and riddle of his 41 first class trips to Birmingham that you paid for.* Daily Mail. 9th February. p. 9.

[259]. PIERCE, Andrew. (2013) *The ex-communist NHS chief, the young wife he fast-tracked and a very lavish lifestyle.* Daily Mail 6 Feb.

[260]. Personal Communication (1978) NWG/JRY

[261]. ADAMS, Stephen (2013) *3.000 More Patients have died Needlessly in Hospital*. The Daily Telegraph. Feb 7. Page 1.

[262]. TIMES (2013) NHS – *No one is Safe*. The Times. 7th February page 1.

[263]. MARTIN, Daniel and BORLAND, Sophie (2013) *Man with No Shame*.
Daily Mail. Feb 7. Page 1.

[264]. GREGORY, Andrew (2013) *1,200 Died in their Care*. Daily Mirror. Feb.7. Page 1

[265]. DOMINICZAK, Peter,.(2013) *Demands grow for Sir David Nicholson to resign over Mid Staffs*. Daily Telegraph. 5 Mar.

[266]. DOMINICZAK, Peter. (2013) *Do not 'denigrate and criticise' NHS pay, Sir David Nicholson says*. Daily Telegraph 5 Nov.

[267]. DONNELLY, Laura and MOORE, Alison, (2011) *NHS fat cats take pay offs – then come back for more*. Daily Telegraph 29 Oct.

[268]. DONNELLY, Laura (2011) *NHS fat cats earn more than David Cameron*.
Daily Telegraph 30 April.

[269]. www//4glengate.net/node/159 (10 March 2007)

[270]. MARTIN, Daniel (2013) *The Management Merry-Go-Round*. Daily Mail. 23 March. Page 10.

[271]. DONNELLY, Laura and MOORE, Alison, (2011) *NHS fat cats take pay offs – then come back for more*. Daily Telegraph 29 Oct.

[272]. MARTIN, Daniel (2013) (op.cit.) (n.54)

[273]. MARTIN, Daniel (2013) *How 2,200 NHS staff were paid off...then re-hired months later*. Daily Mail. 23 March. Page 10.

[274]. Personal Communication (2013) Hospital Porter/JRY December.

[275]. PÉGUY,Charles (1899) *Basic Verities*. Lettre du Provincial, 21 December.

[276]. HAMMOND, Phil and BOUSFIELD, Andrew (2011) *Shoot the Messenger: How NHS Whistleblowers are Silenced and Sacked*. Private Eye. 8-22 July. pp15-22.

[277]. LORD NOLAN. (1995) *Standards in Public Life*. London: HMSO.

[278]. HUNT, G. (1995) *Whistleblowing in the Health Service, Accountable Law and Professional Practice*. London: Edward Arnold.

[279]. CRAFT, N. (1994) *Secrecy in the NHS*. Br Med J 309:1640-1643.

[280]. JOHNSON, Angella (2011) *I was driven out to protect the Great Ormond Street brand, says the whistleblowing paediatrician who could have saved Baby Peter*.
Daily Mail. 30th October.

[281]. HORTON, R. (2011) *A singular lack of foresight*. Lancet; **378**: 14.

[282]. PACK, Mark (2011) *Stinging rebuke for Great Ormond Street's management in The Lancet*. 21 June. http://www.libdemvoice.org/great-ormond-street-hospital-richard-horton-24510.html

[283]. MEIKLE, James (2013) *Hospital faces claim of cancer care cover up.* The Guardian, 5th November.

[284]. *Ibid.*

[285]. YOUNG, JR et al, (2008) *The Hospital Revolution.* Metro. London. The last Chapter, *Disciplining Hospital Doctors in th NHS* contains a cornucopia of lawbreaking by the Stasi.

[286]. DYER, C. (2012) *GMC bans doctors from signing contracts containing "gagging" clauses on issues of public interest.* BritMedJ. 344.

[287]. LINTERN. Shaun (2011) *Mid Staffordshire was a total system failure.*
The Guardian. 7 December

[288]. CALKEN, Sarah, (2011) *Mid Staffs Nurse too scared to walk to car after shift.* Nursing Times. 17 Oct.

[289]. BORLAND, Sophie (2013) *Hospital staff should face jail for covering up mistakes.* Daily Mail. 7th February.page 7.

[290]. HEALTH NEWS Blog (2009) *NHS 'whistleblower' claims hospital bullied him.* Daily Telegraph. 09 Sep.

[291]. CHANDLER, Mark. (2012) *Suspended hospital consultant Dr Ramon Niekrash made to wait over damages claim.* News Shopper. 16th Jan.

[292]. CAMPBELL, Denis (2013) *Doctors pass motion of no confidence in health secretary Jeremy Hunt.* The Guardian. 24 June

[293]. PRICE, Caroline. (2013) *Hunt says 'name and shame' surgeons, NHS 'discriminates' against liver patients and the patch to revolutionise vaccinations.* Pulse. 14 June.

[294]. WINNETT, Robert, MASON, Rowena (2013) *Doctors should be able to veto treatment data until 'happy' with it, say surgeons.* Daily Telegraph 14 Jun.

[295]. CLARK, Steve (2008) *Interview: Jeremy Hunt* Broadcast Magazine www.broadcastnow.co.uk 13 August

CONCLUSION

Nobody in the United Kingdom would doubt for one minute that our once glorious National Health Service is in dire straits. It is definitely very sick and some consultants think that it is terminally ill[296] and might soon be in its death throes.

The British public is acutely aware of the impending demise of a national institution, which it holds so dear that in the opening ceremony to the 2012 Olympic Games (and much to the puzzlement of all the foreigners watching the proceedings), it gave pride of place. The lay people however laid the blame for this malaise firmly at the door of government. Of course, the Department of Health must share some of the guilt, but as a veteran NHS worker, I have no doubt at all that the main villains of the tragedy are the hospital administrators, the so-called "managers". In this book they have been referred to as the Stasi (after the odious East German Secret Police). The one big difference between these two evil groups is that the real Staatssicherheitdienst were chillingly efficient ruthless bureaucrats, but their hospital manager namesakes are a bunch of incompetent clowns.

In the title of the book, the management is compared to a cancer. That is a very apt metaphor because it has certainly acted like a malignant mass growing inside the system, sapping it of all its strength. A cancer continues to grow and grow before the patient realises that something is wrong: most of the public in Britain are blissfully unaware of the real cause of the malaise of the NHS. As a cancer grows, it damages the healthy tissues around it without serving any useful purpose. To the detriment of the professionals, administration has grown bigger and bigger and it has certainly not served any useful function. Quite the reverse; it is pernicious. The anecdotes in this book have surely proved that beyond all reasonable doubt. Most intelligent clinicians believe that the administrators are so useless, it would be better if they were paid to stay at home! But they are worse than that; just like a tumour, their presence is actually harmful to the wellbeing of the whole.

A tumour starts off with a few abnormal cells, which then go on proliferating beyond normal control. It grows and grows until it sometimes becomes bigger than the organ from which it has developed. Cancer ultimately kills the patient by an insidious process of infiltration and spread. The Stasi are certainly guilty of that. Twenty years ago there was just a handful, but now there are countless numbers of them. In the hospital in North Devon where I used to work before I retired, they actually closed an entire 20 bedded ward on the top floor and then filled the space with potted plants and administrators' desks. Now surprise, surprise, they are short of beds.

By paying themselves inappropriate and exorbitant salaries, by their own continuing bungling incompetence and misuse of public money, they have redirected precious funds and have made our once thriving Health Service into an emaciated shadow of its former self, just like the thin cachectic patient suffering from advanced cancer.

Quite often cancer causes haemorrhage or bleeding. As the life blood flows away, it cannot be replaced quickly enough by the ailing body. Doctors and nurses (the life blood of the NHS) are leaving (or taking early retirement) in hitherto unprecedented numbers. The cancer on the top floor has caused that loss.

The only treatment for a cancer is to completely get rid of it by cutting out every bit of it.

I still believe if all (yes, every last one!) of the managers were to be sacked, the overall effect would be an improvement of the service. This change for the better would result from the immediate and overwhelming increase in morale by not only the doctors and nurses but by everyone else in the hospital, who would be overjoyed at getting rid of the hated "managers". The importance of morale in a large corporate organization such as a hospital cannot be overemphasised. In addition to this, of course would be the immense savings. That is not to say I would advocate this harsh expedient, but if I am right that sacking every last one would lead to an improvement, then clearly we need to get rid of the vast majority. Perhaps we could retain half a dozen administrators in the larger hospitals, but we would have to ensure that they were kept firmly under the watchful eye of controlling clinical staff.

The Stasi are control freaks and have bullied and tried to humiliate everyone who actually does some work in the Health Service. This includes everyone from the porters and cleaners and extends to the most senior consultants. All feel absolutely and utterly unvalued. Morale is terrible and work and enthusiasm suffers accordingly.

After the scandal at the Stafford Hospital broke in 2013, the public were amazed to learn that in most hospitals, these administrators are paid higher salaries than the most senior and experienced surgeons. I really hope that they are starting to see the true picture and appreciate who the true culprits are. Very few lay people are aware of the minimal academic qualifications and lack of any proper Civil Service training of these so-called managers. They were incredulous to learn about the bullying tactics they use. Over my fifty years working for the NHS, I have found that the great majority of fellow NHS workers have been pleasant and amiable, often driven by a philanthropy of wanting to help their fellow man. I can honestly say that I have not met more than two managers during this entire period, who fit this category. As it has recently been shown overwhelmingly in Mid Staffs, Colchester, Bolton, Medway, Nuneaton, Morecambe Bay etc.etc.etc.[a], they tend to be bullies who make up for their lack of medical knowledge and competence by exerting their new found power and intimidating the real workers at the hospital.

They certainly tried to bully me.

As an *OldSchool* doctor, I did not take kindly to their intrusion into the hospital scene in the eighties. I took a leaf from the book of the then Prime Minister, Mrs Thatcher. She

---

[a] Basildon, Blackpool, Stoke Mandeville, Burton-on-Trent, Dudley, Blackburn, Lincoln, Whitehaven, Grimsby, Sutton-in-Ashfield, Tameside and Walsall.

did not recognise the IRA (or any other terrorists) and I refused to recognise the new Stalinist health service administrators, who appeared to me to be little better than terrorists. Unfortunately, I was mainly on my own in this respect and most of my colleagues who dared to speak out were ruthlessly suppressed. Political correctness was raising its ugly head at round about the same time and they often used this as a ready excuse to get rid of dissident doctors. They tried this out with me. They suspended me, accusing me of racism. This was a particularly nasty accusation and as they say, *Mud always sticks.*[b] The chief executive was exultant saying to one of my colleagues, "*We've got him now!*" Even though the Race Relations Board and the Devon and Cornwall Constabulary insisted that I was not a racist, the Stasi bully boys persisted in their campaign of spiteful persecution and made me attend a Disciplinary Tribunal (which I attended wearing Nigerian robes).

As it happened, they came out with egg on their face and I enjoyed local folk hero status for a few months. But as the Medical Defence Union once told me, the Stasi never forget or forgive[297] and sure enough, like a savage dog drooling with a bone, they would not let go and a few years later, accused me of *bringing the NHS into disrepute,* after I had spoken out openly at a public meeting about their crass incompetence.[298] At this next enquiry,[299] I pointed out that I had always been a passionate supporter of the Health Service, which I had served faithfully for decades and that it was not me, but the managers themselves who had brought the service into disrepute. They had to let this drop and I was re-instated.

Even when I retired, the local paper published a short article about my 32 years service to the North Devon Hospital.[300] They showed a photograph of me wearing my morning dress and white coat in my out-patient clinic. With me was an old lady, who looked very pleased because she had just been fitted with a hearing aid. The vitriolic Stasi on seeing the picture immediately asked whether I had obtained written consent from the old dear, informing her that her picture would

---

[b] In fact what they usually say is, *Shit always sticks.*

be in the *Journal*. But it was too late; I had retired. They didn't even give me another plastic pen. At least when I had completed the first 25 years they sent me a ball point pen through the internal post. I did think of sending a photograph of me holding this wonderful pen in one hand and in the other the silver pocket watch, which my grandad was given after he completed 25 years at the colliery in Yorkshire. I never quite got round to it; I was probably too busy getting on with my job as a surgeon.

In the last chapter, Albert Schweitzer's self-evident truth about the importance of doctors in running a hospital was invoked: you cannot run a hospital without doctors - but you sure as hell can run one without administrators. The age-old lie is wheeled out over and over again, that since Schweitzer's days, things have changed and *"the doctor is different, the patient is different, and the medicine is different"*.

New and modern technology is cited as another reason why we need managers. However, it has been effectively shown that the administrators know nothing about technology. The sad truth is they know nothing about medicine, they know nothing about nursing; they know absolutely nothing at all about leadership: unfortunately, they do not even know about civil service administrative procedures. As always, your author will be generous and say that perhaps they once knew something about double-entry bookkeeping!

In 2007, the television management guru, Sir Gerry Robinson was set a challenge by the BBC.[c] He went to work in an NHS Hospital (in Rotherham) for six months to try to help reduce the waiting lists. As an outsider, his first impression was surprise at the "power struggle" between doctors and managers. He left *with a very frustrated feeling that actually quite small sums of money properly and sensibly spent could have produced very large results in terms of reduced waiting lists, and actually very large sums of money had been thrown at the NHS and produced very little.* Later in the year, when Brown replaced Blair as Prime Minister, Sir Gerry gave the new PM some public advice. He pointed out that the

---

[c] It was called "Can Gerry Robinson Fix the NHS?"

staggering amounts of money (around £90 billion) thrown at the NHS should really have improved the service but that *sadly and quite frankly,* it had not. He then said that what the NHS really needed was some "*really good managers*". But he did not know where we would get them.

We certainly haven't found any so far.

In 2013, the incompetence and nastiness of the senior Stasi was revealed in the Francis Report, but the man responsible for the *3,000 needless deaths*[301] (Sir David Nicholson) got away with it scot-free,[d] despite calls for his resignation by cabinet ministers. Could any sane person call this top Stasi dubbed by the tabloids as "*the man with no shame*" a *really good manager?* He appeared on the front pages of four major newspapers all on the same day.[e] We have been disgusted by other very senior executives telling diabolical lies and being really nasty to employees by bullying them into lying too.

Sir Bruce Keogh, Medical Director to the Department of Health (*Chief Drain Sniffer*) said that *very significant salaries* should be paid to ensure people of *the right calibre.*[302] He surely cannot mean that we increase the massive salaries which they are getting at present. There is however a ring of truth in what he says. We certainly do need men of the right calibre, but sadly in nearly fifty NHS years, I have never yet come across one manager whom I would consider to have one ounce of leadership qualities. This is the reason why they are universally disliked and have never gained anybody's respect.

The Stasi started to infiltrate traditional hospital medicine during the 1980s. Before then everybody got on well together and morale was good. There were never any problems between the very few hospital administrators and the medical and nursing staff. I found an old 1982 hospital telephone directory and there were only four entries under "Administration". They were Hospital Secretary, Matron, Treasurer and Lady Almoner (AKA Social Worker). In the 2012 directory from the same hospital there are over one hundred.

---

[d] Evidently a *scot* is a *tax*. Literally therefore this means *tax-free.*
[e] 7th February 2013.

During those thirty years they have destroyed completely the time-honoured hospital nursing hierarchy. This was formerly an extremely professional, well-integrated and much respected part of the hospital. They were all highly disciplined and under the leadership of a competent matron. It wasn't too long ago (my parents' generation) that nurses weren't allowed to marry. My father-in-law always used to joke that he could hear the clatter of wedding rings in purses as he approached Charing Cross Station every morning just after the war. (There used to be a hospital just by the railway terminus.) Nowadays and, oh so sadly, nurses appear to be little more than an amorphous group of downtrodden women in blue pyjamas.

They have also had a catastrophic effect in dividing the medical profession. There is now almost a generation of doctors, who never experienced the "Good Old Days" when hospitals were happy places. This new cohort has grown up with the Stasi always there. They have accepted them as it were, because they don't realise that they are not only unnecessary but pernicious. These are the *NewSchool*. Unfortunately they have been reared in this new ethos, which in my opinion is less caring and driven far more by financial considerations and so they recognise it and accept it as normal.

Even their medical school training falls into this category. In some medical schools, there is now no dissection of the cadaver at all, and some students qualify as doctors without ever having placed a foot in the mortuary to see an autopsy. Cadaveric dissection and post-mortem examination were formerly two of the cornerstones of our profession. On qualification, the *OldSchool* doctor became a houseman (even if you were a woman, you were called a houseman) and started the most rigorous and hardworking year of his or her life. It was also probably the best and most fulfilling. You worked very hard, but the experience was phenomenal and at the end you were almost certainly fit for rôle. They always said that at the end of your house years, you probably knew more about everything than you ever would again.

Because the incompetent Stasi have misinterpreted a Common Market rule, which was originally meant to prevent lorry drivers from falling asleep, the *NewSchool* housemen (who now actually are mainly female, but are called F1 doctors) aren't allowed to work so many hours and therefore have to spend two full years (during the second of which they will have become an F2 doctor) and even when they finish that, they almost certainly won't have got as much experience as an *OldSchool* houseman did anyway. Worse than that, the doctors' messes and hospital bars have been mostly closed.

When the hospital was your home, it instilled a different feeling of loyalty towards it. You felt part of it. Consultants too had a different loyalty to their hospital. An appointment *On the Staff of a Hospital*[f] was usually for the whole of your professional life. It was always written into your contract that you were obliged to live within a ten-mile radius of the place. This was often erroneously thought to be so that you could get in quickly when you were called for an emergency, but the origin in fact dates back further than that (and indeed further back than the days of telephones). It was so that you were perceived as part of the local community and had a loyalty to it. This is no longer the case. The last chap who was appointed as my consultant colleague in Barnstaple, lived forty miles away from our hospital in Exeter. This of course was far from ideal when it came to his nights on-call for emergencies. After a couple of years, he left and took another job hundreds of miles away in Scotland. The surgeon who replaced him doesn't live near the hospital either; he lives in Taunton, which is also forty miles away. The old ethic of having loyalty to the local community certainly seems to have gone by the board.

When I was appointed as a consultant, my old boss always said that it was paramount that I got on with my partners, because a professional partnership had all the disadvantages of marriage but without the option of divorce. He was right. It was very difficult to swap jobs in those days, unless there could be seen to be an exceptional reason. My contract was of course life-long or certainly up to retirement age, although being a consultant surgeon is such a stressful occupation that a

---

[f] This term was used solely for the consultant physicians and surgeons at that hospital.

very significant proportion do not live to draw their pension. Happily, I did.

Consultant contracts now however are increasingly becoming limited to say two years. What of course the Stasi would really like is for us to turn up every morning and stand outside the hospital gate, cap in hand, waiting for some manager to come along with a list of jobs and choose from the assembled surgeons and physicians just who would be required for the operating lists and outpatient clinics that particular day. The unfortunates who were not chosen could then pull their cloth caps back on and miserably shuffle away back home (or to the dockside pub, like in the old grey and white[g] films).

Doctors had never realized what draconian changes the administrators would enforce and now it all seems too late. One of the most disturbing features is that there appears to be no solution; there is no going back. Not only medicine but also the whole of society has changed. The replacement of professionalism by managerialism has overthrown a wonderful system, which had slowly developed over generations. Moreover, during that process of evolution it had blossomed and improved. Less than two generations ago, doctors had an ethos of duty - and with that duty went a degree of privilege. Patients on the whole would respect their medical attendants: it went without saying . They would, however, implicitly expect their doctor to make a visit in the middle of the night if necessary: that too went without saying. There was an old fashioned Boy's Own Paper sense of chivalry.

Sadly, that professionalism has now been dismantled and what is perhaps saddest of all is that, like Vesalius in his sixteenth century anatomy theatre, it is we doctors who have been duped into dismembering it! If we had only shown solidarity in the 'eighties, and just refused to have anything to do with them; if in effect we had not *collaborated*.[h] They

---

[g] US gray and white

[h] In France during, and after the Second World War, *collaborators* had their heads shaven and branded on the scalp with the sign of a swastika; in Northern Ireland, during the Troubles, colleens who collaborated with British soldiers were similarly shorn, then stripped and tied to lamp-posts where they were *tarred and feathered* (a punishment first accorded to

appealed to our baser instincts and offered financial incentives: we prostituted ourselves and took the bait. It is now far too late to take united action against them, and besides, doctors will never all agree now to present a united front - they are far too individualistic.

I was giving a talk at a book fair in 2011 and I was asked what I thought about the then Minister of Health, Andrew Lansley's proposals – that the numbers of top-heavy NHS management should be drastically cut. I remember that my answer really disappointed the man who had asked this question. I invoked the old Arabic proverb that *a man does not cut off his own head* and pointed out that the only people empowered to sack managers were other managers. The politicians wouldn't do it. I told him that I was most pessimistic and that I would only believe it if and when it happened.

At that stage not even I was expecting just how doggedly tenacious they would hold on. Let me refer (again) to Sir David Nicholson. Even when four national newspapers demanded his resignation on their front pages and forty two MPs (including several cabinet ministers) insisted that he resign, he still stuck to his office like mud to the proverbial blanket.[i] He simply ignored the lot of them, insisting that he was needed by the service. The Arabs were of course right; this was certainly one man who *not going to cut off his own head.*

Lansley's other suggestions in his almost unintelligible proposals are to use GPs as hospital commissioners. I do not think that they will ever actually take the bull by the horns and get rid of all the incompetent Stasi. They probably won't be empowered to. I am similarly pessimistic about this making any effective change at all.

---

thieves on Crusaders' boats). Your author would not of course suggest that all medical directors should suffer this indignity: suffice it that they are branded as wilfully treacherous individuals devoid of all moral worth and totally unfit to be received into the society of worthy men who prize honour and virtue above the external advantages of rank and fortune.

[i] I have cleaned this metaphor up a bit for my younger readers.

Of course, when I have made somewhat controversial statements about the decline of the NHS, I have been asked what if any solution I would propose. After all I once used to be commanding officer of an efficient Army field hospital, so it is a reasonable question. The sad truth of the matter is that I think the buffoons who have been in charge for the last few decades have taken us, as it were beyond the event horizon[j] and we are about to enter a frightening and inevitable black hole.

Unfortunately not all cancers can be cut out. It is important for a surgeon to realise when a malignant disease is incurable and I really think that this one is. If the cancer could somehow be successfully extirpated, perhaps a possible solution would be to reinstitute a revised form of an old administrative system, which worked very well in the past. In the pre-NHS days, before Aneurin Bevan, a very senior and well-respected consultant was appointed by his colleagues as Medical Superintendent of the hospital. He was not retired from his clinical consultancy and was still busy working. What I would suggest might just work is that that a newly retired consultant, respected and elected by his peers (i.e. other medically qualified consultants at that same hospital) should be appointed for a finite term of office (certainly no longer than a period of three years). The Ancient Greeks realized that if one person is in power for too long, things start to go badly wrong.[k]

I would not suggest that he need be full time: indeed, it would be much better if he only went in for a few hours a week to sort things out (preferably just before they went wrong). He would have the absolute respect of everyone in the hospital and also the community. He would have the personal experience of many years of hospital work and above all he would be a *doctor* with all that implies. Physicians are usually

---

[j] In quantum physics, an *event horizon* is the point of no return at which the gravitational pull becomes so great that escape is impossible; not even a ray of light can ever get out. The most common case for an event horizon is the one surrounding a *Black Hole*.

[k] The Greeks had Pericles; we have had Mr Blair (and Mrs Thatcher).

highly intelligent and hard-working individuals, who place the well-being of the patients who have entrusted themselves into their care above all other considerations, particularly those of money and financial reward. They have served the whole of their working life with that ethic in the forefront of their minds. On the whole and even in the twenty-first century, society still respects its doctors.

When I have dared to suggest this in the past[303] (and only then because I was otherwise accused of non-constructive criticism) I was told that it would be "turning the clock back over fifty years!" Perhaps so, but it would be going back to a time when people were glad to work in hospitals, which in turn were efficient, clean and happy places to work. It would be a return to a time when doctors trusted other members of the hospital staff and felt respected and valued by the community in which they worked. They might even stop retiring years before their time!

I have now retired altogether and would not cherish the prospect of ever going back to NHS in its current form. I think it is sad the clock cannot be turned back to this excellent system of hospital management, but as the poet once said:

The Moving Finger writes; and having writ,
Moves on: nor all thy Piety or Wit
Shall lure it back to cancel half a Line,
Nor all thy Tears wash out a Word of it.[304]

REFERENCES

[296]. TAYLOR, K (2006) *Bringing managers to book for what they do.* Hosp.Doct.26th July. p.26.

[297]. PERSONAL COMMUNICATION (1987) JRY/KJS

[298]. DAILY TELEGRAPH REPORTER (2011) *Swastika doctor in trouble again.* Daily Telegraph. 25 March p.16.

[299]. CHURCHILL, Laura (2011) *Hospital consultant's views branded wholly offensive.* North Devon Journal 24 March, p.3.

[300]. TOPPS, Will (2013) *Popular health figure is relieved to leave the NHS.* North Devon Journal. June 13. p.4.

[301] ADAMS, Stephen (2013) *3.000 More Patients have died needlessly in Hospital.* Daily Telegraph. Feb 7. Page 1.